Effective Planning and Administration of Early Education Programs

© 2014 Penn Consulting (Training and Publishing). This book is available in print at most online retailers. All rights are reserved. No part of this book may be reproduced or transmitted in any form or by any means, electronic or mechanical, including photocopying, recording, or by an information storage and retrieval system; or used for advertising or promotional purposes, general distribution, creating new collective works, or for resale without permission in writing from the copyright owner and publisher. Exceptions are the reproduction of forms, handouts, policies, or procedures contained herein solely for use within the site-of-purchase facility or by a reviewer who may quote brief passages in a review to be printed in a magazine, newspaper, or on the web. For information, please contact Penn Consulting at 678.557.8684, penntraining@yahoo.com, or apenn@pennconsulting.org.

Library of Congress Cataloging in publication data
Penn, Althea
Effective Planning and Administration of Early Education Programs/Althea Penn – 1st ed.
p.cm.
Includes biographical references.
School management and organization – United States.
School supervision –Unites States.

Attention corporations, universities, colleges, and professional organizations: Quantity discounts are available on bulk purchases of this book for educational, gift purposes, or as premiums for increasing magazine subscriptions or renewals. Special books or book excerpts can be created to fit specific needs. For further information, please contact Althea Penn, Penn Consulting (Training and Publishing) at apenn@pennconsuting.org.

Copyright © 2014 Penn Consulting (Training and Publishing)
All rights reserved.
ISBN-13: 978-1500631178
ISBN-10: 1500631175

Effective Planning and Administration of Early Education Programs

Introduction

This manual will provide the information and encouragement necessary for early childhood education professionals to implement a high quality educational program for young children (birth through age twelve). As professional development, the course is approved for program administrators and early childhood educators pursuant to the University of Georgia's training approval contract, Bright from the Start: Georgia Department of Early Care and Learning, and Georgia Department of Education's Office of Professional Learning. This course fulfills the forty hour training requirement for program administrators and teachers of early care and education and school-age care programs. It also meets the competency goals and indicators set forth in Rules and Regulations for Day Care Centers 290-2-2-09. (2014) Participants demonstrate an application of effective school leadership behaviors and practices that support proficiency in all of the Georgia Department of Education's School Keys of Excellence. Course assessments utilize the Georgia Leader Keys Performance Appraisal System leading to individual professional growth goals. The manual accompanies the online or classroom face-to-face training. Any owner, board member, administrative staff member (e.g. Principal, Director, Afterschool coordinator, Extended Care Supervisor, summer enrichment Program Coordinator, Bookkeeper, Administrative Director, Athletic Program Director, and so forth), or program supervisor that makes decisions needs to complete the course. Upon completion participants receive a Georgia program administration credential.

The primary course objective is to equip participants with child care program planning and administration knowledge and skills (e.g. licensing, legal issues, child development, developmentally appropriate practices, marketing, budget, maintenance, staff development, parental/community relations, ethics, professionalism, diversity) in order to improve the quality of educational programs for young children. Programs which use the model provided will be structured to meet National Health and Safety Performance Standards for Educational Settings (2012) which are provided by the American Academy of Pediatrics (as well as the accreditation standards of most organizations (e.g. Southern association of Colleges and Schools (SACS), National Association for the Education of Young Children (NAEYC), and the Association of Christian Schools International (ACSI)).

About the author

This course is facilitated by Althea Penn, of Penn Consulting (Training and Publishing). Penn Consulting is a full service education consultation organization that provides professional and organizational development services. Althea has a passion for children and those who serve them. She has over thirty years of experience in education and early education management serving as a teacher, Children's Ministry pastor, and principal. She has earned a Masters degree in Education Administration, certification as an Early Childhood Educator, and the National Administrator Credential. This well-rounded background equips her to share with fellow educators as she regularly conducts high quality early childhood professional development seminars and leadership workshops. Althea is an inspirational communicator and has served as a conference speaker for *The Georgia Preschool Association, the National Black Child Development Institute, Kid's Advocacy Coalition, Quality Care for Children, The Association of Christian Schools International* and other organizations which share her passion for children and her colleagues. As an educational consultant she has trained thousands of board members, owners, and program directors of preschools and private schools. She has also provided guidance in the accreditation (NAEYC, SACS, GAC, and ACSI) and licensing process.

Althea also holds a Bachelor of Applied Science in Organizational Leadership degree. As an Organization Development Practitioner (ODP), she designs and delivers strategic interventions to organizations interested in creating high performing, inclusive, and culturally effective workplaces. This includes drafting legal documents (articles of incorporation, bylaws, and the like.), business plans, grants, handbooks (parent and personnel), administrative forms, websites, brochures, and so forth. Her insight helps achieve long-term, sustainable change by working at all levels of an organization. As a coach, she supports leaders and individuals in discovering and aligning people, performance, and payoffs for results in their personal and professional lives. She is married to her best friend and high school sweetheart. They are the parents of two beautiful daughters who have also become certified educators. You can usually find her curled up with a book and her grandchildren.

This course is facilitated by Althea Penn, M. Ed.Adm., N.A.C., PDS, ODP, and Educational Consultant.

Table of Contents

- Introduction 3
- About the author 4
- Administrative Professional Development Learning Objectives and Competencies 8
- Course materials 8
- Registration 8
- Course procedures 9
- Syllabus - Course Outline 12
- Session 1 The School Leader and Program Philosophy 14
- My Purpose 14
- Minimum Qualifications of the Program Director 21
- Director's School Year Task Time Line 23
- NAEYC Code of Ethical Conduct and Statement of Commitment 27
- Professional Ethics: Applying The NAEYC Code 37
- Session 2 Principles of Child Growth and Development 39
- Stages of Child Development 43
- Writing your personal philosophy of education statement 53
- Sample Developmental History and Background Information Form 54
- Child Care Programs and Philosophy of Early Childhood Education 57
- Child Care In The U.S.: A Brief History 60
- Common Characteristics of High Quality Early Childhood Education Programs 65
- Session 3 Strategic Planning 66
- Business Plan 66
- Developing a Parent Handbook or Family Manual 69
- Sample Parent Orientation Agenda 70
- Session 4 Programs for Infants and Toddlers (birth through three years of age) 72
- Sample equipment list 77
- Vendors 79
- Session 5 Programs for Preschool Students (three to five years of age) 80
- Playground Grants 83
- List of curriculum providers 83
- Session 6 Programs for School-age children (five to twelve years of age) 84
- Common elements 84
- The Afterschool Alliance 85
- Marketing 86
- Sample Daily Schedules 88
- Toddler Daily Schedule (13 months to 35 months) 89
- Extended Care Daily Schedule 91
- Federal Copyright Act 94
- Session 7 Recruiting and Hiring Staff 95
- Minimum credential recommendations 95
- Substitute Employees 96
- Students in Training 97
- Personnel Policies 99
- Federal and state employment laws 100
- Employment Law 104
- Insurance 104
- Staff Records 109
- Reference Checks 110
- Job Offer Letter 114
- Sample Job Announcement and Application/Selection Process 117

Employment Agreement 118
Supervision and Evaluation 118
Discipline-suspension and termination 119
Grievance Procedures 120
Wage Conversion Table 121
Attendance 122
Orientation 123
Child Abuse and Neglect Prevention 125
Session 8 Supervising and Developing Staff 127
Professional Development Plan 130
Session 9 Recruiting, Training, and Supervising Interns and Volunteers 132
Parent volunteers 132
Student interns 132
Teacher aides 132
Session 10 Budget 134
Sample Budget Form 136
Operating Budget Worksheet 137
Funding Agencies 138
Session 11 Maintenance, Health and Safety 141
Injury control precautions 141
Playground Safety 143
Selecting an Appropriate Sanitizer 145
Sample Emergency Procedures 146
First Aid Kits 148
Avoid plant poisoning 148
Animals in educational settings 149
Transportation Safety 149
Common Childhood Illnesses Detection and Prevention 152
Cleaning Up Body Fluids 153
Choking Hazards 204
Recognizing and Reporting Child Abuse and Neglect 205
Types of Abuse 206
Child Care Safety Checklist 208
Session 12 Food and Nutrition Services 210
Session 13 New School Year Checklist 215
Internet Resources 215
Session 14 Family and Community Involvement 218
Session 15 Accreditation and Networking 222
Professional Development Course Evaluation 227
References 228

© 2014 Penn Consulting

Effective Planning and Administration of Early Education Programs

This forty clock hour training meets the following **Bright from the Start: Georgia Department of Early Care and Learning (DECAL) Director's Training Requirements**:

It reflects state (DECAL) rules and regulations for early learning centers specific to director responsibilities and facility management

It promotes effective communication, interpersonal skills, and good rapport between program director, parents, and staff

It enhances business management skills and legal knowledge of the program director

It educates and equips the program director on how to define, research, identify, and implement various types of resources

It enhances leadership abilities, child, family and staff advocacy, and the promotion of ethical guidelines in the work place

It promotes sound fiscal management practices and oversight under a program director's control

It promotes a basic knowledge of child development and developmentally appropriate best practices based upon scientific research

It addresses diversity and linguistic awareness in the learning center *(documents published in different languages)*

It empowers the director to offer support and skills to assist parents or guardians with providing quality care for children

Administrative Professional Development Learning Objectives and Competencies:
Demonstrate the skills and knowledge necessary to coordinate an effective child development program. ADM-1

Demonstrate the ability to develop (business, personnel and parent/child) policies and procedures and effectively communicate them to parents, staff and community. ADM-2

Complete a feasibility study and plan for marketing their program in the community at large. ADM-3

Demonstrate knowledge of employment law in developing personnel policies, systems, and the ability to articulate the rights of the employee and the rights of the employer. ADM-4

Demonstrate knowledge of facility management regulations which meet state and national safety standards. ADM-5

Demonstrate legal knowledge regarding regulatory standards, custody issues, mandated reporting, confidentiality, labor, and anti-discrimination laws. ADM-6

Improve public relation skills and develop community collaboration. ADM-7

Develop a financial plan including a start-up budget and three year projection, in addition to reviewing various accounting methods. ADM-8

Develop relationships with organizations which encourage professional development and a long term professional development plan. ADM-9

The Professional Development Competencies were developed by the Georgia Childhood Care and Education Professional Development System, a project of the Georgia Association on Young Children and the Collaborative Leadership Team, funded (in part) by the Bright from the Start through the federal Child Care and Development Block Grant.

Course materials: Materials provided may be copied, unless otherwise noted, for use within the individual center setting. Charts and graphs may be altered to suit the needs of the center. Copyrighted materials include the information needed to request permission or the limitations on their usage. Students will need to download the Director's Training manual. They may also purchase an Administrative Toolkit with form templates on CD at www.pennconsulting.org. The paperback book Early Education Program Administration Toolkit: is available at www.amazon.com.
Participants seeking accreditation by NAEYC or ACSI will need the following optional supplies: 2"
Presentation Binder/Notebook   12 Section Divider Tabs
File Folders (25 minimum)   Portable File Folder Bin File Folder Labels

Registration: Program administrators may view the class schedule or register for the online or classroom (face-to-face) class at www.pennconsulting.org.

© 2014 Penn Consulting

Course procedures: (for Directors that are completing the online or classroom course)
It is recommended that students have good basic academic skills or enroll in basic skills courses to work on improving their reading, writing, and math skills. Students should be confident about computer (Microsoft Office: Word and PowerPoint, accessing Adobe PDF files) and study skills. Students will need access to a computer, email, and the Internet for forty hours. All assignments are submitted online. Internet access through a JavaScript enabled web browser (i.e. Mozilla Firefox 3.0 or higher, etc.) is necessary.

Class Attendance: Students must document 40 clock hours of formal child care administrative education, in the 15 subject matter areas. In order to receive a certificate of completion students must complete all assignments. There are no makeup assignments. The online course is self-paced and all assignments are due within six weeks of admission to class.

Withdrawals: A student may withdraw her/himself at any time, however, the registration fee is nonrefundable and nontransferable. Child development instructors may choose to withdraw a student if the student does not meet the course requirements. Students are urged to consult with their instructor or an advisor before making schedule changes.

Incompletes: An incomplete means that there are extenuating circumstances which have prevented you from completing the class within the indicated time-frame. *An "I" will be given upon the request of the student only if at least 50% of course work has been completed in a satisfactory manner.* You will then have a limited amount of time to complete the course requirements. An automatic F results when the course is not completed as agreed upon.

Professional behavior: in all respects is expected. You are in a professional training program designed to train you to become a top professional in the field. Courtesy and respect should be shown toward colleagues and the instructor. In this class students are expected to use proper web course Netiquette (a word that is a combination of Inter*net* and et*iquette*). This means that the students in this class will be courteous and use common sense while posting or emailing assignments or projects. If a student violates the netiquette code, he/she may be removed from the class.

The following web etiquette procedures apply for all students:
1. Submit your own work (postings, attachments, assignments). Plagiarism will not be tolerated and will result in a failing grade. You may not submit another program's handbooks, brochures, or business plan.
2. Avoid typing in all caps. In this class, typing in caps means that you're screaming or shouting.
3. Avoid inserting pictures or colors to your postings or attachments unless the professor requires it. This increases the size of the file, and it is too difficult for some students to open large files.
4. Treat the *Discussion Forum* as a serious communication tool. Post data that is relevant to the item up for discussion.
5. Post directly to the *Discussion Forum*. Do not submit attachments to the *Discussion Forum (unless requested by the instructor)*. Attachments are only used for submitting assignments to the professor.
6. Read the syllabus several times in order to determine due dates for all readings, assignments, and/or quizzes.
7. Check emails **often** for updates, changes and clarifications.
8. Complete all assignments by the due dates.
9. Complete all assignments regardless of computer problems.

Work Standards: Any work not turned in or presented within six weeks of class start date will not be accepted. Any written work must be typed in at least a 12 point font, proofread [spelling and word usage errors will negatively affect the project grade] double-spaced, well-written, and neat. All work is expected on the specified date and time. Sources must be cited in all assignments using the APA (American Psychological Association) style. Please refer to the Purdue Online Writing Laboratory for further information. http://owl.english.purdue.edu/owl/resource/560/01/

Disability statement: Penn consulting is committed to the equal and excellent education of all students including students with disabilities. In compliance with Section 504 of the Rehabilitation Act of 1973 and the Americans with Disabilities Act of 1990, "otherwise qualified" students with disabilities are protected from discrimination and may be entitled to certain reasonable accommodations intended to ensure equal access to higher education. All students requiring accommodations must provide appropriate documentation of their disability that supports the need for the requested accommodations. Students requiring accommodations for a disability should inform the instructor at the close of the first day of class or as soon as possible.

Student Assessment: Students are assessed using the following methods:
- Competency based practical applications:

Writing a business plan
Conducting a feasibility study
Preparing a one year budget (three, five, and ten year projections are recommended)
Designing a parent and personnel handbook
Writing a job description
Writing a job announcement
Diagramming an organizational chart
Downloading required Department of Labor Posters (minimum wage, OSHA, unemployment insurance, etc.)
Planning Daily Class Schedules
Planning one week of menus
- Open-ended essay discussion questions
- Student activity and/or observations with written feedback

Honor Policy: Academic integrity is maintained through the Honor System. The Honor System imposes on each student the responsibility for his or her own honest deportment and assumes the corollary responsibility that each one will report any violations of the Honor Code about which he or she has information.

Academic dishonesty includes the following examples, as well as similar conduct aimed at making false representation with respect to academic performance:
1. Cheating on an examination.
2. Collaborating with others in work to be presented, all work must be completed by the student.
3. Plagiarizing, including the submission of others' ideas or papers, whether purchased, borrowed, or otherwise obtained, as one's own. When direct quotations are used in themes, essays, documents, and other similar work, they must be acknowledged according to the APA style of documentation. This does not include templates or sample policies provided by the instructor.
4. Stealing examination or course materials.
5. Falsifying records, laboratory results, or other data.
6. Submitting, if contrary to the rules of a course, work previously presented in another course.
7. Knowingly and intentionally assisting another student in any of the above, including assistance in an arrangement whereby any work, classroom performance, examination, or other activity is submitted or performed by a person other than the student under whose name the work is submitted or performed. **Any suspected infraction of the above Honor Code may result in dismissal from the training program.**

Additional Policies
1. A professional support system is in place to ensure teacher success in delivering the online course and students have access to training and /or information to assist them in navigating the online environment
2. as well as access to technical assistance via www.collaborizeclassroom.com. The support team is available to provide technical assistance between 8:00 AM and 5:00 PM Pacific Time, Monday through Friday (excluding major holidays). Students must have basic computer skills with Microsoft Word, PowerPoint, Adobe PDF, etc.

3. The online teacher provides appropriate feedback, guidance, and direction and responds to student inquiries within 24 hours (M-F)

4. Student and teacher dialogue online in the collaborize classroom (online platform), questions and discussions are encouraged throughout the course.

5. Throughout the course, the teacher regularly conducts discussion-based assessments with students. These conversations occur regularly in the course and are part of the assessments and grading for each session. This teacher/student discussion provides opportunity for students to share what they have learned, to demonstrate mastery of the content, and provide the opportunity to verify the authenticity of the student's work. The instructor possesses extensive classroom and administrative experience. Her expertise will be used as a guide in identifying the level of originality in student work. Students will also sign an honor code.

We suggest strongly that you download and set up the Mozilla Firefox browser for this purpose only. We have found that this browser works best with our system. If you are in the US, go to this link http://www.mozilla.com/en-US/firefox/.

If you do not want the browser in English, go to this link and choose your language: http://www.mozilla.com/en-US/firefox/all.html.
When you download, a pop-up should ask you if you want to run, save or cancel. Choose **RUN**. Continue through the steps of downloading and installing Firefox. It might ask if you want to make Firefox your default browser. Usually the answer is **no** if you use Internet Explorer for all other searching. **If you are successful, the Firefox icon should appear on your desktop.**

Effective Planning and Administration of Early Education Programs

Syllabus - Course Outline
1. The School Leader and Program Philosophy: Session one reviews the crucial role of transformational leadership in the quality of educational organizations. We will review the professional competencies recommended by the United States Department of Education and the National Association for the Education of Young Children, in addition to the standards required by Bright from the Start (DECAL). Directors will review the history of early childhood education; examine milestones of development for children; and how the principles of child growth and development relate to the various theories of child development.
2. Methods, Activities, Programs, and Practices (MAPP): Program administrators will review legal structures, the various types of centers and the Bright from the Start rules and regulations which govern licensing such as ratios, discipline, etc. Participants will draft a business plan based upon the philosophy and mission statement of their program.
3. Strategic Planning: Participants will develop a draft of a parent handbook based upon Bright from the Start regulations, ethical business practices and set goals for implementation of their business plan.
4. Programs for Infants and Toddlers (birth through three years of age): Participants will review NAEYC guidelines for developmentally appropriate practices for infants and toddlers and develop daily class schedules, classroom layouts and equipment purchase requisitions (esp. discipline and exclusions policies).
5. Programs for Preschool (Three to five years of age): In session five, participants will review various curriculum models, NAEYC guidelines for developmentally appropriate practices for preschool age children and develop daily class schedules, classroom layouts and equipment purchase requisitions (esp. discipline and exclusions policies).
6. Programs for School-age children (Five to twelve years of age): Participants will review requirements for a cognitively and socially engaging school age care program. We will develop a program appropriate for each age group including equipment and supplies, daily schedule, marketing material (flyer, postcard and brochure using Microsoft Office publisher templates)
7. Recruiting and Hiring Staff: Participants will review sample job descriptions and staffing models. We will develop recruitment, interviewing, screening, and hiring policies and discuss staff retention factors. We will discuss Georgia Department of Labor and OSHA employee and employer rights. Participants will review the Bright from the Start Applications and Criminal Records Check Applications.
8. Supervising and Developing Staff: Participants will review Bright from the Start training requirements and contrast those with accreditation standards. Participants will review sample staff evaluation instruments and procedures. Participants will outline a professional development plan and organizational chart.
9. Recruiting, Training, and Supervising Interns and Volunteers: Participants will review and develop job descriptions for student teachers and volunteers. We will also design teacher/staff recruitment brochures or flyers. Participants will use the internet to find professional development opportunities and develop a personnel handbook draft.

10. Budgeting Basics: Participants will review recommendations for start-up and annual budgets and how to estimate monthly cash flow in order to make projections and complete the accompanying budget form. The group will also discuss funding sources (e.g. the various state and federal grants available) and review Bright from the Start's grant application.
11. Maintenance, Health and Safety: Participants will develop an Emergency Plan of Action and Exclusion Policies based upon Bright from the Start's recommendation and Model Child Care Policy recommendations by the American Academy of Pediatrics. Participants will contact local emergency care provider for letter indicating services provided. Participants will develop floor and site plans along with plans for facility maintenance. Participants will utilize internet resources to assist with classroom design.
12. Food and Nutrition Services: Participants will review USDA Food Service Guidelines and budgeting recommendations. We will review Bright from the Start and the Board of Health food preparation guidelines. Interested participants will complete Bright from the Start Nutrition Program Applications. Students will complete menus, shopping lists and a budget for the first month.
13. New School Year Checklist: Participants will complete the Bright form the Start licensing operation plan and develop necessary forms (i.e. employment application packets and new hire forms including W-4, G-4, I-9, health assessment, etc., Curriculum overview, class schedules, Health policies, Fee schedules and children's records forms). Participants will develop recruitment and enrollment procedure; and plan Parent and Staff Orientations based upon Bright from the Start requirements.
14. Family and Community Involvement: In session fourteen participants will discuss ways to communicate the vision to parents and the community, empowering parents through involvement. Students will review advisory board bylaws and develop family and parent education programs. Students will develop and review handbooks and marketing materials.
15. Accreditation and Networking: Participants will review child care related websites, periodicals, software and institutional assessment (self-study) tools, including Bright from the Start's self-study.

Session 1 The School Leader and Program Philosophy
My Purpose
Icebreaker Activity

An important key to any successful journey is to start with the end in mind. This is true whether the journey is something like a long planned vacation or like the initiation of a new business enterprise or restructuring of an existing business. A vision is the concept of what you really want your school to be and achieve. It captures the imagination of the leader and provides a focus for efforts. An educational organization's mission describes what the business does and what client it serves. A mission is more specific than the vision in that it establishes the guidelines of how the business fulfills its vision. The vision and mission are supported by core values.

Core values are what support the vision, shape the culture and reflect what the educational organization values. They are the essence of the school's identity – the principles, beliefs or philosophy of values. Many program administrators focus mostly on the technical early education or management competencies but often forget the underlying competencies that make it all run smoothly — core values. Establishing strong core values provides both internal and external advantages to the organization and its stakeholders (students, parents, staff, community leaders, and others).

Take a moment to review the following vision and mission statement. Notice the characteristics of a mission (reflects purpose, goals, objectives and values of your organization, brief) and vision (influences decisions, fosters commitment & understanding, narrows focus) statement. Notice the guiding principles of the organization as well. Answer the questions below and share your statements with the class.

Sample statements of Children's Healthcare of Atlanta
Mission
To enhance the lives of children through excellence in patient care, research and education.

Vision
To be the model for addressing children's health needs by defining, then providing or advocating for: accessible, innovative and excellent patient care; integrated teaching and research; and partnerships in wellness and prevention programs.

Values *(Core beliefs which drive your program mission and vision.)*

Integrity - Being honest, ethical and committed to all we do

Respect - Appreciating all people, work and ideas

Nurturing - Fostering the care, growth and development of the individual

Excellence - Delivering the highest level of care and service

Teamwork - Working together to achieve our goals.

Take a look at a few vision statements from child care programs and schools. Identify key words that indicate a vision that is supported by core values and program goals:

1. Vision statement: Crème is not your typical child care or preschool, but rather an early learning center designed to make the most of the windows of opportunity in a child's brain development for math, science, music, art, second language acquisition and other subjects.

2. Mission statement: We exist to deliver innovative, high quality education services for children in partnership with parents, schools, and communities in order to inspire the love of learning through engaging programs and unique opportunities. Believing that we are accountable, we conduct ourselves with integrity and foster a collaborative, respectful environment which leads to growth for our clients, our company, and our employees.
3. Where lifetime learning begins.®

Sample Goals: In the toddler program, we build on skills learned in the infant program and provide a safe and happy environment for toddlers to become more independent. Problem solving, concept formation, cooperation and self-help skills are also introduced.

Consider the following questions when writing your statements:
Mission-
Consider the population to be served, what are their needs? What are the long term goals or desired results of your program?
What are your program's objectives or tasks you wish to accomplish? This concise list should include words such as support, provide, advocate, help, offer, and assist.
Who are your key team members?
What are their previous accomplishments?
Vision-
How will you reach your accomplishment?
List three to five characteristics you desire that your program reflect that will distinguish it from others (culture, staff, families, curriculum, governance and discipline policies).

Values-
Everyone has a personal philosophy of education which is based upon your personal values, list seven of yours. Your assumptions about the nature of the student, teacher and the educational process will greatly influence your program's goals and objectives.

Be as concise as possible 25 words or less.

Core values:

Mission statement:

Vision statement:

"The key to the ability to change is a **changeless sense of who you are, what you are about and what you value**." -Stephen R. Covey

Welcome to the wonderful world of early childhood education! Research indicates a program director's knowledge and skills have a strong correlation and direct impact on the quality and effectiveness of a program. A competent director possesses expertise in the following areas: Pedagogy, Business Management, Human Resources, Development, and Networking. Job responsibilities generally include, but are not limited to the following: Developing the overall mission, goals and philosophy of the program; Curriculum development, selection and implementation; Establishing and maintaining financial budgets, policies, fundraising and records, including invoicing parents, payroll; Recruiting, screening, training, scheduling, supervision and evaluation of instructional and administrative personnel; Facility management; and Developing partnerships with parents and the community. Program directors may have different roles and responsibilities which are determined by the program's type and/or sponsorship.

Every program is as unique as the individuals administering the program, your philosophy or beliefs about the learning process, the nature of the learner, the instructional process and the role of parents will determine your program's goals and objectives. It is important that you consider the purpose for your program and the influence you wish to have upon society. This manual will support your efforts to define the methods, activities, programs and practices you plan to implement, as well as greatly improve the quality of your program. We will review current research and sources of information that will be helpful in planning a successful program.

It is a good idea to assess your leadership skills and knowledge to determine the staff and resources needed to complement your management style. We suggest two free online personal leadership style assessment tools which will help you to identify your strengths and weaknesses and understand your communication style. This information will help as you develop your leadership style and team. Visit either website www.crown.org. (personality i.d.) or www.injoy.com (REAL- relationship, equipping, attitude, and leadership).

Transformational leadership: "...occurs when one or more persons engage with others in such a way that leader, and followers raise one another to higher levels of motivation, and morality…" and is seen as a process by which change (transformation) is introduced to individuals and/or organizations. This view is fairly well supported in the more recent literature (Bennis and Nanus, 1985; Van Eron, 1995; Conger, 1989; Kouzes & Posner, 1995; Wheatley, 1994; Kent, Crotts, & Azziz, 2001) Transformational leadership promotes high achievement in every early education program stakeholder. Kouzes and Posner recommend transformational leadership practices which "leaders use to transform values into actions, visions into realities, obstacles into innovations, separateness into solidarity, and risks into rewards" (2007, p. 1). Their leadership challenge encourages: modeling the way, inspiring shared vision, challenging the process, enabling others to act, and encouraging the heart. Developing the people you serve should be a high priority. Strong individuals make strong families and contribute to strengthening organizations and communities.

Review the following article from The Education Resources Information Center (ERIC) (sponsored by the Institute of Education Sciences (IES) of the U.S. Department of Education), and contrast it with Bright from the Start's (DECAL) child care director's training and qualifications requirements and their impact upon the quality of programs.

Child Care Directors' Training and Qualifications. ERIC Digest.
ERIC Identifier: ED301363 **Publication Date:** 1988-00-00 **Author:** Jorde-Bloom, Paula

The director's role in the early childhood center is central and complex. While there is agreement about the need for highly trained personnel to serve as directors, there is a surprising lack of agreement about directors' training and minimum qualifications. This digest provides an overview of the competencies needed for effective center administration and summarizes state regulations governing minimum qualifications.

THE MULTIFACETED ROLE OF THE CHILD CARE DIRECTOR

The skills and competencies needed to effectively administer a child care center vary according to the age and background of the children enrolled, the services provided, the philosophical orientation of the program, the local sponsorship of the center, and program size. Directors of very small programs may have few administrative tasks and may serve as a classroom teacher part of the day, while directors of large programs may have to coordinate multiple sites and funding sources and a large staff. Researchers and teachers agree that four major task performance areas are encompassed in the director's role:

ORGANIZATION, LEADERSHIP AND MANAGEMENT. Directors are expected to:
* assess program needs,
* articulate a clear vision,
* implement goals,
* evaluate program effectiveness,
* recruit, train, and supervise staff,
* translate program goals into well-written policies and procedures,
* know about leadership styles and group behavior,
* understand their professional identity and responsibility,
* be alert to changing demographics, social and economic trends, and developments in the field.

CHILD DEVELOPMENT AND EARLY CHILDHOOD PROGRAMMING. Directors need to: assess each child's needs and assist staff in planning developmentally appropriate experiences. Their organizational skills can be used to implement effective systems to keep track of enrollment, attendance, and anecdotal data. Directors need to understand:
* developmental patterns in early childhood and their implications for child care,
* environmental psychology and the arrangements of space and materials that support development,
* health, safety, and nutrition in care programs.

FISCAL AND LEGAL CONSIDERATIONS. Directors are expected to:
know federal, state, and local regulations governing child care centers, and be able to develop a budget, set tuition rates, prepare financial reports, maintain insurance coverage, and use fundraising and grantsmanship to secure funding from various sources.

BOARD, PARENT, AND COMMUNITY RELATIONS. Directors need to be able to:
* articulate a rationale for program practices to the advisory board, owner, or sponsor,
* interpret child development for parents and others in the community,
* regularly contact professional organizations, congressional representatives, public schools, the media, community service and other groups,
* understand the dynamics of family life,
* be aware of community resources that can support efforts in marketing and in serving parents.

STATE REGULATIONS GOVERNING MINIMUM QUALIFICATIONS

There are no federal regulations governing the qualifications of directors. Standards are mainly determined by state regulatory bodies. In most states, regulation of child care personnel is tied to center licensing and falls under the auspices of the Department of Public Welfare or the state's equivalent to the Department of Child and Family Social Services. Among states, regulations for almost every requirement differ with striking diversity (Morgan, 1987). The regulations are neither consistent nor specific.

Requirements for child care personnel are not uniformly regulated, as are requirements for entry into primary education positions (Berk, 1985). Some states do not differentiate personnel roles in child care settings, and place directors in the broad category of "child worker". Others define a second level of teacher more highly qualified in child development than other teachers, but do not necessarily designate this person to fill the role of director. States that set requirements for directors often use quite different terms to define the director's role.

BACKGROUND QUALIFICATIONS. The minimum age for directors is set at 18 or 21 in most states. Some states require demonstrated proficiency in basic literacy skills. In 9 states, directors are not required to have any relevant qualifying education. Several states require high school education, but only if the centers employ someone else to be responsible for programmatic aspects (Morgan, 1987). Directors are required to be well-qualified in child development in 26 states, and 10 require substantial coursework. Only 6 states require directors to have had courses in administration. Ongoing training for directors is required by 12 states (Morgan, 1987).

EXPERIENCE AND FORMAL EDUCATION QUALIFICATIONS. In the past, states often equated a year of experience with a year of college. But research has shown that education in early childhood or child development has a far stronger positive impact than years of experience on teacher behavior and student achievement. States are increasingly linking levels of experience to formal educational requirements.

CURRENT LEVELS OF TRAINING AND EXPERIENCE

Child care directors are overwhelmingly (88-92%) female. They are experienced, averaging over 9 years in the field of early childhood. The baccalaureate is held by 78%, and 38% have a master's or doctorate. The level of formal training appears to have increased in the last 15 years.

Child care directors are typically promoted to their positions from the ranks of teachers. Of the directors Norton and Abramowitz (1981) surveyed, 78% were head teachers or assistant directors before they assumed their positions. Interest and experience, rather than formal training, seem to be the primary criteria for promotion. Directors with concentrated course work in child care management are rare. Most have put together a patchwork of coursework, in-service professional development, and on-the-job training. Only recently have intensive graduate programs in child care administration appeared (Jorde-Bloom, 1987; Manburg, 1984).

CONCLUSION

Current trends reflect awareness of the importance of the child care director. Several states are making a concerted effort to increase minimum qualifications. A tendency toward professionalization is emerging. Directors are receiving more education, increasing participation in professional organizations, and using training opportunities to increase their expertise in administration.

Copyright information: ERIC Digests are in the public domain and may be freely reproduced and disseminated in any format. On the Web, it is permissible to link to Digests or to post copies on other sites without express permission. Text from ERIC Digests on this site are in the public domain and may be used however you like. -funded by the Office of Educational Research and Improvement (OERI), of the U.S. Department of Education (ED).

The leadership role played by the program director is critical. Administrators wear many different hats during the school day, but the most effective school leaders are not only managers and disciplinarians but also instructional leaders for the learning community. Successful program directors provide a common vision of what good instruction looks like, support teachers with the help and resources they need to be effective in their classrooms, and monitor the performance of teachers and students, with an eye always on the overall goal—to create school cultures or environments in which all children can achieve to their full potential. The program administrator must demonstrate competency in each of the four major task areas discussed above.

Organization leadership and management: All stakeholders (parents, students, volunteers, community leaders and the like) should have in hand the objectives for the program clearly documented and easy to follow. Expectations for each professional should be clearly documented and easily understood. Class procedures should be decided by the lead teachers with the administration having approved. Schedules for additional activities being led by specialty teachers should be precise and create a smooth transition from one part of the children's day to the next. An administrator should make sure all policies and procedures are clearly defined in a manual that is easily accessible to teachers, including an emergency manual. These manuals should be reviewed prior to a school year beginning, making sure there are no doubts or confusion amongst staff members as to their roles and what is expected of them. Orientation should be provided for parents, students, and volunteers.

Leadership should be what defines an administrator. Anything an administrator expects of their staff must be supported by the administrator with a willingness to give support in any way necessary. An administrator doesn't have to be the expert on each subject (like teaching an algebra class or specific age group), however, an administrator must be able to give guidance on how to approach various types of learning styles, provide advice on discipline, provide guidance for teachers of exceptional learners (esp. students with disabilities or atypical development). This support should be embraced with positive encouragement and compliments whenever possible. An administrator should be willing to eagerly step into unexpected situations and fill gaps immediately. A leader must rise above the emotion of situations and offer answers and advice with confidence and certainty.

A transformational school leader is also able to conduct a SWOT analysis at any given time in the school year and make the necessary changes. A SWOT analysis is an institutional assessment tool that identifies the **s**trengths, **w**eaknesses, **o**pportunities and **t**hreats of an educational organization. Specifically, SWOT is a strategic planning model that assesses what an organization can and cannot do as well as its potential opportunities and threats. The method of SWOT analysis is to take the information from an environmental analysis and separate it into internal (strengths and weaknesses) and external issues (opportunities and threats). Once this is completed, the leader uses the SWOT analysis to determine what actions (or changes) may assist the school in accomplishing its objectives, and what obstacles must be overcome or minimized to achieve desired results.

Child Development and Early Childhood Programming: Directors are to help staff facilitate the planning and implementation of different yet age, need and developmentally appropriate activities, learning methods, and daily routines for children. They help to create environments and room layout that are age appropriate and engaging with a blend of learning and play experiences for the developmental stage and age group of each class. They are responsible to see to it that materials are age appropriate and in their proper location for each class. They ensure the safety of the center in the classrooms, on the playground or anyplace a child might be while in their care. It is also their responsibility to see to it that children are served well-balanced and appetizing meals. It is the director's job to make sure all learning experiences and environments are accommodating to each child's individual needs.

*[Handwritten note: 5 c's of program mgmt.
1 – character
2 – caring
3 – commitment
4 – confidence
5 – communication]*

© 2014 Penn Consulting

Fiscal and Legal Considerations: Directors must be knowledgeable of the state, local and federal laws governing their center and employees. They must be able to plan, budget and maintain a fiscally fit organization, perform the required financial bookkeeping and payroll functions, generate the reports from bookkeeping and for payroll reporting as well as payment of payroll taxes. It is also their responsibility to ensure insurance coverage is up to date. Knowledge of grants or other funding sources is a possible Director responsibility. An administrator should research and globally communicate with others in the field to become well versed and familiar with various programs so the program that will best suit your community needs will be in place. Flexibility is necessary for any program to be successful as no program can be cookie cutter perfect. One must be able to see the strengths and weaknesses of the program and evaluate how it is meeting the needs of your community. Once this evaluation is complete, changes should be considered and implemented when there is a certainty that this change is in the best interest of the program's goals. All legal matters pertaining to the building, the land and the program are an administrator's responsibility. It is important to know all the appropriate resources for obtaining and becoming familiar with federal and state labor laws, licensing regulations, and health and safety standards.

While the administrator is responsible for the financial obligations of the program and the annual budget, if one is not comfortable with numbers they must secure a board of directors that is willing to work side by side with them to secure an appropriate and viable budget for the program. Working together as a team with an understanding that priorities will be governed by the administrator, will ensure that this method works.

Board, Parent & Community Relations: Directors should be able to communicate with parents in relation to the care given to and proper for their child. They should be familiar with and able to communicate with the media, government officials, local businessmen, other schools or groups of people regarding the center. Having a good understanding of how to present the center and what to keep confidential is a must. Communicating with the community and parents on a weekly or monthly basis empowers both parents and stakeholders to feel included and knowledgeable about their school. When people feel a part of something and when they feel their being a part matters to those at the helm, it creates a strong relationship consisting of respect, confidence and support.

Minimum Qualifications of the Program Director
Georgia Bright from the Start (DECAL) Rules and Regulations: 591-1-1-.31 Staff.
Director.
A center must have a director who is responsible for the supervision, operation and maintenance of the center. The director must be on the center's premises. If the director is absent from the center at any time during the hours of the center's operation, there shall be an officially designated person on the center site to assume responsibility for the operation of the center, and this person shall have full access to all records required to be maintained under these rules.
Qualifications of Director. The director must meet the minimum qualifications listed below:
Be at least twenty-one (21) years of age;
Possess at least one of the following sets of minimum academic requirements and qualifying child care experience at the time of employment:
Child Development Associate (CDA) credential issued by the Council for Professional Recognition;
Child Development and Related Care diploma from a vocational institute accredited by the Commission on Colleges of the SACS; or similar credential where the course of study includes an intensive practicum in child care as part of the curriculum and which is approved by the Department; and six months of exp;
Technical Certificate of Credit (TCC) in ECE or CD and six (6) months of experience;
Technical Certificate of Credit (TCC) in Infant and Toddler and six (6) months of experience;
Technical Certificate of Credit (TCC) in Program Administration and six (6) months experience;
Technical Certificate of Credit (TCC) in School Age and Youth Care and six (6) months of experience;
Technical College Diploma (TCD) in ECE or CD and six (6) months of experience;
Forty-hour (40) director training course approved by the Department and has been employed for a minimum of five (5) years as an on-site child care learning center director or as an on-site group day care home director;
Associate's degree in ECE or CD and six (6) months of qualifying child care experience;
Paraprofessional Certificate issued by the GA Professional Standards Commission and 6 months exp;
Twenty-five (25) quarter hours or fifteen (15) semester hours from an accredited college or university in ECE or CD and six (6) months of qualifying child care experience;
Bachelor's degree in a field other than ECE or CD and three (3) months of qualifying child care experience;
Bachelor's degree from an accredited college or university in ECE or CD;
Master's degree from an accredited college or university in ECE or CD;
Have current evidence of successful completion of a biennial training program in cardiopulmonary resuscitation (CPR) and a triennial training program in first aid provided by certified or licensed health care professionals and which covers the provision of emergency care to infants and children;
Participate in the orientation and training required by these rules;
Not be suffering from any physical handicap or mental health disorder that would interfere with the applicant's ability to perform adequately the job duties of providing for the care and supervision of the children enrolled in the center in accordance with these rules;
Never have been shown by credible evidence, e.g., a court or jury, a Department investigation or other reliable evidence to have abused, neglected or deprived a child or adult or to have subjected any person to serious injury as a result of intentional or grossly negligent misconduct. The Department may request an oral or written statement to this effect at the time of application or at any other time. Upon said request, the director or staff shall provide this statement to the Department;
Not have a criminal record; and
Not have made any material false statements concerning qualifications requirements either to the Department or to the proposed or current licensee or commission holder.
A copy and/or written verification of the credential or degree awarded to the director by the technical college, university, school or Department-approved trainer listed in 591-1-1-.31(1) (b) 3. (i) through (xiii)

National Association for the Education of Young Children (NAEYC) Minimum Qualifications for Directors:

In order to attain NAEYC accreditation, the director must demonstrate one of the following criteria:

1. BA and 9 hours of college-level coursework in administration, leadership or management and 24 hours of college-level course work in ECE, CD, elementary education or early childhood special education
2. Documents indicating a plan in place to meet the above qualifications within five years
3. Documents meeting an appropriate combination of formal education, work experience, and relevant training and credentials as outlined in the alternative pathways table (must score 100 points)

Source: NAEYC (n.d.). *Candidacy Requirements Related to Staff Qualifications.* Retrieved from http://www.naeyc.org/academy/pursuing/edquals/candidacy

In summary, Georgia has a much more varied path to becoming a director than NAEYC. In Georgia, education requirements range from a high school diploma with child care experience to a college degree. NAEYC requires a bachelor's degree as well as 24 credit hours in ECE/CD/EE/SE.

Most states require directors to have experience in early childhood education. Some states or employers require preschool and childcare center directors to have a nationally recognized certification such as the Child Development Associate (CDA) certification. The states that require advanced degrees have higher rankings in education at all levels.

Association of Christian Schools International (ACSI) Minimum Qualifications for Directors:

In order to attain ACSI accreditation, the K-12 chief administrator and all K-12 principals must hold an ACSI administrative certificate. (E/S)
Early Education Director: The director of the early education program has professional training as evidenced by having obtained a minimum of a bachelor's degree in early childhood education/child development (or its equivalent) from an accredited institution. The director must also demonstrate a working understanding of business practices as evidenced by nine credit hours of college course work in administration/business (or its equivalent). The coursework includes training in leadership development and supervision of adults.

Source: ACSI (n.d). *ACSI Accreditation Manual* Retrieved from http://www.acsiglobal.org/accreditation

Program Director Training and Qualifications Contrast Chart

ERIC Digest/NAEYC criteria	ACSI criteria	Bright from the Start (DECAL)

Reflect

Tabitha had been hired to direct a private preschool and elementary school program. After a few months under her direction, the staff began to complain to the board of directors. They felt Tabitha was not supportive and did not seem to know or even care what was happening in the classrooms. The chairman of the board was surprised since Tabitha had excellent recommendations from her previous positions. However, the board members knew that it had been difficult to find qualified directors for the schools and centers in the county and was reluctant to try to replace her.

An independent consultant was asked to spend two weeks working with Tabitha and the staff to try to resolve the problems. The consultant found that Tabitha spent very little time with teachers or in the classrooms. She was most often in her office situated behind the secretary's area.

1. What factors do you think might cause Tabitha to behave as described?
2. Can you suggest ways to help Tabitha?
3. Was the board right in hiring the consultant, or would you have done something different?

Director's School Year Task Time Line

To effectively manage a program, program administrators must juggle everything from budgeting to supervising food service. With tasks ranging from analyzing attendance data to handling high level student discipline issues under their umbrellas of responsibility, delegation proves an important leadership tool. If early education leaders don't effectively delegate responsibilities, they will become overburdened and bogged down, unable to complete any of their assigned tasks with much success. In order for everyone to reach their full potential, the leader should delegate responsibilities to competent individuals.

Directors complete a wide variety of tasks each year. The schedule depends on the center. In year-round centers, the budget/program year may begin in January. However, for many centers, the year begins in autumn when some children leave for kindergarten or first grade. Some directors find that enrollment is reduced in summer when older siblings may be available to care for young children. (Click & Karos, 2010)

Annual Tasks
Prior to Beginning of New Program Year

Prepare budget and get board approval (if needed).
Determine salaries for coming year.
Prepare staff contracts for coming year.
Assign teachers and children to groups and classrooms.
Interview substitutes and prepare sub list.
Recruit and orient volunteers.
Update policies and procedures.
Update marketing plan.
Confirm that all child and staff records are complete and up to date.
Order equipment and supplies.
Replace outmoded, underused, or faulty equipment.
Set up reminders on computer for renewal of the following:
Individual medical forms (child and staff)
Licenses (child care license, NAEYC accreditation renewal, food service, fire department license, first aid, communicable diseases, CPR, child abuse training, staff teaching licenses/certificates, bus driver's chauffeur's license, bus license)
Insurance coverage

Check supply of forms needed throughout year.
Arrange for extra services such as medical, dental, social services if these are to be provided.
Set up calendar for coming program year, including items such as:
Staff meetings and appreciation events
Staff supervision and conferences
Parent conferences
Parent meetings
Meetings with assistant director, educational coordinator, accountant, bookkeeper, other staff who assist with administration of center
Meetings with board of directors and with chairman
Meet with banker to discuss money saving products
Periodic maintenance (heating/air-conditioning, appliances, computers, bus, security system)
Preparation of proposals for ongoing funding, such as for Head Start and United Way, and for special funding
In-service training for self and staff
Confer with student teachers and college supervisors.
Attend courses, professional conferences, and workshops.
Participate in professional organizations.
Make arrangements for special activities for children and families.
Conduct open house for potential clients.
Cleanout files and emails.
Document passwords.
Turn past due accounts receivable over to collections.
Review business goals and adjust (marketing, profitability, and the like).
Cancel unread publications.

Beginning of Program Year
Place new equipment and supplies.
Arrange with colleges for student teachers.
Conduct opening parent meeting.

End of Program Year
Clean, repair, and inventory equipment and supplies.
Conduct staff evaluations.
Prepare self-evaluation.
Arrange for program evaluation (may be done biannually).
Check with creditors for better rates or discounts.
Check interest rates on credit cards and savings.
Assist teachers in evaluating children's progress and in holding parent conferences.
Recognize volunteers.
Prepare annual report.
Thoroughly check building and grounds for needed maintenance and arrange to have work done.

Monthly Tasks
Review budget.
Prepare financial reports.
Report to board of directors (if applicable).
Plan menus.
Order nonperishable food.
Order supplies.
Read professional journals.

Check building, grounds, and equipment and schedule required maintenance.
Review teachers' classroom plans (may be done weekly).
Review attendance records.
Prepare billing.
Make payments.
Complete forms required by funders.
Prepare family newsletter.
Conduct fire drill.
Backup computer files.
Scan and destroy (three year old) records that are archived.

Weekly Tasks
Prepare payroll.
Supervise staff (observe and confer).

Quite a few of the duties above can be delegated to an assistant director, bookkeeper, or the administrative assistant. That person can check records for expiration dates (e.g. immunization) and enrollment applications for critical data. The administrator should inspect these once a quarter or so. Qualified teachers may conduct peer weekly observations in addition to team leaders. An instructional supervisor or board member may help with performance evaluations. Although the program administrator or supervisor will conduct the annual appraisals, the administrator may use data collected from numerous sources throughout the school year. The bookkeeper could order supplies with specified vendors, a list of contact people, and pre-approved spending limits. Administrators are always accountable for their subordinate's actions; however, we must give them some ownership of or investment in the organization.

Identify and list tasks that can be delegated.

Commitment to Professionalism

Early childhood education is an interesting profession. To become an early childhood professional, educators will need education and training to provide them with the necessary skills, vocabulary, and concepts. In order to understand the field of early childhood education, you will also need to know something about its history. Because history is an important part of being socialized into a profession, teachers should carefully review early childhood education's past. Early educators must learn the language of the profession and understand how the profession is organized and regulated. Early childhood educators know what it means to behave in a professional manner. They understand the importance of confidentiality. They never talk about one family to another or spread gossip. They have an attitude that shows they take their profession seriously. They are dedicated to working with children and families, using the skills and knowledge they have gained through preparation and training. Interpretations of high quality child care differ from place to place. We must become more united as a profession and possibly requirement membership in professional organizations that promote professionalism.

Early childhood professionals are lifelong learners. They continually pursue professional development and create professional goals for themselves, using on-the-job evaluations and feedback, as well as self-assessment, to determine future directions for learning. They understand and follow the requirements set by Bright from the Start. They adhere to the adult-child ratios, group size, and space requirements determined to be minimum standards and realize that optimum or national standards are what they should strive for.

In an article titled "Early Childhood Education as an Emerging Profession: Ongoing Conversations," Stephanie Feeney and Nancy Freeman (2002) write of their attempts to define ethics as applied to early childhood education. Feeney first began studying ethics in the 1980's because she realized that ethics was important to a profession. While at the University of Hawaii she met Kenneth Kipnis and shared with him her interest in developing a statement of ethics.

He and other philosophers have been instrumental in helping early childhood educators understand how their profession is different from other occupations. Feeney learned that sociologists characterize their profession by the following criteria:

- "Requirements for entry, i.e. some selection procedure."
- "Specialized knowledge and expertise."
- "Prolonged training based on principles that involve professional judgment for their application."
- "Standards of practice that assure that every practitioner applies standard procedures in the exercise of professional judgment."
- "Distance from clients. Professionals don't 'get their hands dirty'—there are intermediaries who insulate them from those they serve and who act as gatekeepers limiting client's access to professional practice."
- "Commitment to a significant social value. The goal of a profession is altruistic; it is intended to meet a need in society, not to generate profit."
- "Recognition as the only group who can perform its societal function."
- "Autonomy—a profession makes its own standards, enforces itself."
- "A profession has a code of ethics. When society allows a profession to have a monopoly on a particular service they must be assured that the practitioners will behave in accordance to high moral standards. A code of ethics assures then that it will do so."

Feeney and Freeman have continued to discuss how the term professionalism applies to those who work in early childhood education. (Click and Karos, 2010)

REFERENCES
Feeney, S. (1995). Professionalism in early childhood teacher education: Focus on ethics. Journal of Early Childhood Teacher Education, 16(3),13-15.
Feeney, S. & Freemen, N.K., (2002). Early childhood education as an emerging profession: Ongoing conversations. Child Care Information Exchange, January/February, 38-41.
Katz, L.G. (1995). Talks with teachers of young children. Norwood, NJ: Ablex.
Stonehouse, A. (1994). Not just nice ladies. Castle Hill, New South Wales, Australia: Pademelon Press.

DISCUSSION
1. Is early childhood education a profession according to the above criteria? If so, why? If not, why not?
2. Which of the statements do you disagree with? Which do you agree with?
3. Compare this statement of professionalism with the NAEYC Code of Ethics.
4. Read the Feeney and Freemen article for their insights on early education as a profession.

NAEYC Code of Ethical Conduct and Statement of Commitment

A position statement of the National Association for the Education of Young Children
Revised April 2005

Core Values
Standards of ethical behavior in early childhood care and education are based on commitment to the following core values that are deeply rooted in the history of the field of early childhood care and education. We have made a commitment to
- Appreciate childhood as a unique and valuable stage of the human life cycle
- Base our work on knowledge of how children develop and learn
- Appreciate and support the bond between the child and family
- Recognize that children are best understood and supported in the context of family, culture, community, and society
- Respect the dignity, worth, and uniqueness of each individual (child, family member, and colleague)
- Respect diversity in children, families, and colleagues
- Recognize that children and adults achieve their full potential in the context of relationships that are based on trust and respect

Conceptual Framework
The Code sets forth a framework of professional responsibilities in four sections. Each section addresses an area of professional relationships: (1) with children, (2) with families, (3) among colleagues, and (4) with the community and society. Each section includes an introduction to the primary responsibilities of the early childhood practitioner in that context. The introduction is followed by a set of ideals (I) that reflect exemplary professional practice and a set of principles (P) describing practices that are required, prohibited, or permitted.

The ideals reflect the aspirations of practitioners. The principles guide conduct and assist practitioners in resolving ethical dilemmas. Both ideals and principles are intended to direct practitioners to those questions which, when responsibly answered, can provide the basis for conscientious decision making. While the Code provides specific direction for addressing some ethical dilemmas, many others will require the practitioner to combine the guidance of the Code with professional judgment.

The ideals and principles in this Code present a shared framework of professional responsibility that affirms our commitment to the core values of our field. The Code publicly acknowledges the responsibilities that we in the field have assumed and in so doing supports ethical behavior in our work. Practitioners who face situations with ethical dimensions are urged to seek guidance in the applicable parts of this Code and in the spirit that informs the whole. Often, "the right answer"-the best ethical course of action to take-is not obvious. There may be no readily apparent, positive way to handle a situation. When one important value contradicts another, we face an ethical dilemma. When we face a dilemma, it is our professional responsibility to consult the Code and all relevant parties to find the most ethical resolution.

Section I:
Ethical responsibilities to children
Childhood is a unique and valuable stage in the human life cycle. Our paramount responsibility is to provide care and education in settings that are safe, healthy, nurturing, and responsive for each child. We are committed to supporting children's development and learning; respecting individual differences; and helping children learn to live, play, and work cooperatively. We are also committed to promoting children's self-awareness, competence, self-worth, resiliency, and physical well-being.

Ideals
1. To be familiar with the knowledge base of early childhood care and education and to stay informed through continuing education and training.
2. To base program practices upon current knowledge and research in the field of early childhood education, child development, and related disciplines, as well as on particular knowledge of each child.
3. To recognize and respect the unique qualities, abilities, and potential of each child.
4. To appreciate the vulnerability of children and their dependence on adults.
5. To create and maintain safe and healthy settings that foster children's social, emotional, cognitive, and physical development and that respect their dignity and their contributions.
6. To use assessment instruments and strategies that are appropriate for the children to be assessed that are used only for the purposes for which they were designed, and that have the potential to benefit children.
7. To use assessment information to understand and support children's development and learning, to support instruction, and to identify children who may need additional services.
8. To support the right of each child to play and learn in an inclusive environment that meets the needs of children with and without disabilities.
9. To advocate for and ensure that all children, including those with special needs, have access to the support services needed to be successful.
10. To ensure that each child's culture, language, ethnicity, and family structure are recognized and valued in the program.
11. To provide all children with experiences in a language that they know, as well as support children in maintaining the use of their home language and in learning English.
12. To work with families to provide a safe and smooth transition as children and families move from one program to the next.

Principles
1. Above all, we shall not harm children. We shall not participate in practices that are emotionally damaging, physically harmful, disrespectful, degrading, dangerous, exploitative, or intimidating to children. This principle has precedence over all others in this Code.
2. We shall care for and educate children in positive emotional and social environments that are cognitively stimulating and that support each child's culture, language, ethnicity, and family structure.
3. We shall not participate in practices that discriminate against children by denying benefits, giving special advantages, or excluding them from programs or activities on the basis of their sex, race, national origin, religious beliefs, medical condition, disability, or the marital status/family structure, sexual orientation, or religious beliefs or other affiliations of their families. (Aspects of this principle do not apply in programs that have a lawful mandate to provide services to a particular population of children.)
4. We shall involve all those with relevant knowledge (including families and staff) in decisions concerning a child, as appropriate, ensuring confidentiality of sensitive information.
5. We shall use appropriate assessment systems, which include multiple sources of information, to provide information on children's learning and development.
6. We shall strive to ensure that decisions such as those related to enrollment, retention, or

assignment to special education services, will be based on multiple sources of information and will never be based on a single assessment, such as a test score or a single observation.

7. We shall strive to build individual relationships with each child; make individualized adaptations in teaching strategies, learning environments, and curricula; and consult with the family so that each child benefits from the program. If after such efforts have been exhausted, the current placement does not meet a child's needs, or the child is seriously jeopardizing the ability of other children to benefit from the program, we shall collaborate with the child's family and appropriate specialists to determine the additional services needed and/or the placement option(s) most likely to ensure the child's success. (Aspects of this principle may not apply in programs that have a lawful mandate to provide services to a particular population of children.)
8. We shall be familiar with the risk factors for and symptoms of child abuse and neglect, including physical, sexual, verbal, and emotional abuse and physical, emotional, educational, and medical neglect. We shall know and follow state laws and community procedures that protect children against abuse and neglect.
9. When we have reasonable cause to suspect child abuse or neglect, we shall report it to the appropriate community agency and follow up to ensure that appropriate action has been taken. When appropriate, parents or guardians will be informed that the referral will be or has been made.
10. When another person tells us of his or her suspicion that a child is being abused or neglected, we shall assist that person in taking appropriate action in order to protect the child.
11. When we become aware of a practice or situation that endangers the health, safety, or well-being of children, we have an ethical responsibility to protect children or inform parents and/or others who can.

Section II:
Ethical responsibilities to families

Families are of primary importance in children's development. Because the family and the early childhood practitioner have a common interest in the child's well-being, we acknowledge a primary responsibility to bring about communication, cooperation, and collaboration between the home and early childhood program in ways that enhance the child's development.

Ideals
1. To be familiar with the knowledge base related to working effectively with families and to stay informed through continuing education and training.
2. To develop relationships of mutual trust and create partnerships with the families we serve.
3. To welcome all family members and encourage them to participate in the program.
4. To listen to families, acknowledge and build upon their strengths and competencies, and learn from families as we support them in their task of nurturing children.
5. To respect the dignity and preferences of each family and to make an effort to learn about its structure, culture, language, customs, and beliefs.
6. To acknowledge families' childrearing values and their right to make decisions for their children.
7. To share information about each child's education and development with families and to help them understand and appreciate the current knowledge base of the early childhood profession.
8. To help family members enhance their understanding of their children and support the continuing development of their skills as parents.
9. To participate in building support networks for families by providing them with opportunities to interact with program staff, other families, community resources, and professional services.

Principles
1. We shall not deny family members access to their child's classroom or program setting unless access is denied by court order or other legal restriction.

2. We shall inform families of program philosophy, policies, curriculum, assessment system, and personnel qualifications, and explain why we teach as we do-which should be in accordance with our ethical responsibilities to children (see Section I).
3. We shall inform families of and, when appropriate, involve them in policy decisions.
4. We shall involve the family in significant decisions affecting their child.
5. We shall make every effort to communicate effectively with all families in a language that they understand. We shall use community resources for translation and interpretation when we do not have sufficient resources in our own programs.
6. As families share information with us about their children and families, we shall consider this information to plan and implement the program.
7. We shall inform families about the nature and purpose of the program's child assessments and how data about their child will be used.
8. We shall treat child assessment information confidentially and share this information only when there is a legitimate need for it.
9. We shall inform the family of injuries and incidents involving their child, of risks such as exposures to communicable diseases that might result in infection, and of occurrences that might result in emotional stress.
10. Families shall be fully informed of any proposed research projects involving their children and shall have the opportunity to give or withhold consent without penalty. We shall not permit or participate in research that could in any way hinder the education, development, or well-being of children.
11. We shall not engage in or support exploitation of families. We shall not use our relationship with a family for private advantage or personal gain, or enter into relationships with family members that might impair our effectiveness working with their children.
12. We shall develop written policies for the protection of confidentiality and the disclosure of children's records. These policy documents shall be made available to all program personnel and families. Disclosure of children's records beyond family members, program personnel, and consultants having an obligation of confidentiality shall require familial consent (except in cases of abuse or neglect).
13. We shall maintain confidentiality and shall respect the family's right to privacy, refraining from disclosure of confidential information and intrusion into family life. However, when we have reason to believe that a child's welfare is at risk, it is permissible to share confidential information with agencies, as well as with individuals who have legal responsibility for intervening in the child's interest.
14. In cases where family members are in conflict with one another, we shall work openly, sharing our observations of the child, to help all parties involved make informed decisions. We shall refrain from becoming an advocate for one party.
15. We shall be familiar with and appropriately refer families to community resources and professional support services. After a referral has been made, we shall follow up to ensure that services have been appropriately provided.

Section III:
Ethical responsibilities to colleagues
In a caring, cooperative workplace, human dignity is respected, professional satisfaction is promoted, and positive relationships are developed and sustained. Based upon our core values, our primary responsibility to colleagues is to establish and maintain settings and relationships that support productive work and meet professional needs. The same ideals that apply to children also apply as we interact with adults in the workplace.

A-Responsibilities to co-workers
Ideals
1. To establish and maintain relationships of respect, trust, confidentiality, collaboration, and cooperation with co-workers.
2. To share resources with co-workers, collaborating to ensure that the best possible early childhood care and education program is provided.
3. To support co-workers in meeting their professional needs and in their professional development.
4. To accord co-workers due recognition of professional achievement.

Principles
1. We shall recognize the contributions of colleagues to our program and not participate in practices that diminish their reputations or impair their effectiveness in working with children and families.
2. When we have concerns about the professional behavior of a co-worker, we shall first let that person know of our concern in a way that shows respect for personal dignity and for the diversity to be found among staff members, and then attempt to resolve the matter collegially and in a confidential manner.
3. We shall exercise care in expressing views regarding the personal attributes or professional conduct of co-workers. Statements should be based on firsthand knowledge, not hearsay, and relevant to the interests of children and programs.
4. We shall not participate in practices that discriminate against a co-worker because of sex, race, national origin, religious beliefs or other affiliations, age, marital status/family structure, disability, or sexual orientation.

B-Responsibilities to employers
Ideals
1. To assist the program in providing the highest quality of service.
2. To do nothing that diminishes the reputation of the program in which we work unless it is violating laws and regulations designed to protect children or is violating the provisions of this Code.

Principles
1. We shall follow all program policies. When we do not agree with program policies, we shall attempt to effect change through constructive action within the organization.
2. We shall speak or act on behalf of an organization only when authorized. We shall take care to acknowledge when we are speaking for the organization and when we are expressing a personal judgment.
3. We shall not violate laws or regulations designed to protect children and shall take appropriate action consistent with this Code when aware of such violations.
4. If we have concerns about a colleague's behavior, and children's well-being is not at risk, we may address the concern with that individual. If children are at risk or the situation does not improve after it has been brought to the colleague's attention, we shall report the colleague's unethical or incompetent behavior to an appropriate authority.
5. When we have a concern about circumstances or conditions that impact the quality of care and education within the program, we shall inform the program's administration or, when necessary, other appropriate authorities.

C-Responsibilities to employees
Ideals
1. To promote safe and healthy working conditions and policies that foster mutual respect, cooperation, collaboration, competence, well-being, confidentiality, and self-esteem in staff members.
2. To create and maintain a climate of trust and candor that will enable staff to speak and act in the best interests of children, families, and the field of early childhood care and education.
3. To strive to secure adequate and equitable compensation (salary and benefits) for those who work with or on behalf of young children.
4. To encourage and support continual development of employees in becoming more skilled and knowledgeable practitioners.

Principles
1. In decisions concerning children and programs, we shall draw upon the education, training, experience, and expertise of staff members.
2. We shall provide staff members with safe and supportive working conditions that honor confidences and permit them to carry out their responsibilities through fair performance evaluation, written grievance procedures, constructive feedback, and opportunities for continuing professional development and advancement.
3. We shall develop and maintain comprehensive written personnel policies that define program standards. These policies shall be given to new staff members and shall be available and easily accessible for review by all staff members.
4. We shall inform employees whose performance does not meet program expectations of areas of concern and, when possible, assist in improving their performance.
5. We shall conduct employee dismissals for just cause, in accordance with all applicable laws and regulations. We shall inform employees who are dismissed of the reasons for their termination. When a dismissal is for cause, justification must be based on evidence of inadequate or inappropriate behavior that is accurately documented, current, and available for the employee to review.
6. In making evaluations and recommendations, we shall make judgments based on fact and relevant to the interests of children and programs.
7. We shall make hiring, retention, termination, and promotion decisions based solely on a person's competence, record of accomplishment, ability to carry out the responsibilities of the position, and professional preparation specific to the developmental levels of children in his/her care.
8. We shall not make hiring, retention, termination, and promotion decisions based on an individual's sex, race, national origin, religious beliefs or other affiliations, age, marital status/family structure, disability, or sexual orientation.
9. We shall be familiar with and observe laws and regulations that pertain to employment discrimination. (Aspects of this principle do not apply to programs that have a lawful mandate to determine eligibility based on one or more of the criteria identified above.)
10. We shall maintain confidentiality in dealing with issues related to an employee's job performance and shall respect an employee's right to privacy regarding personal issues.

Section IV:
Ethical responsibilities to community and society
Early childhood programs operate within the context of their immediate community made up of families and other institutions concerned with children's welfare. Our responsibilities to the community are to provide programs that meet the diverse needs of families, to cooperate with agencies and professions that share the responsibility for children, to assist families in gaining access to those agencies and allied professionals, and to assist in the development of community programs that are needed but not currently available.

As individuals, we acknowledge our responsibility to provide the best possible programs of care and education for children and to conduct ourselves with honesty and integrity. Because of our specialized expertise in early childhood development and education and because the larger society shares responsibility for the welfare and protection of young children, we acknowledge a collective obligation to advocate for the best interests of children within early childhood programs and in the larger community and to serve as a voice for young children everywhere.

The ideals and principles in this section are presented to distinguish between those that pertain to the work of the individual early childhood educator and those that more typically are engaged in collectively on behalf of the best interests of children-with the understanding that individual early childhood educators have a shared responsibility for addressing the ideals and principles that are identified as "collective."

Ideal (Individual)

1. To provide the community with high-quality early childhood care and education programs and services.

Ideals (Collective)
1. To promote cooperation among professionals and agencies and interdisciplinary collaboration among professions concerned with addressing issues in the health, education, and well-being of young children, their families, and their early childhood educators.
2. To work through education, research, and advocacy toward an environmentally safe world in which all children receive health care, food, and shelter; are nurtured; and live free from violence in their home and their communities.
3. To work through education, research, and advocacy toward a society in which all young children have access to high-quality early care and education programs.
4. To work to ensure that appropriate assessment systems, which include multiple sources of information, are used for purposes that benefit children.
5. To promote knowledge and understanding of young children and their needs. To work toward greater societal acknowledgment of children's rights and greater social acceptance of responsibility for the well-being of all children.
6. To support policies and laws that promote the well-being of children and families, and to work to change those that impair their well-being. To participate in developing policies and laws that are needed, and to cooperate with other individuals and groups in these efforts.
7. To further the professional development of the field of early childhood care and education and to strengthen its commitment to realizing its core values as reflected in this Code.

Principles (Individual)
1. We shall communicate openly and truthfully about the nature and extent of services that we provide.
2. We shall apply for, accept, and work in positions for which we are personally well-suited and professionally qualified. We shall not offer services that we do not have the competence, qualifications, or resources to provide.
3. We shall carefully check references and shall not hire or recommend for employment any person whose competence, qualifications, or character makes him or her unsuited for the position.
4. We shall be objective and accurate in reporting the knowledge upon which we base our program practices.
5. We shall be knowledgeable about the appropriate use of assessment strategies and instruments and interpret results accurately to families.
6. We shall be familiar with laws and regulations that serve to protect the children in our programs and be vigilant in ensuring that these laws and regulations are followed.
7. When we become aware of a practice or situation that endangers the health, safety, or well-being

of children, we have an ethical responsibility to protect children or inform parents and/or others who can.
8. We shall not participate in practices that are in violation of laws and regulations that protect the children in our programs.
9. When we have evidence that an early childhood program is violating laws or regulations protecting children, we shall report the violation to appropriate authorities who can be expected to remedy the situation.
10. When a program violates or requires its employees to violate this Code, it is permissible, after fair assessment of the evidence, to disclose the identity of that program.

Principles (Collective)
1. When policies are enacted for purposes that do not benefit children, we have a collective responsibility to work to change these practices.
2. When we have evidence that an agency that provides services intended to ensure children's well-being is failing to meet its obligations, we acknowledge a collective ethical responsibility to report the problem to appropriate authorities or to the public. We shall be vigilant in our follow-up until the situation is resolved.
3. When a child protection agency fails to provide adequate protection for abused or neglected children, we acknowledge a collective ethical responsibility to work toward the improvement of these services.

Glossary of Terms Related to Ethics
Code of Ethics: Defines the core values of the field and provides guidance for what professionals should do when they encounter conflicting obligations or responsibilities in their work.

Values: Qualities or principles that individuals believe to be desirable or worthwhile and that they prize for themselves, for others, and for the world in which they live.

Core Values: Commitments held by a profession that are consciously and knowingly embraced by its practitioners because they make a contribution to society. There is a difference between personal values and the core values of a profession.

Morality: Peoples' views of what is good, right, and proper; their beliefs about their obligations; and their ideas about how they should behave.

Ethics: The study of right and wrong, or duty and obligation, that involves critical reflection on morality and the ability to make choices between values and the examination of the moral dimensions of relationships.

Professional: The moral commitments of a profession that involve moral reflection that extends and enhances the personal Ethics   morality practitioners bring to their work, that concern actions of right and wrong in the workplace, and that help individuals resolve moral dilemmas they encounter in their work.

Ethical: Behaviors that one must or must not engage in. Ethical responsibilities are clear-cut and are spelled out in the Responsibilities - Code of Ethical Conduct (for example, early childhood educators should never share confidential information about a child or family with a person who has no legitimate need for knowing).

Ethical Dilemma: A moral conflict that involves determining appropriate conduct when an individual faces conflicting professional values and responsibilities. (Feeney & Freeman, 2005) (Kipnis, 1995)

[handwritten: Getting employees to go through & sign.]

Statement of Commitment

As an individual who works with young children, I commit myself to furthering the values of early childhood education as they are reflected in the ideals and principles of the Code of Ethical Conduct. To the best of my ability I will:

- Never harm children
- Ensure that programs for young children are based on current knowledge and research of child development and early childhood education.
- Respect and support families in their task of nurturing children.
- Respect colleagues in early childhood care and education and support them in maintaining the NAEYC Code of Ethical Conduct.
- Serve as an advocate for children, their families, and their teachers in community and society.
- Stay informed of and maintains high standards of professional conduct.
- Engage in an ongoing process of self-reflection, realizing that personal characteristics, biases, and beliefs have an impact on children and families.
- Be open to new ideas and be willing to learn from the suggestions of others.
- Continue to learn, grow, and contribute as a professional.
- Honor the ideals and principles of the NAEYC Code of Ethical Conduct

[1] Culture includes ethnicity, racial identity, economic level, family structure, language, and religious and political beliefs, which profoundly influence each child's development and relationship to the world.
[2] There is not necessarily a corresponding principle for each ideal.
[3] The term family may include those adults, besides parents, with the responsibility of being involved in educating, nurturing, and advocating for the child.
[4] This Statement of Commitment is not part of the Code but is a personal acknowledgement of the individual's willingness to embrace the distinctive values and moral obligations of the field of early childhood care and education. It is recognition of the moral obligations that lead to an individual becoming part of the profession.

Group Activity: Professional Ethics: Applying The NAEYC Code

Review the situations on the pages that follow. Use the NAEYC Code for guidance in figuring out what you might do if faced with each situation. (Kidder, 1995)

Which principles apply in this situation? To whom do you have responsibilities?
What guidance can you find in the Code? List the relevant items from the Code and their letters (be sure to look in all four parts and at Ideals and Principles)

Based on your analysis of the guidance from the Code what do you think "the good early childhood educator" should do in this situation?

The Process of Resolving an Ethical Dilemma

- Identify the problem
- Decide if it involves ethics
— Is it a dilemma or responsibility?
— Can it be finessed?
- Look for guidance in the NAEYC Code
— What are the conflicting values?
— How should they be prioritized?
- What is the most ethically defensible course of action?

Professional Ethics: Applying The NAEYC Code

Write the letter for the item you wish to explore further in the space below. Use the NAEYC Code for guidance in figuring out what you might do if faced with each situation.

The Situations:

A. The program you teach for is under pressure to use "standardized paper-and-pencil" tests. You've been told that two tests have been chosen and you'll receive training on how to administer them. Your observation recordings will no longer be used to assess children's progress. You've heard that for these tests you must remove the child from the classroom and take him to another room to test him. You're worried that many children will find this to be stressful, and you're also concerned about leaving your aide alone with all the other children in the group for long periods of time.

B. You've been teaching in a multi-cultural, multi-lingual program for many years. You speak English and Spanish and you've used both languages in your classroom—for conversing with children and other adults, for labeling the bookshelves, etc. You also have several Vietnamese children who do not speak English in your group. You've asked their parents to teach you some words in Vietnamese so that you can help children with routines and in their play—words such as "bathroom," "outside," "inside," and "lunch." Several parents whose home language is Spanish are concerned that their children will not learn English if you keep speaking Spanish in the classroom. And, the Vietnamese families do not want their children speaking Vietnamese in the classroom. They want you to have "English lessons" for the toddlers and preschoolers.

C. Your program uses a standardized test for assessing children's progress. You've been given a copy of the test and told that you must drill children on these items throughout the year so that they all will do well on the test.

D. A parent calls to express concern that her three-year-old daughter is permitted to walk the short distance to the bathroom without an adult accompanying and waiting for her. You reassure her that the security in your center is good, but she insists that her child must be individually escorted to the bathroom.

E. Families who previously had children enrolled in a nearby preschool have told you stories of what happened to their children in that center. They describe dirty sheets on the cots, harsh punishments including withholding food, and ratios of twenty children to one adult. One day you drive by and see a lot covered with asphalt and dry grass. There are a few rusting pieces of playground equipment. Several children are standing along the chain link fence looking at the cars going by. There are no adults in sight.

F. The mother of a child in your school is a single parent. She has fallen behind on her tuition payments and is currently 2 months in arrears. She was arrested on drug charges about a month ago. Right now she is in jail trying to make bail. The child is staying with the maternal grandmother who works and brings him to the center. Several families are waiting for a space in the center. They are financially qualified and anxious for their children to be enrolled. Should the center's policy for prompt payment of tuition be disregarded, upheld, or revised?

G. A parent in our program has deep Biblical values and believes in "sparing the rod, spoiling the child." Her child who is almost two years old has been consistently hitting other children in your group. When you shared with her other alternatives to disciplining at home visits, she responded by saying, "I only listen to my pastor."

H. A parent asks if he can bring a young sibling to a parent workshop even though there is a policy that younger siblings should not be brought to school. You have had problems with parents violating the no sibling rule but you also think this parent could benefit greatly from the content of the workshop.

I. There is a long waiting list for enrollment at your center. Many families have been waiting for more than six months. You get a call from the president of your board explaining that his son's family has just moved back to your community and that he would like you to enroll his three-year-old grandson in the center immediately. He tells you that he will make a generous donation to the fund for the new playground if you comply with this request.

J. Two staff members in your center have indicated their interest in the lead teacher position that just opened up in the four-year-old classroom. One has been a loyal staff member for over fifteen years but she has little formal training. She is nice to children but doesn't really understand how to provide appropriate curriculum. The other candidate has a degree in early childhood education and has worked at the center for less than two years. She relates well to the children and is very skilled in planning appropriate and creative curriculum.

K. Your center has a strict no-sugar policy. The Parents' Handbook makes it clear you expect birthdays and other special events be celebrated with healthy snacks. A mother who has been coming to the center for only two months and speaks little English arrives on her child's birthday with an expensive cake she purchased from the local bakery. You know the cake stretched her budget and represents her earnest hope that a festive birthday celebration will help her child enter the social mainstream of the class—he is having some difficulty making friends and fitting in.

(S. Feeney, N. Freeman, & P. Pizzolongo, 2008)

Session 2 Principles of Child Growth and Development

A competent and effective program administrator understands the importance of developing instructional programs and learning communities that promote optimal child development, healthy families, and strong communities. Administrators must be knowledgeable about the various theoretical positions and factors which influence child development (e.g. environment, culture and brain development). It is important to recognize the physical, cognitive, language, emotional, aesthetic, and social developmental milestones of children (prenatal through adolescence). The knowledge of current research in brain-based instruction (neuroscience) and its applications in early childhood development programs are crucial to the development of one's philosophy of education. There are many resources for use in development of your program's pedagogy. Excerpts regarding each of eight child development and learning theories are taken from Natural wonders: A guide to early childhood education. This detailed publication was created by the Minnesota Early Childhood Environmental Education Consortium. It can be downloaded free of charge from their website for use in staff training and development. We will review and discuss the following theories and principles of child growth and development: Developmentally Appropriate Practice, Developmental Stages, Constructivism, Egocentrism, and Multiple Intelligences, Teaching the Whole Child, Diverse Learning and Play. (Minnesota Children's Museum, 2002)

Child development expert Dr. Laura Berk defines physical development as, "Changes in body size, shape, appearance, functioning of body systems, perceptual and motor capacities, and physical health." Her definition of child development is: "a field of study devoted to understanding all aspects of human growth and change from conception through adolescence" (Berk, 2012). There are numerous domains of development (e.g. creative, physical, cognitive, language, social, emotional, and so forth). Throughout the course we will see ways a child's development may be delayed or hindered. A recent study by Georgia State University scholars found that forty percent of our child care programs are of such poor quality that they actually hinder the development of children.

Healthy child development is dependent upon positive social interactions which are intentional and holistic. In the U.S., nearly seventeen percent of all children experience some form of developmental or behavioral disability. Recognizing a problem (e.g mild to severe developmental disabilities, attention deficit disorder, autism, visual impairments, sensory processing issues, specific learning or behavioral disabilities, traumatic brain injury, emotional disturbance, Tourette syndrome, and the like) early is a key to success for parents and early educators across the nation. Adults should use positive and caring behaviors in all settings throughout the day. This would include modeling appropriate classroom behaviors, engaging in positive adult-child interactions, and fostering appropriate peer-to-peer interactions.

Reflect: Answer these questions and respond to the replies of two cohort members.

What are your assumptions about child growth and development?

How does learning or the development of knowledge and skills come about?

During a child's early years of development, what is the adult's role relative to:

    a)   Physical development

    b)   Social development

    c)   Emotional development

    d)   Cognitive development

    e)   Language development

    f)   Moral development

    g)   Creative development

(Click & Karos, 2010)

Section I: Understanding Young Children - Developmentally Appropriate Practice

What does it mean?

Developmentally appropriate practice (...) is an early childhood education standard that was first described by the National Association for the Education of Young Children. According to ....., developmentally appropriate practice is matching the learning environment—the physical set-up, materials, schedule, curriculum, teaching methods, and so forth—to the developmental levels of children. It means understanding the developmental changes that typically occur from birth through age eight (and beyond), variations in development for individuals and how we can best support their learning and development during these years.

There is no magic formula for developmentally appropriate practice. Educators make decisions day by day, minute by minute, based on knowledge of how children develop and learn, the individual children and families in question and the environmental, social and cultural context (Bredekamp & Copple, ...).

Developmentally appropriate practice in early childhood environmental education means making program choices that emphasize and support both the individual and collective abilities of children.

Why is it important?

Developmentally appropriate practice is based on decades of research and knowledge of how children grow and develop and are guidelines by which we can measure our effectiveness. The power of developmentally appropriate practice lies in the educator's ability to make choices and decisions about what is best for the children and families he or she serves. We all know that educational practices are most effective when they are attuned to the way children develop and learn—that is, when they are developmentally appropriate.

What are the benefits of using developmentally appropriate practice?

Children have **better comprehension and retention**.
Because material is presented in a manner best **suited to their developmental stage**, the material is absorbed better than it would have been if it was designed for older children.
There are **fewer struggles to get children to engage** in the program.
Material presented in a developmentally appropriate manner is more interesting to students and **naturally grabs their attention**.
Children and adults can **learn together**.
Following a child's lead often takes us in a much **more interesting** direction than any adult prescribed curriculum.
More diverse programming can **reach more students**.
Creating developmentally appropriate materials requires more **diverse forms of interaction and presentation and reaches more diverse learning styles.**

Why don't educators use developmentally appropriate practices?

We tend to stay with a teaching style we are most comfortable with.
We tend to rely heavily on props, scripts or visual aides to do the teaching instead of allowing for more personal discovery, interaction and relationship building.
We tend to focus more on sharing facts than on the process of learning.

What are possible behavior issues related to developmentally appropriate practice?

Often there are perceived behavior concerns when, in fact, the opposite is usually the case. In developmentally appropriate programs, children have more freedom to think and do for themselves. Providing well-structured programs with the freedom to make choices actually keeps behavioral issues to a minimum. There are usually more behavior-based problems in programs that are rigidly didactic, require children to sit and listen for long periods of time or don't encourage open ended exploration. However, it may be necessary to change approaches for certain individuals, cultures and or abilities. Some children may require more structure, fewer options or less stimulation. Developmentally appropriate practice is by definition, tailoring programs to meet the needs of particular individuals and groups. (Minnesota Children's Museum, 2002)

Want to know more?
Bredekamp, S & Copple, C. 1997, *Developmentally Appropriate Practice in Early Childhood Programs*, revised edition. Washington D.C.: National Association for the Education of Young Children. Excerpts available at newhorizons.org/naeyc.html

Section 2: Understanding Young Children - Developmental Stages
What does it mean?
Psychologist Jean Piaget first described young children as having a unique set of physical, cognitive, social and emotional attributes that differentiates them from any other age group. He described the constructivist theory—that children construct knowledge out of their exploratory actions on the environment. This theory forms the basis of the modern interactive, hands-on approach to learning.

Piaget also described how children's thinking changed over time. By observing children's behavior, he noted four distinct stages: sensorimotor, preoperational, concrete operational and formal operational. (See accompanying chart.)

Why is it important?

Young children think differently than adults. Because of this, we have difficulty interpreting their actions, emotions and reactions. They have little concept of the past, present and future; they confuse reality with fantasy; they think that everyone feels, thinks and acts like they do. It is essential for us to understand not only how young children think but why they think what they do and change our methods accordingly.

What are the benefits to recognizing developmental stages and characteristics?

Knowing your audience.

Knowing how young children think and feel is essential to developmentally appropriate practice and good teaching in any setting.

It helps us respond to children appropriately. Our first response to a child's burst of illogical thought is too often to either correct them or dismiss it as cute. However, if we respond by asking questions, we can find out a lot about the mysteries of learning and thought.

What are the challenges to recognizing developmental stages and characteristics?

It's difficult for adults to really think like children. Once you've gone through the developmental stages yourself, it's nearly impossible to backtrack. Try to imagine having no concept of the past, present and future or believing in the tooth fairy. The best we can do is to incorporate theory into our teaching practices and try to remember what life was like without logical thought.

Why don't we recognize developmental stages and characteristics more?

We weren't taught to recognize these stages. Unless you've taken classes specifically for early childhood education, it's likely you weren't exposed to the developmental theories of learning in young children. It takes practice to recognize certain characteristics. It's hard to master the mysteries of young children when you teach them infrequently. But once you catch on, the payoffs are immense.

What are possible behavior issues related to not recognizing developmental characteristics?

Unrealistic expectations.
Expecting too much or too little from children almost guarantees difficult or "inappropriate" behavior. The more you know about children's abilities the better chance you'll have for a successful program. (Minnesota Children's Museum, 2002)

Want to know more?
Miller, Karen. 2001 *Ages and Stages: Developmental Descriptions And Activities, Birth through Eight Years.* Beltsville, MD: Telshare Publishing.

Stages of Child Development

Jean William Fritz Piaget's Cognitive Development Stages (4 Stages)
1. Sensorimotor stage (Infancy) — *Object Permanence – Accomplishment (2)*
2. Pre-operational stage (Toddler and Early Childhood) *(6)*
3. Concrete operational stage (Elementary and early adolescence) *(11)*
4. Formal operational stage (Adolescence and adulthood) *(19)*

Erik Erikson's Childhood and Society Social Development 1963 (8 Stages)
1. Birth to 18 Months-Trust vs. Mistrust -**Hope**
2. 18 Months to 3 Years-Autonomy vs. Shame –**Right use of Will**
3. 3 to 5 Years -Initiative vs. Guilt –**Self Confidence**
4. 6 to 12 Years-Industry vs. Inferiority -**Competence**
5. 12 to 18 Years-Identity vs. Role Confusion -**Loyalty**
6. 18 to 35-Intimacy and Solidarity vs. Isolation -**Commitment**
7. 35 to 55 -Productivity vs. Self absorption -**Learning**
8. 55 to Death-Integrity vs. Despair -**Wisdom**

Current research concerning pre-operational stage of cognitive development:

Egocentric, Animistic, and Magical Thinking	Can adjust language to others and take others' perspectives in simple situations. Animistic thinking comes from incomplete knowledge of objects.
Illogical Thought	Can do simplified conservation Can reason by analogy Use causal expressions
Categorization	Everyday knowledge is categorized.
Appearance versus reality	Make-believe helps children tell the difference.

Faith based programs strive to promote spiritual formation and faith development in addition to healthy child development. This is considered teaching the whole child. Leaders in the field define faith development as: *the process of God working through committed teachers using biblical methods and truthful curriculum materials to bring forth disciples who possess a biblical world view, godly character and academic skills necessary to fulfill God's calling and live for His glory.*

Ages and stages of development to be considered by faith based programs:
John H. Westerhoff Faith Development Theory (1976) (4 stages)
1. Experienced Faith (Early Childhood): This is what 'we' do. This is how 'we' act.
2. Belonging Faith (Childhood and Early Adolescence): This is what 'we' believe and do. This is 'our' group/church
3. Searching Faith (Late Adolescence): Is this what 'I' believe?
4. Owned Faith (Early Adulthood): This is what 'I' believe.

James W. Fowler's Faith Development Theory (1995) (6 stages)
Summarized by C. McCullough in *Heads of Heaven, Feet of Clay* (Pilgrim, 1983)
1. Intuitive-Projective (Early Childhood): *The Innocent*-God is often associated with parents or parental figures
2. Mythic-Literal (School Years): *The Literalist*-what emerges is the idea of fairness
3. Synthetic-Conventional (Adolescence): *The Loyalist*-the individual is basically a conformist, there is a deep hunger for acceptance by peers, and the individual believes what the church believes
4. Individuative-Reflective (Young Adult, Plus): *The Critic*-there is a movement from conformity to individuality as in a student going away to college
5. Conjunctive (Mid-life and Beyond): *The Seer*-one's faith expression is no longer that of parents, church, or tradition, but becomes one's own, so that persons in this stage have the ability to see and evaluate other perspectives
6. Universalizing (Exceedingly Rare): *The Saint*-one is motivated by the guiding sense of a supreme authority in all aspects of life.

Lawrence Kohlberg's Philosophy of Moral Development (1981) (6 Stages)
1. Pre-Conventional - Obedience and punishment orientation
2. Pre-Conventional - Self-interest orientation
3. Conventional - Interpersonal accord and conformity to social norms
4. Conventional - Authority and social-order maintaining orientation
5. Post-Conventional - Social contract orientation
6. Post-Conventional - Universal ethical principles

Section 3: Understanding Young Children - Constructivism

What does it mean?

One of the most widely used theories describing how young children learn is the constructivist theory by Jean Piaget. It states that all knowledge comes from an individual's interaction with the environment. Piaget proposed that children construct knowledge out of their exploratory actions—either physical (manipulation of objects) or mental (wondering about something). Exploration is then focused on constructing or making sense of the world by actively interpreting experiences. They will often make up or construct answers to their many questions in an attempt to make sense of something that is puzzling them. Because they lack the ability to think logically, these "naïve" theories can be interesting and lead to creative conclusions. For example, a four-year-old may conclude that the sun goes down because she goes to bed, and in her limited experience this seems true. Attempting to correct her with a scientifically accurate explanation will probably be fruitless because she's in the throes of preoperational, illogical thought. The educator's job is to provide her with rich experiences, ask thought-provoking questions like "Does it go down when I go to bed?" encouraging her to revise her theories and most of all, to trust the process.

Why is it important?

Understanding and promoting constructivism is fundamental to teaching young children. It can also be the most challenging to teachers and environmental educators. We are scientists, eager to share our own knowledge of the outdoors. It is easy to lose sight of the importance of the individual experience and opportunity for creative thought. The preoperational child needs to make the transition into logical thought. Effective educators need to facilitate and support children's learning at the children's level not the educator's. In the words of Jean Piaget, "Every time we teach a child something, we keep him from inventing it himself . . . that which we allow him to discover himself will remain with him."

What are the benefits of constructivism?

It is active, hands-on learning at its best.
It is the heart and soul of environmental education.

Why don't we use constructivism more?

We may be afraid children aren't learning anything or are learning the wrong things.

Children are learning beings. It is not possible for them to go through an experience and not learn from it. However, mastery and understanding take a long time, and there is a lot for
a little person to learn. For example, it'll probably take more than an afternoon with even the most talented educator for a young child to truly understand the life cycle of the frog.

It takes time and effort to learn the process.

Just like breaking a bad habit, it takes practice and careful thought to encourage creative thinking. But it's all worth it when you see that light bulb go on!

What are possible behavior issues related to constructivism?

Children feel trusted.

Children recognize that their ideas are respected and not trivialized. This can lead to mutual trust and excitement about learning.

Give an inch and they'll take a yard.

Be prepared for creativity and experimentation to explode! Your tolerance levels for messiness and noise might be challenged but if you relinquish a little control, the rewards are priceless. (Minnesota Children's Museum, 2002)

Want to know more?
DeVries, Rita, et.al. 2002 *Developing Constructivist Early Childhood Curriculum: Practical Principles and Activities.* New York: Teachers College Press.

Forman, George & Kuschner, David. 1983. *The Child's Construction of Knowledge: Piaget For Teaching Children.* Washington D.C.: National Association for the Education of Young Children.

Forman, George & Hill, Fleet, 1984. Constructive Play: Applying Piaget In The Preschool. London: Addison-Wesley.

Section 4: Understanding Young Children - Egocentrism
What does it mean?

When talking about young children, egocentrism does not mean selfish or arrogant. Rather, it means that a child experiences everything from only one point-of-view—his or her own. They assume everyone else sees, feels and experiences things just as they do. Much of the way children behave can be attributed to their egocentrism and their inability to see things from another's perspective. For instance, in describing a sibling's birthday party, a three-year-old might describe it like this. "My sister had a birthday yesterday and I had birthday cake and I went to Chuck E. Cheese and I ate fish pizza and then I threw-up." Nothing is more important to young children than sharing things that are personally happening to them.

Why is it important?

Egocentrism is the cornerstone of how young children think.

Understanding the limits to how young children think enables us to tailor our programs to meet their needs. Lecturing young children on the wonders of the water cycle has nothing to do with them personally. However, playing in rain puddles and catching raindrops on their tongues has everything to do with them.

What are the benefits to recognizing egocentrism? Fewer behavior problems.

Recognizing egocentrism and planning accordingly can make a large difference in your programs. For example, if you plan on illustrating plant adaptations to a group of four-year-olds by asking for one volunteer to stand up in front and put on pieces of a plant costume, you'll soon have .. preschoolers wondering when it will be their turn. Most would be so focused on their own desire to dress up they couldn't listen to or enjoy another's experience. Allowing every child to simultaneously act out a sprouting plant with all its parts is a more effective way to participate for preschool children.

Why don't educators recognize egocentrism more?

Our own egos get in the way.

We tend to be so focused on our own agendas and teaching everything we know about our subject, we forget to make it relevant to young children. The best way to make it relevant to them is by including each individual and their whole bodies in the experience.

We don't make the time.

In trying to do too many things in a short period of time, we don't allow for young children to share things with us. For example, when reading storybooks, we tend to dislike interruptions from children because it slows us down. From their point of view however, sharing their thoughts as they occur is just as important as listening to the story.

What are possible behavior issues related to egocentrism?

Children may have difficulty waiting their turn or sharing. This may result in excessive fidgeting, talking or disruption. Avoid activities that only one or two children can do while others wait their turn. Emphasize activities that everyone can do at once and make sure you have an abundance of materials to avoid the hoarding instinct. Children have an intense, yet skewed, sense of fairness. Make sure there is enough of the same thing for everyone. For example, you've discovered that you don't have enough Teddy Grahams for the whole group so you add regular graham crackers, figuring they are just about the same thing. Any three-year-old can and probably will tell you, " That's not fair." In other words, everyone should get the same amount of the exact same thing. If it's not possible for everyone to have exactly the same thing, let children choose their own items. (Minnesota Children's Museum, 2002)

Want to know more?
Elkind, David. 1989.Child Development and Education: A Piagetian Perspective. Oxford University Press.

Peterson, Rosemary & Felton, Victoria. 1986. Piaget Handbook For Teachers and Parents. Early Childhood Series. NY: Teachers College Press.

Section 5: Understanding Young Children - Teaching to the Whole Child
What does it mean?

For children to learn effectively and joyfully, they must be engaged. It is impossible to separate the cognitive, physical and social and emotional aspects of development when discussing and planning activities and programs for young children. Children are learning about everything, all the time and with every fiber of their being. If you want something to stick in the brain, it must first go through the body and heart.

Why is it important?

This is the prime time in life when all three aspects of development converge and must be treated with equal importance and relevancy. Learning how to make friends and maintain friendships is just as important as learning how to count or read. For typically developing children neither can be accomplished without moving and mastering one's own body in space.

What is important about the mind, heart and body of preschoolers?

The mind - As discussed previously, a major characteristic of the preschooler is egocentricity.

They have difficulty taking another's point of view and think everyone thinks, sees and acts like they do. They frequently talk to themselves or to their toys rather than to each other. They may think that inanimate objects such as trees or stuffed animals have human feelings and desires. They are bound by their perceptions of the world and therefore can think in only concrete terms. One way children begin to broaden their egocentric perceptions is by adopting roles and acting out make-believe scenarios and stories. This helps them see things from different perspectives. Because preschoolers lack logical thought, they often confuse appearance and reality. Toddlers and preschoolers often think that a Halloween mask changes the identity of the person wearing it and believe that a straight stick partially submerged in water actually gets bent because it appears that way. They begin to reason by making simple, but often mistaken associations between ideas.

For example, a child may think that the sun goes down because it's time to go to bed.

The heart - The social and emotional life of preschoolers is filled with constant challenges. They are navigating their way through a sea of social rules and contexts and finding out through trial and error which rules work. They struggle with recognizing, accepting and expressing feelings as well as responding to the feelings and needs of others. Developing strategies for initiating and maintaining play with other children is a major challenge and gradually moves from solitary to cooperative play. Providing children with the time, place and freedom to interact with each other is essential to good preschool programming in any setting.

The body - Preschool children are learning about how their bodies move and becoming aware of how to manage this movement. They need lots of experiences with lots of different objects and types of movement to master a wide variety of physical skills. Gross motor experiences such as running, balancing, climbing, throwing, kicking, swinging and so forth, enhance physical and motor fitness. Fine motor control is developed through manipulating small objects like blocks, puzzles, beads and play dough as well as pointing. A well-rounded program includes a balance of gross motor and fine motor activities.

What are the benefits to teaching to the whole child?

When you attend to the whole child, you will engage children more fully and make a greater impact on their thinking. If you work with young children, you are going to deal with their physical, social, and emotional needs whether you plan to or not. By taking the whole child into consideration when planning, your plans are not derailed by these needs. Working with joyful children is fun!

Attend to their social needs, and enjoy watching them make connections with you and each other.

Deal with their physical needs, and watch them learn to keep their balance when walking over varied terrain, handle tweezers and other tools for researching nature, and manage eye-hand coordination to use magnifying glasses.

Attend to their emotional needs, and experience emotional connection with children and their connection with nature.

Why don't we teach to the whole child more often?
If teachers don't have background in child development, they may not understand the importance of including emotional, social, and physical needs as well as cognitive needs.

Young children's emotions can be overwhelming.

Rather than getting emotionally involved with children, some people find it easier to pretend they don't have feelings.
If your experience is with older children, you are less accustomed to dealing with other aspects of development. Older children find it easier to compartmentalize their learning.

Teachers tend to think of teaching content as being their job and do not understand the need to engage all areas of development to help children learn.

What are possible behavioral issues related to teaching to the whole child?

If children are allowed or encouraged to interact with each other, conflicts will come up. They will come up anyway, but this allows the instructor to maintain some control though anticipating problems and planning for their resolution. When children are allowed physical outlets, they need to move enough to satisfy their needs before they are ready to sit still again. Instead of unfocused, short-term running around, involve children physically in learning for longer periods of time.

Encouraging children to express their feelings takes time. You can't let one child make a personal connection out-loud ("My dog died just like the dog in the story!") and not expect the other children to also express their feelings.

Plan time for this to happen.

If children develop an emotional connection with you, you may experience conflicts with them. Addressing children's feelings creates more complex relationships, even if you only know them for a few hours. (Minnesota Children's Museum, 2002)

Want to know more?
Gurewitz, Sydney.1983 *The Sun's Not Broken, A cloud's Just in the Way*. Mt. Rainier, MD: Gryphon House.

Griffen, Elinor Fitch. 1982. Island of Childhood. New York: Teacher's College Press.

Section 6: Understanding Young Children - Multiple Intelligence Theory

What does it mean?

Multiple Intelligence (…) is a theory developed by Dr. Howard Gardner of Harvard University. He theorized that people have at least eight different intelligences. Every person has capabilities in each area but some areas are stronger than others. The following are the eight intelligences:

Logical-mathematical (numbers, reasoning)
Linguistic (reading, talking)
Bodily-kinesthetic (moving, doing things with your body)
Musical (songs, patterns, sound)
Interpersonal (understanding other people and social interactions)
Intrapersonal (self knowledge)
Spatial (drawing, mapping)
Naturalist (understanding of the physical world, nature)
He considers that existential and moral intelligence may also be worthy of inclusion. (2011)

Why is it important?

Young children do not compartmentalize their learning. Just focusing on science curriculum without looking at all ways children can develop understanding makes the program less effective.

As educators we can use this concept to see children as individuals with specific areas of strengths and limitations and adjust our teaching accordingly. In doing so, we can combine many of the intelligences into one activity and meet several children's needs at a time.

What are the benefits to teaching to multiple intelligences?

You can reach more children in less time.
Informal educators rarely get to know individual children well because our contact is limited. If subjects are taught in many ways, we will reach more children than the traditional methods of teaching—using lectures, books or demonstrations.
It makes planning easier.
Using multiple intelligence helps to provide variety in programming options. Why don't educators use multiple intelligence theory more?
We think of ourselves as scientists.
Teachers often focus their lessons on getting children to understand concepts and facts. As a consequence, we often plan for one intelligence, neglecting the others. We're unfamiliar with multiple intelligence theory.
We often do what is comfortable and familiar rather than try new techniques.

What are possible behavior issues related to multiple intelligence theory?

If children are truly engaged, they are less likely to behave inappropriately.
By offering a variety of activities that address many of the multiple intelligences, educators should experience fewer behavior issues. (Minnesota Children's Museum, 2002)

Want to Know More?

Campbell, Linda & Dickinson, Dee. 1999 Teaching And Learning Through Multiple Intelligence. Upper Saddle River, N.J.: Prentice Hall.

Dr. Howard Gardner, a Harvard professor and psychologist, developed the theory of multiple intelligences in his book Frames of Mind (1983). This book took a new look at the way humans process, retrieve, and use information and developed new ways of thinking about the human capacity to learn and interact in the world. In 1999 Gardner wrote Intelligence Reframed, Multiple Intelligences for the 21st Century to provide an opportunity to reflect on the impact and changes that have happened as a result of his earlier work.

Dr. Gardner defined an intelligence as a "biopsychological potential to process information that can be activated in a cultural setting to solve problems or create products that are of value in a culture." He asserted that everyone has the basic potential for many intelligences, even those that are not valued in a particular culture. Personal choices, educators, families, and other environmental factors can stimulate the potential development of intelligence. The charts that follow indicate strategies for employing this knowledge.

Multiple Intelligences Definitions and Examples:

LINGUISTIC
To think in words and to use language to express and understand complex meanings
Sensitivity to the meaning of words as well as the order of words, their sounds, rhythms, and inflections
To reflect on the use of language in everyday life
Linguistic Sensitivity: Skill in the use of words for expressive and practical purposes
Reading: Skill in reading
Writing: Ability and interest in writing projects such as poems, stories, books, or letters
Speaking: Skill in oral communication for persuasion, memorization, and description
LOGICAL-MATHEMATICAL
To think of cause and effect and to understand relationships among actions, objects, or ideas
To be able to calculate, quantify, consider propositions, and perform complex mathematical or logical operations
Inductive and deductive reasoning skills, as well as critical and creative problem-solving
Problem Solving: Skill in organization, problem solving, and logical reasoning; curiosity and investigation
Calculations: Ability to work with numbers for mathematical operations such as addition and division
MUSICAL
To think in sounds, rhythms, melodies, and rhymes
To be sensitive to pitch, rhythm, timbre, and tone
To be able to recognize, create, and reproduce music by using an instrument or the voice
To listen actively
Musical Ability: Awareness of and sensitivity to music, rhythms, tunes, and melody
Instrument: Skill and experience in playing a musical instrument
Vocal: A good voice for singing in tune and along with other people
Appreciation: Actively enjoys listening to music
BODILY-KINESTHETIC
To think in movements and to use the body in skilled and complicated ways for expressive as well as goal-directed activities
Sense of timing and coordination
Physical Skill: Ability to move the whole body for physical activities such as balancing, coordination, and sports
Dancing, Acting: To use the body in expressive, rhythmic, and imitative ways
Working with Hands: To use the hands with dexterity and skill for detailed activities and small work
INTERPERSONAL
To think about and understand another person
To have empathy and recognize distinctions among people and to appreciate their perspectives with a sensitivity to their motives, moods, and intentions
Includes interacting effectively with one or more people among family, friends, or working relationships

© 2014 Penn Consulting

Understanding People: Sensitivity to and understanding of other people's moods, feelings, and point of view
Getting Along with Others: Able to maintain good relationships with other people, especially friends and siblings
Leadership: To take a leadership role among people through problem solving and influence
INTRAPERSONAL
To think about and understand oneself
To be aware of one's strengths and weaknesses and to plan effectively to achieve personal goals
Includes reflecting on and monitoring one's thoughts and feelings and regulating them effectively
Knowing Myself: Awareness of one's own ideas, abilities; personal decision-making skills
Goal Awareness: Awareness of goals and self-correction and monitoring in light of a goal
Managing Feelings: Ability to regulate one's feelings, moods and emotional responses
Managing Behavior: Ability to regulate one's mental activities and behavior
SPATIAL
To think in pictures and to perceive the visual world accurately
To be able to think in three dimensions and to transform one's perceptions and recreate aspects of one's visual experience via imagination
To work with objects
Imagery: Use of mental imagery for observation, artistic, creative, and other visual activities
Artistic Design: To create artistic designs, drawings, paintings, or other crafts
Construction: To be able to make, build, or assemble things
NATURALIST
To understand the natural world including plants, animals, and scientific studies
To be able to recognize and classify individuals, species, and ecological relationships
To interact effectively with living creatures and discern patterns of life and natural forces
Animal Care: Skill for understanding animal behavior, needs, characteristics
Plant Care: Ability to work with plants (i.e., gardening, farming, and horticulture)
Science: Knowledge of natural living energy forces, including cooking, weather, and physics
Adapted from Enhancing Education, http://enhancinged.wgbh.org/research/multi/examples.html
SPIRITUAL OR EXISTENTIAL INTELLIGENCE
The potential to engage in thinking about cosmic issues, which might be motivated by pain, powerful personal or aesthetic experiences, or life in a community, that highlights spiritual thinking and experience.
An awareness of oneself with respect to the furthest reaches of the cosmos, the infinite and the infinitesimal, and the related capacity to locate oneself with respect to such existential features of the human condition as the significance of life, the meaning of death, the ultimate fate of the physical and the psychological worlds, and such profound experiences as love of another person or total immersion in a work of art.
Children with this intelligence are philosophers and wonderers. They question everything they encounter.

Adapted from Learning Contracts and Menus
http://www.decd.sa.gov.au/northernadelaide/files/links/Blooms_Gardner_Handout.pdf

Section 7: Understanding Young Children - Diverse Learners

What does it mean?

In order to create the best possible experience for children, diversity can and should be addressed and planned for. Diversity includes race, language, socio-economic status, disability and even learning style. A quality program will take these areas of diversity into account and will make every effort to address them sensitively. Programs that strive to create an environment and curriculum that is inclusive go beyond the surface level of "political correctness" and understand that it is in all children's best interest to be provided with a larger, more accurate picture of the world.

This means being aware that all students are not coming from homogenous backgrounds with the same base of knowledge. It means making a genuine effort to create programs that connect familiar things to children.

Educator Emily Styles of the Seeking Education, Equity and Diversity (2002) project encourages teachers to develop experiences for students that create both windows and mirrors. Mirrors are opportunities for children see their own experiences reflected. Windows allow them to see the experiences of others. Activities or experiences that may be a window for one child could be a mirror for another. If children do not see themselves in an educational experience, they are less likely to retain the information.

Connecting learning that occurs in your programs to children's home and community experiences is respectful and sets a foundation for learning.

Why is it important?

The United States' population is becoming increasingly diverse. Some of the most obvious and quantifiable changes are happening in the racial makeup of our nation. The Bureau of Educational Statistics predicts that by 2030 children of color will make up over half of the students in U.S. schools. A Children of 2010 report published in the Los Angeles Times (March 1999) predicted that by 2052 no single ethnic group will constitute a majority of the U.S. population. These statistics have enormous significance for all educators. If the goal of an environmental education program is to create a positive connection between children and the environment, not taking diverse factors into account can sabotage the goal.

What are the benefits of diverse learning?

Providing experiences that children can connect to prior knowledge increases their learning.
We know from research in educational psychology and brain function that children learn new things based on what is already established.
New knowledge is categorized into what already makes sense.
Learning that is isolated from what is familiar or known is less likely to be long term.

Early childhood pioneer Lev Vygotsky stated the idea of socio-cultural development, in which learning and psychological developments occur through experiences that happen in a social and cultural context. Although this is now a widely accepted concept, many educators overlook the experience of a student that may be different from their own experiences. By making an extra effort to provide an inclusive experience, the learning becomes more meaningful for all students.

Why don't educators take diversity into account more often?

Educators may see multicultural education as a separate field from environmental education. This couldn't be farther from the truth. The future of our planet is a concern for all people and learning to make connections with the natural world is crucial for all people to ensure its survival.

Educators think that a great deal of background knowledge is needed.

While there is a wealth of information about diverse populations and about how to work most effectively with diversity, the most important piece is awareness. Educators who are aware that diversity exists and who make an effort to be inclusive are taking an essential first step.

Educators feel uncomfortable talking about diversity.

Young children are aware of differences in people. When these differences are ignored or overlooked, they get the message there is something wrong with the differences. The more that human diversity is discussed and celebrated, the more children will understand and feel comfortable with the diversity around them.

Educators think taking diversity into account is only necessary if there is a noticeably diverse group.

Inclusive education is the best practice no matter what the group. A child in summer camp may be in a much more homogeneous group during summer than she is in her public school during the rest of the year.

What does representing diversity look like?

Represent reality and avoid stereotypes.

Books and materials used (posters, photographs, music, props and so forth) should show a diverse group of people. Addressing diversity does not mean that every program and every project has to have a specific cultural focus, but the underlying message must be one of inclusion.

Varying levels of comfort and knowledge are accepted.

For example, a child living in an apartment building may have had minimal contact with the world outside of his or her apartment. Venturing out into a non-urban area might be frightening. Another child from the same building may have no fears of the same area. Inclusive instructors provide a variety of ways to participate and value all kinds of knowledge.

Welcome diversity.

Educators should find out as much as possible about the children attending a program and adapt accordingly. This could be as simple as learning some common Hmong pronunciations of children's names or giving a welcome greeting in one of the children's home languages. (Minnesota Children's Museum, 2002)

Want to know more?

Derman-Sparks, Louise.1989 The Anti-Bias Curriculum: Tools for Empowering Young Children. Washington D.C.: National Association for the Education of Young Children.

Menkart, D., Lee, E., Okazawa-Rey, M.1998 Beyond Heroes and Holidays: A Practical Guide to K-12 Anti-Racist, Multicultural Education and Staff Development. Washington D.C.: Network of Educators on the Americas.

Section 8: Understanding Young Children - Learning through Play

What does it mean? Play is the natural activity of children. It is a mental or physical activity whose sole conscious aim is amusement, relaxation, enjoyment and/or self-expression. Researchers have described six elements of play, known as the disposition of play (Rubin as referenced in Rodgers and Sawyer, ...):

.. Play is intrinsically motivated.
.. Play is relatively free of externally imposed rules.
.. Play is carried out as if the activity were real.
.. Play focuses on the process rather than any product.
.. The players dominate play.
.. Play requires the active involvement of the player.

Why is it important?

The most important things in life are learned through play. Although play is often considered frivolous or ineffective, play actually benefits children's learning in several ways. Physical play is necessary for children to learn through their kinesthetic intelligence. During play, children form their own context from things they are learning and experiencing in everyday life. Imaginative play allows children to become someone or something else, to do things they've never done before or have seen others do often.

Play allows children to explore lines of thought, either extending or breaking patterns. It gives children opportunities for success with a minimum of risk or penalties for mistakes.

Play is where it all comes together—the mind, heart and body are fully engaged and —voila— learning happens!

What are the benefits of play?

Playing is fun.
Play is open ended and not goal oriented. Everyone can do it.
Play naturally falls to the level, or varying levels, of participants. Learning can be spontaneous.
Children will introduce new ideas based on what they are experiencing at that moment. Play can relieve children's stress.
Stress can build up from too many teacher-directed activities, emotional or social tension and worry.
Play can be used as a release, distraction or as a means to work out stressful scenarios.

Why don't educators use play more often?

Play is not seen as effective.

Educators often worry that children are not learning if they are playing. They may feel a need to control what children are learning by lecturing or providing study sheets.

There isn't time in the schedule.

If it feels like there is no time to play, reexamine the schedule. How much time is spent in teacher-directed activities? In transitioning from one activity to another? In explaining rules and directions? Play should be at the heart of every program.

What are possible behavior issues related to play?

Inevitable conflicts between children.

When two or more children play together there are bound to be conflicts. Resist the

temptation to rush in and solve the problem for them unless there is danger of people or property getting hurt. Instead, help children

Solve their problems by helping them express how they feel and what they need. (Minnesota Children's Museum, 2002)

Want to know more?
Jones, Elizabeth & Reynolds, Gretchen. 1992. *The Play's The Thing.* NY: Teachers College Press.
Rogers, Cosby & Sawyers, Janet K. 1988 *Play in the Lives of Children*. Washington D.C.: National Association for the Education of Young Children.

Smilansky, Sara & Shefatya, Leah. 1991 *Facilitating Play*. Psychosocial and Educational Publications.

Van Hoorn, Judith, et al. 1999. *Play At The Center Of The Curriculum.* Saddlebrook, NJ: Prentice Hall.

INTERNET ACTIVITY:
Log onto this website to view the new Georgia Early Learning and Development Standards: http://www.gelds.decal.ga.gov/Resources.aspx . NAEYC published a position statement on the risk and benefits of early learning standards. Please check it out at this link: http://www.naeyc.org/files NAEYC also recently published their thoughts on Common Core Standards. The University of North Carolina at Chapel Hill has made some blanket recommendations concerning early learning standards which are insightful. Please check them out here: http://ectacenter.org/topics/earlylearn/earlylearn.asp
Define GELDS and describe how they are to be used in the classroom.

Georgia's early learning and developmental standards are approaches toward teaching and learning that center on the foundational behaviors, dispositions and attitudes that young children bring to social interactions and learning experiences. The standards identify typical developmental levels which include children's demonstration of initiative and curiosity and their motivation to participate in new and varied experiences and challenges. These behaviors are fundamental to children's abilities to take advantage of learning opportunities and to set, plan and achieve goals for themselves. This tool also includes children's level of attention, engagement and persistence as they do a variety of tasks. These factors are consistent predictors of early academic success (Duncan et al., 2007). Finally, children's creativity, innovative thinking and flexibility of thought allow them to think about or use materials in unconventional ways and to express thoughts, ideas and feelings in a variety of media. Hopefully this tool will increase the quality of learning experiences we offer in our programs daily. Teachers should use the standards to identify teaching and learning objectives for lessons. Objectives are one of the four primary components of an effective lesson plan. Methods, assessment of learning and evaluation are the remaining three components.

Please keep in mind, as we have, that every child is unique. That is why these standards are designed to be flexible enough to support children's individual rates of development, approaches to learning, and cultural context. Early learning standards and developmental goals will help you better understand what you may expect to see in a child's learning and development, as well as what you can do to encourage learning in everyday experiences. Their comprehensive nature promotes positive outcomes for all children birth through three-years-old. In conjunction with Georgia's Pre-K Content Standards for four-year-olds and the Department of Education's Georgia Performance Standards for K-12, early educators now have access to a continuum of information for children of all ages. The program administrator's role in overseeing academic curriculum development and instruction is essential to an organization's ability to meet its objectives. We must be knowledgeable about early learning standards and methods for assessing child development and academic achievement. Programs should seek parental insight into developmental levels of children in order to properly place them in groups which will meet their needs.

Visit the following website and print the Developmental Milestone Checklist for Three year olds: http://www.cdc.gov/NCBDDD/autism/freematerials.html

Research your state's early learning standards. List goals for development for a toddler. Then identify activities and materials required. This can be in a lesson plan format.

Example: The goals for a child's development fall into one of five areas. They are: 1. Physical Development and Motor Skills (PDM) 2. Social and Emotional Development (SED) 3. Approaches to Play and Learning (APL) 4. Communication, Language and Literacy (CLL) and 5. Cognitive Development and General Knowledge (CD). The following are the goals for a toddler along with the activities and materials needed for this development:

Some of the PDM goals for a toddler are:
PDM 3: Intentional actions/movement; controls head/body; pulls up; walks holding onto objects; picks up/place items; tries to copy actions like kicking/throwing. Discover and learn about their body's capability by crawling in/out of varying spaces, backs down objects, chairs or stairs.
- **Materials**: boxes, tunnels, tables, foam climbing objects or chairs
- **Activities**: follow the leader, musical movement direction, puppet or stuffed animal leading in activity, holding child through action for demonstration

PDM 4: Exploring/experiencing environment through five senses. They'll reach, catch, grab, hold, hug, pet, squeeze or shake items; engage in finger play.
- **Materials**: soft toys, soft easy to handle balls, water, play dough, jello, pudding, cooked pasta or rice, finger paints, graham cracker crumbs, bubbles.
- **Activities**: Trade animals around a circle and perform an action. At designated area pick a few items for exploration such as pudding and graham cracker crumbs.

PDM 5: Greater bodily control and balance developed by climbing, throwing, kicking, bending, squatting, standing, walking and running as well as moving back and forth or side to side and dancing.
- **Materials**: Open space, safe climbing objects that are appropriate size
- **Activities**: Demonstrate, assist and encourage in each activity on different surfaces and with different objects; games or one on one activity; following directions for balancing. Dance and twirl keeping balance.

PDM 6: Control of hands & fingers by grabbing/holding items and using rightly; points or pokes, using fingers independently.
- **Materials**: chunky crayons, spoons, stackable toys, books, bubbles
- **Activities**: Holding/using crayon purposefully, stack items, turn book pages, pop bubbles.

Some of the SED goals for a toddler are:
SED 1: Identify self in a mirror or picture. Makes activity choices, material selections, teacher preferences, food choices, and comfort preferences.
- **Materials**: mirrors; pictures of the child placed in room; new and familiar foods
- **Activities**: Show child their reflection/picture and ask "Is this ___?" say "I see you ___." Present foods with joy and expectancy so they are more open to foods.

SED 2: Communicates choice through facial expressions, gestures, and noises.
- **Activities:** Reaches to be held; holds cup or plate up when wanting more; brings book to teacher to read; shows dislike through of others using or having their things.
- **Materials:** books, plates, cups

Some of the APL goals for a toddler are:
APL 1: Sensory exploration and creation water tub or table, pudding or jello art,
- **Materials**: cups, sponges, containers, water, pudding, jello, camera.
- **Activities**: demonstrate moving water from one place/container to another with a sponge and let them do so. Give them pudding or jello on a plastic tray to create expressive art. Take a picture of their work for posting in the room.

APL 2: They look for new objects and are drawn to toys with differing sounds
- **Materials**: New toys, toys that make sound and have movement or interact, batteries!!!
- **Activities**: Rotate toys or bring in new ones from other areas. Introduce & demonstrate several interactive toys at one time.

APL 3: Persist with a single activity/toy, repeating an action as long as it interests them;

© 2014 Penn Consulting

o **Materials**: puzzles, small items and container items; rolling toys with different action movement possibilities; books; dolls & clothes easy to remove and replace
o **Activities**: putting puzzles together; filling and dumping objects; reading favorite book over and over; practice undressing and dressing dolls or stuffed animals; have a race with different objects on different surfaces.

Some of the CLL goals for a toddler are:
CLL 4: Toddlers spontaneously experiment vocally by making their voices loud or soft, repeating a word or two, babbling, repeating a single syllable.
o **Activities**: read books in various ways, slow or fast, soft or boisterous, squeaky or gruff.
o **Materials**: Books with varying characters, situations, surroundings.
CLL 5: Make noises associated with items/animals in books, toys, videos.
o **Activities:** Play with vehicle, dolls, toys that make noises,
o **Materials:** Vehicles, toys, and dolls that make noises.
CLL 6: Through rhyming songs/finger play they are developing an awareness of phonics.
o **Activity:** Rhymes, finger play activities
o **Materials:** Activities for teacher to engage toddlers in these at appropriate times.
CLL 8: They become aware of books, ask to have a book read to the them, identify pictures, assist with holding book or turning pages.
o **Materials**: Variety of easy to handle, various size books.
o **Activities**: Reading

Some of the CD goals for a toddler are:
CD-MA1: Learning to recognize and say numbers in order through rhymes, stories or activities.
o **Activities**: Count aloud how many children served, plates on table, hands in the air, feet dancing,
CD-MA2: Toddlers begin to compare, understand, and show their understanding of amount as teachers routinely remind them through counting one or two items like nose, eyes, ears, shoes, feet, hands or toys.
o **Activities**: Fun and playful repetition of counting these things. Counting can be accompanied by steps, jumps, claps etc.
CD-MA3: Begin to understand/communicate measurements, distances, time and weight about their surroundings.
o **Materials**: Similar toys of the differing sizes and weights, measuring tools, pictures of adult/juvenile animals and humans; morning and night pictures; varying block sizes; varying cups sizes; varying weights of similar objects.
o **Activities**: point out measurements of portions before/after eating; count toys – few or many; let them feel the weight difference of objects; show difference in size of parent/child animals; difference of morning and night time; block sizes; heavy/light toys; big/little glass with a little or a lot of water.
CD-MA4: Sort and classify simple objects
o **Materials**: Nesting cups, different sized, shaped and colored blocks or plastic pieces
o **Activities**: Teacher directed or student driven measuring, comparison. Clean up - put like toys together.
CD-MA5: Toddlers explore/ learn to recognize/and understand up/down, under/over, around, high/low.
o **Activities:** Teachers can point out "we sit on the chair," "our feet are in our shoes," "walk around their area," or "we lay on our mat," "we slide down," "the tree grows up," "we go under/through."
CD-MA6: Toddlers learn to recognize basic shapes and their properties.
o **Materials:** Pictures of shapes and things that are those shapes around room. Puzzles and books with shapes and pictures of things that are those shapes.
o **Activities:** Looking at and reviewing shapes and finger tracing shapes in different aspects and as they are found in different objects.
CD-SC2: Toddlers learn movement in water play

- **Activities**: pouring, funneling, dipping, splashing water; dig, pack, scoop, pour, manipulate, build, mash or paint with sand or mud.
- **Materials**: Cups, funnels, floating objects, sponges, scoops, shovels, spoons, buckets, forms

CD-SC4: Toddlers learn slow and fast movement as they push and move objects or observe/engage in games moving slow/fast. They learn to hop like a frog, waddle like a duck, buck like a bronco, etc.
- **Materials**: Video or picture cards of animals in motion
- **Activities**: Watch videos or view pictures and act out animal movements.

CD-SC5: Toddlers can and need to be exposed to people and living things common to their environment. Through real-life items, pictures or songs about these living aspects we create a better learning environment for these children.
- **Materials**: Clothing or items from different cultures.
- **Activities:** Dress up like children in other countries, play with musical instruments from other countries.

CD-SS1: Toddlers begin to understand and identify their family which is shown in them calling family by their place – momma, daddy, bubba, sissy, grandma, aunt and names of siblings. Also notice differences in the physical attributes of others from themselves.
- **Materials**: Pictures of their family or different families, different ages, ethnicities, attributes.
- **Activities**: Look at and talk in one word descriptive about beautiful differences and similarities of people. Point out family members – mommy, daddy, baby, brother etc.

CD-SS4: Associate people with their jobs or tools with the jobs they accomplish.
- **Materials**: Life like items safe for play; pictures of real people performing real jobs
- **Activities**: Play like a fireman, businessman, president, singer as seen in a picture in class.

CD-CR2: Artistically growing, exploring and expressing themselves.
- **Materials**: sidewalk chalk, contact paper, pudding, chunky crayons, easel, paper.
- **Activities**: Allow to create and express artistically on ground outdoors or easel inside.

CD-CR3: Toddlers imitate sounds they hear such as learning animal sounds, mumbling noises that sound like the words to a routine song they hear or noises of things in their community such as bells, whistles, alarms, vehicles, lawnmowers, trains.
- **Activities**: Make noises of these items as they are seen in books or pictures.

CD-CR4: Listen to short stories with props, movements or sounds and respond. Learning to experiment with voice tones, strengths and to imitate sounds.
- **Activities:** Read books or tell stories with voices of characters, climaxing and slowing at integral parts, making animal, emotion or vehicle noises. Using books with recordings or sound.
- **Materials:** Books with accompanying CD, books with varying animals, situations, families, experiences so teacher can express new and different experiences to children.

CD-CP3: Toddles are beginning to understand how to problem solve with different items. They may use a cup to dig dirt when there is no shovel or switch hands when having trouble with one.
- **Activity:** Digging in dirt with different objects
- **Materials:** shovels, cups, spoons, scoops, bowls and dirt.

TERMS AS DEFINED in Webster's 1828 Dictionary

PHILOS'OPHY, n. [L. philosophia; Gr. love, to love, and wisdom.]
Literally, the love of wisdom. But in modern acceptation, philosophy is a general term denoting an explanation of the reasons of things; or an investigation of the causes of all phenomena both of mind and of matter. When applied to any particular department of knowledge, it denotes the collection of general laws or principles under which all the subordinate phenomena or facts relating to that subject, are comprehended. Thus, that branch of philosophy which treats of God... is called theology; that which treats of nature, is called physics or natural philosophy; that which treats of man is called logic and ethics, or moral philosophy; that which treats of the mind is called intellectual or mental philosophy, or metaphysics.
1. The objects of philosophy are to ascertain facts or truth, and the causes of things or their phenomena; to enlarge our views of God and his works, and to render our knowledge of both practically useful and subservient to human happiness.
2. True religion and true philosophy must ultimately arrive at the same principle.
3. Hypothesis or system on which natural effects are explained.
4. We shall in vain interpret their words by the notions of our philosophy and the doctrines in our schools.
5. Reasoning; argumentation.
6. Course of sciences read in the schools.

EDUCA'TION, n. [L. educatio.] The bringing up, as of a child, instruction; formation of manners. Education comprehends all that series of instruction and discipline which is intended to enlighten the understanding, correct the temper, and form the manners and habits of youth, and fit them for usefulness in their future stations. To give children a good education in manners, arts and science, is important; to give them a religious education is indispensable; and an immense responsibility rests on parents and guardians who neglect these duties.
TE'ACHING, ppr. Instructing; informing. TE'ACHING, n. The act or business of instructing.
1. Instruction. LEARNING, ppr. lern'ing. Gaining knowledge by instruction or reading, by study, by experience or observation; acquiring skill by practice.

LEARNING, n. lern'ing.
1. The knowledge of principles or facts received by instruction or study; acquired knowledge or ideas in any branch of science or literature; erudition; literature; science. The Scaligers were men of great learning. [This is the proper sense of the word.]
2. Knowledge acquired by experience, experiment or observation.
3. Skill in anything good or bad. (Webster, 1828)

Writing your personal philosophy of education statement:
Why do you teach?
What do you believe is important to teach?
What is the nature of the learner (student)?
What is the role of the teacher?
Why are your educational objectives important?
How do you teach?
How do you know whether you are meeting your objectives?
Identify the three learning theories that are aligned with your program's goals.
Identify a curriculum that implements learning activities based upon one of the listed theories
Be sure to consider the goals and objectives of your program: development of the whole child…sensitivity and creativity…self-esteem…self-direction in learning…thinking skills…academic skills…

Sample Developmental History and Background Information Form

Child's name: _____ DOB: _____

Age began sitting: _____ crawling: _____

walking: _____ talking: _____

Any speech difficulties: _____
_____

Special words used to describe needs: _____
_____

Health
Any known complication at birth? _____
_____

Serious illnesses and/or hospitalizations: _____
_____
_____

Special physical conditions, disabilities: _____
_____
_____

Allergies i.e. asthma, hay fever, insect bites, medicine, food reactions: Pediatrician needs to submit a care plan for admission to class) _____
_____

Regular medications: _____
_____

Eating Habits
Child eats with hands (yes or no): _____ spoon: _____ fork: _____
Special characteristics or difficulties: Favorite foods:
_____
_____

Foods refused:
_____

© 2014 Penn Consulting

Toilet Habits
How does child indicate bathroom needs (include special words)? _____

_____

_____

Is your child ever reluctant to use the bathroom?

_____

_____

Does your child have accidents?

_____

_____

Sleeping Habits
Does your child become tired or nap during the day (include when and how long)?

_____

When does your child go to bed at night?_____and get up in the morning?
_____

Describe any special characteristics or needs (stuffed animal, backrub, story, mood on waking, etc.):
_____

_____

Social Relationships
How would you describe your child's temperament? (Mood, Adaptability, Activity Level, Distractibility, Intensity or Energy Level, Regularity, Sensory Threshold, Approach/withdrawal, Persistence)

_____

_____

Previous experience with other children/early childhood programs:

_____

_____

Reaction to strangers:
_____

Able to play alone:

_____

Describe your child's interest in playing with other children:

_____

Favorite toys and activities:

_____

© 2014 Penn Consulting

Fears (the dark, animals, etc.):

_____

_____

_____

How do you comfort child?

_____

_____

_____

What is the method of behavior management/discipline at home?

_____

Describe your child's schedule on a typical day?

_____

_____

_____

_____

_____

Is there anything else you would like us to know about your child?

_____

_____

_____

_____

Parent/Guardian Signature: _____

Date: _____

Session 2 Methods, Activities, Programs, and Practices (MAPP)

Child Care Programs and Philosophy of Early Childhood Education

A recent study conducted by Georgia State University's Education Policy Group, Andrew Young School of Policy Studies found that "(1) Georgia women exceed the national average in workforce participation, increasing demand for child *care*; (2) Georgia lags significantly behind the other states in providing child *care* subsidies to families whose children are at highest risk of poor outcomes and in setting standards to improve quality; (3) with 25% of Georgia children living in poverty, the cost of high quality *care* would be prohibitive for families even if it were widely available; and (4) Georgia ranks poorly on measures of child *care* quality, particularly on child to staff ratios, although the state performs relatively well in the area of wages for child *care* workers." (Regional Child *Care* Trends: Comparing Georgia to Its Neighbors. Waits, Lauren; Monaco, Malina; Beck, Lisa; Edwards, Jennifer, 2001). Georgia's leadership has implemented the following interventions (through Georgia's Early Learning Initiative, GELI) in an effort to improve the quality of services provided to our children:

- SMART Start Georgia's salary supplement program
- SMART Start Georgia's academic scholarship assistance for early childhood education professionals seeking credentials
- A QRS or "tiered reimbursement" system which rewards high-quality child care providers
- Training and technical assistance for providers in those low-income level counties.
- On July 1, 2014, DECAL launched *Awards for Early Educators* to reward eligible directors, assistant directors, teachers, and assistant teachers who earn an early childhood education credential. Eligible credentials must be earned between January 1, 2014 and June 30, 2017.

Awards for Early Educators rewards three levels of credentials. Eligible applicants may receive a one-time award at each of three levels. Awards range from $1,200 to $2,500:
1st Level - $1,200 (Awards Technical Certificate of Credit and CDA)
2nd Level - $1,500 (Awards Technical College Diploma and Associate's Degree)
3rd Level - $2,500 (Awards Bachelor's or Master's Degree)
Additional information and applications can be found at http://www.decalscholars.com/ on their new website for SCHOLARSHIPS, INCENTIVES, and now *Awards for Early Educators*. Applicants must meet all eligibility requirements. Questions? Visit the above website or contact Care Solutions at 1.800.227.3410 or 770.642.6722 with specific questions about this time-limited opportunity.

Although there are several classes of early childhood programs (Public schools, Private control (e.g. nursery schools, parent cooperatives, business operated programs and programs sponsored by churches, service organizations and charities), Federal programs (e.g. Head Start), National private agency programs (e.g. Montessori) and University laboratory programs (e.g. nursery, kindergarten and primary level schools)), Bright from the Start regulates the following four types of programs:
Day care center — a place operated by a person or organization that cares for 19 or more children. Centers must be approved by the BFTS before opening and reviewed each year for their license to be renewed.
Group day care home — a place where seven to 18 children are cared for. These homes must be approved before opening and must be licensed each year by the state.
Family day care home — a private home where three to six children are cared for by a person who is not related to the children. These homes must register with the state.
Informal provider — a private home where one or two children or related children are cared for. These are not required to register with BFTS, but if the provider receives a child care subsidy from DFCS, BFTS staff visit the home to check basic health and safety items, and the provider is must submit a criminal background check.

© 2014 Penn Consulting

After deciding which type of program you want to offer it is import to seek legal counsel with experience in the child care industry. Your attorney can advise you on the best legal structure for your program. It is important to consider your source of funding when selecting a legal structure. There are three types of private ownership: proprietorship, partnership and corporation.

Sole proprietorship	Incorporation	Partnership
Owned by one person	Legal entity (for-profit or not-for profit basis May be independent or divisions of a parent corporation	Two or more owners Divides profits and losses among partners
File business and personal tax returns simultaneously	May be eligible for tax exempt status (NFP) and other incentives Higher taxes	File IRS form 1040 and form 1065
Name reservation/registration	Articles of Corporation, Bylaws, Minutes of Incorporator's Meeting, Name reservation	True Name Certificate Limited Partnership Certificate Partnership Agreement
Full decision making authority	Decision making board of directors	Limited transferability of partner's interest General-coequal authority to make binding decisions Limited-liable to the extent of financial or service contribution
Owner assumes full personal liability for debts, taxes, regulatory fees, breaches of contract, tort	Credibility and personal assets are protected if the business fails or is sued. Board members can be held liable for fraud or failure to pay withholding taxes.	More financial resources and complementary skills Each partner is responsible for partnership's debts
Simplest and least expensive	Exists as a legal entity perpetually unless dissolved by the board of directors or a court	Partnership dissolves upon the death of a partner

The following IRS regulations apply to all programs regardless of legal structure:
1. Filing form SS-4 Application for a Employer Identification Number
2. Filing annual tax returns. Employers file quarterly tax returns, IRS form 941. Sole proprietors and partnerships report income on the appropriate schedule with IRS Form 1040 or 1065. For profit corporations file IRS form 1120 and not for profit corporations file IRS form 990.
3. Filing federal IRS form W-4 and state Georgia form G-4 withholding exemption certificates for employees, in addition to Social Security Administration form W-2 and W-3.

> The Internal Revenue Service offers free or low cost Small Business Tax Workshops which help child care professionals understand and fulfill their federal tax responsibilities. The workshop is also available on DVD or online in streaming video (Virtual Small Business Workshop). The workshops provide a general overview of taxes in addition to more detailed topics such as retirement planning and recordkeeping.

CHILD CARE IN THE US: A BRIEF HISTORY

The beginning of the day care movement originated with the welfare and reform movements of the 19th century. "Day care grew out of a welfare movement to care for immigrant and working class children while their impoverished mothers worked (Scarr & Weinberg, 1986, p. 1140)." The day care centers of today evolved from these day nurseries which began in Boston in the 1840's.

The early nurseries cared for children of working wives and widows of merchant seamen who were an economically deprived and disadvantaged group in society. Settlement houses were especially active in promoting day care for immigrant children. Jane Adams, a well known reformer in her era, developed nurseries for poor children who needed supervision and care while their parents endeavored to survive in a new land. "Day care," according to Scarr and Weinberg (1986), "was founded... as a social service to alleviate the child care problems of parents who had to work, and to prevent young children from wandering the streets (p. 1141)."

GOVERNMENT SPONSORSHIP

Child care in the United States has, like many other national enterprises, has been a melting pot of ideas and interests. During the Great Depression, day care was sponsored by the Federal Government. This sponsorship was motivated by a desire to employ out-of-work adults, however, not from a belief in early education.

During World War II, the Federal Government sponsored day care for 400,000 preschool children. Again, this was not done because Congress perceived day care to be beneficial for children, but because the mothers of these children were needed to work in industries producing war materials. Ironically, after the war, the Federal government abdicated all support for day care and instructed women to quit working, go home, and take care of their children. Many women, however, chose not to accept that advice. The ranks of working women have been steadily increasing since World War II (Scarr & Weinberg, 1986).

PRIVATELY SPONSORED CHILD CARE CENTERS

In addition to the Federal sponsorship of child care during World War II, a unique program began in Portland, Oregon in 1943. The Kaiser shipyards opened a child care center at the entrance of each of their two shipyards. In building the centers, they hoped to reduce the rate of absenteeism among their working mothers. Henry Kaiser built the centers, which were the world's largest child care centers and were in operation 24 hours a day. These centers had a nurse on site for children who were ill, and also provided hot meals for mothers to take home with them. The centers were models of child-centered construction, built around a courtyard with wading pools. The playrooms branching off of the courtyards had large windows and window seats that allowed children to watch the construction taking place in the yards. Cost of the care was shared by parents and the Kaiser company. In the two years they were open they served 3,811 different children (Gordon & Browne, 1996).

After the war these centers closed, but today more and more businesses are following Kaiser's example and are providing on-site child care centers for their employees. New innovations in corporate day care settings are also being tried. Stride Rite Corporation began their day care center in 1971 and have now opened an intergenerational center which provides services to toddlers and preschoolers, as well as the elderly (Berenbeim, 1992). Two Marriott hotels in Atlanta have joined forces with the Omni hotel to build a 24 hour a day, subsidized child care center. The center will offer family-support services, including immunizations, linking parents with social workers, and offering parenting classes. Eighty percent of their 250 slots are reserved for children from low-income families (Shellenbarger, 1994).

CHILD CARE TODAY

During the last half century there has been a substantial increase in the labor force among women who have children under the age of 18. In 1940 only 8.6% of mothers with children younger than 18 were in the work force (Bridgman, 1989). According to the U.S. Bureau of Labor Statistics, 50% of women with children younger than three years of age were working in 1985. This represents a 33% increase over 1975 figures and a 47% increase over 1965 figures (Hofferth, 1987). According to the 1996 Yearbook on *The State of America's Children,* 57% of the women with children younger than three are now in the workforce and 60% of women with children younger than six. According to their figures, however, only one in seven of the child care centers these children attend and one in 10 family child care homes are considered to be high enough quality to enhance children's development (Children's Defense Fund, 1996).

There is a real need then, not just for child care, but for quality child care. The advice that Galinsky and Phillips (1989) give to parents in need of child care is: "If you have been wondering how your children will turn out...it is your relationship with your child and the child care you select that matter (p. 115)." Help for improving the quality of care provided to our nation's youngest citizens is again coming from a variety of sources.

Corporations are helping to fund a number of projects, as well as providing child care subsidies and services. For example, Levi Strauss is not only helping to subsidize care for its low income families, but is also offering grants to improve the quality of childcare programs in their community. The American Business Collaboration, which includes 144 employers, has been backing improvements in both local and state child care programs. Along with AT&T, this Collaboration has awarded grants to over 500 day care facilities that are working toward attaining accreditation from the National Association for the Education of Young Children (Shellenbarger, 1994).

Help to improve childcare for families has also come from groups such as The National Association for the Education of Young Children, The Children's Defense Fund, and the Association for Childhood Education International. The quest for quality childcare must become one of the top priorities for our entire nation, though. Only then will we be able to meet the growing need for quality childcare in the future.

SOURCES
Berenbeim, R. E. (1992). Corporate Programs for Early Education Improvement. Report Number 1001. New York: The Conference Board.
Bridgman, A. (1989). Early Childhood Education and Childcare. Arlington, VA: American Association of School Administrators.
Children's Defense Fund (1996). The State of America's Children Yearbook, 1996. Washington, DC: Children's Defense Fund.
Galinsky, E. & Phillips, D. (1988) The day-care debate. Parents, 63, 114-116. Gordon, A., & Browne, K.W. (1996). Beginnings and Beyond. Albany, NY: Delmar. Gotts, E.E. (1988). The right to quality child care. Childhood Education, 64, 269-273.
Hofferth, S.L. (1987). Implications of family trends for children: A research perspective, 44, 78-84. Scarr & Weinberg. (1986). The Early Childhood enterprise: Care and education of the young. American Psychologist, 41, 1140-1141.
Shellenbarger, S. (1994). Companies help solve day-care problems. The Wall Street Journal, July 22, 1994.

National Network for Child Care - NNCC. Part of CYFERNET, the National Extension Service Children Youth and Family Educational Research Network. Boschee, M.A., & Jacobs, G. (1997). Childcare in the United States: Yesterday and today. Internet. National Network for Child Care. (www.nncc.org).

The child care industry has changed drastically from what it used to be. Child care centers are now early learning centers. In the past, child care centers provided mostly babysitting but these days, parents have high expectations for what their child can and should learn before they go to Kindergarten. Additionally, research shows that children are capable of learning what was being taught at a later age earlier. Due to the increase in demand for child care, there has been a proliferation of child care options from which parents can choose. In addition to traditional day care centers, flexible child care options such as drop-in care, mommy morning out and parents' night options are now available. Advances in technology are changing many aspects of the child care experience including increasing security of childcare facilities, increasing communication with parents about their children and changing how curriculum is being delivered in the classroom, to name a few.

Are you looking for information and resources about childcare industry trends in the United States? If that is the case, the Child Care Aware and National Child Care Information and Technical Assistance Center websites are great places to begin.

On this website you can find information on childcare centers, **child development**, early child education, and about **children and health**. What is more, http://childcareaware.org/ offers details regarding projects and about school age programs. Furthermore, helpful information about **child protection** is available.

The National Child Care Information Center (NCCIC), a project of the Child Care Bureau, Administration for Children and Families (ACF), U.S. Department of Health and Human Services (HHS), is a national resource that links information and people to complement, enhance, and promote the child care delivery system, working to ensure that all children and families have access to high-quality comprehensive services.

ICF has operated the National Child Care Information and Technical Assistance Center (NCCIC) since 1994, providing broad information on early and school age care and education through its website, toll-free line, and email service on behalf of the Office of Child Care.

ICF also offers more individualized support to federal grantees administering programming at the state level using Child Care Development Fund dollars. Through NCCIC, ICF provides on-site technical assistance, training, meeting facilitation, and information sharing. In addition, ICF researchers and analysts develop customized information summaries and publications useful to state and national policymakers.

You may log on to the following websites to see the latest research and industry trends:

National Child Care Information and Technical Assistance Center   http://www.nccic.org*
The State of Georgia Families 2010
http://www.fcs.uga.edu/ext/pubs/state/2010/Chattooga%20County%202010%20Fact%20Sheet.pdf
Child Care Aware http://childcareaware.org/
Annie E. Casey Foundation Kids Count Data http://www.aecf.org/kidscount/factsheets/ga.pdf

*Federally funded programs often lose their funding and website domains may change. Conduct a Goggle search for the title of the document in order to locate archived files.
Internet Activity: Search the internet for "child care industry trends". Are they stable or declining in your area?

http://www.anythingresearch.com/industry/Child-Day-Care-Services.htm
http://www.ibisworld.com/industry/default..aspx?indid=1618
http://childcare.about.com/od/evaluations/tp/trends.html
http://www.collegegrad.com/industries/edhea01.shtml
http://www.naccrra.org/sites/default/files/default_site_pages/2012/full2012cca_state_factsheetbook.pdf
http://www.dol.gov/dol/aboutdol/history/herman/reports/futurework/report/chapter1/main.htm
http://www.qualitycareforchildren.org/uploaded-files/Quality%20Care%20for%20Children_2013%20White%20Paper.pdf
http://www.sbdcnet.org/small-business-research-reports/daycare-business-2012

Knowing the number of children in your zip code, the number of licensed centers and their capacity to serve those children, the median household income, the parents' current child care arrangements, their degree of satisfaction with their current arrangements, what they presently pay for care, what they would be willing to pay and whether they would enroll their child in your program once established, is necessary to the overall planning process. The SBA reports that 50% of programs started today will not last one year because of a failure to complete the feasibility study and determine relative market share. They also indicate that 90% of programs that start this year will not exist in five years due to poor management practices. The effort put forth in strategic planning can make all the difference. Determine what **methods, activities, programs, and practices (MAPP)** will enable your program to achieve its objectives and list them below:

Type of program (Pre-K , Kindergarten, Montessori, Nursery, Day Care and Early Learning Center, Head Start, Private, Public, Group, Center)

_____

Target Audience:

Ages Served_____Months of Operation_____Hours _____

Location_____Other identifiers _____

Legal Structure _____

Write a brief philosophy statement which explains your beliefs regarding why your program is necessary and how it will impact the lives of your target audience.

Objectives:
☐ Specific nature of the program
☐ Describe how you will meet the needs of your target audience
☐ What are the expected outcomes
☐ How will you measure results
☐ Realistic staffing needs assessment
☐ Timetable

Potential locations _____ Consider locale: urban 1 mile radius, rural 5 mile radius, suburban 3 mile radius

Income level _____

Avg. # of children/household within targeted age range _____

Median household annual income _____

Determine relative market share: # of licensed slots available + # of slots in your center/# of slots needed = rms _____

Population projections _____

Level of government/community support/subsidy programs _____

Average cost of care _____

List other services in the community (schools, after care, family services, health departments, DFACS, corporations which provide reimbursement, children's clothing stores, children's hospitals, etc.):

Common Characteristics of High Quality Early Childhood Education Programs
1. Parental involvement and engagement through education and service (i.e. offering parenting seminars, parent night out, etc.)
2. The programs activities are determined by research proven best practices and interventions and parental input which exceed licensing standards.
3. The program regularly participates in self-studies or evaluation of standards of care provided.
4. The program is financed by both public and private sources (i.e. parents, employers, government, foundations, businesses within the community and other civic groups.
5. The program's administration operates within a budget and financial records are audited annually.
6. The program's participants are advocates for higher standards of care and funding in federal, state and local policy.
7. The program complies with licensing regulations and is regularly monitored for high standards.
8. The early learning objectives are communicated to all instructional personnel and families through various means.
9. The program's staff is highly qualified and credentialed.
10. The program provides funding for continuing professional development and increases compensation as the staff increases levels of training.
11. The program networks with local resource and referral agencies.
12. The staff implements developmentally appropriate practices.
13. The program provides well-lighted, spacious and well-equipped classrooms, outdoor play areas and common areas which encourage family support.
14. The facility is well maintained and provides security for staff and children.
15. The program collaborates with the community to enhance the quality of its program and the community at large.

Session 3 Strategic Planning

It is vitally important that your program have specific goals to guide decision making.
Program goals need to be specific, measurable and achievable. Remember to align your goals with your values. There should be a realistic timeframe for the achievement of both long and short- term goals. Consider appropriate goals in light of the following areas:

1. Setting or environment (provide a safe and nurturing community of learners)
2. Skills Development (promote optimal intellectual growth of every child through multi- sensory learning experiences)
3. Curriculum (promotes development of the whole child-emotional, social, cognitive, spiritual, and physical)
4. Collaboration (families are engaged in community service to improve the quality of life for children)
5. Staff (supported through pre-service and ongoing education and a pleasant work environment)

Business Plan
A business plan clearly sets out the objectives of your educational institution. It communicates to lenders, grant makers, and other stakeholders exactly how the business intends to operate and how it will become profitable and sustainable. The plan must be credible, clear, and authoritative. You should cite specific "sources" of information that are within in the plan. Be sure to include tables and graphs that clarify numerical data. The plan should be 10-15 pages in length (excluding the introduction and any supporting documents) and it should be typed (single or double spaced) without grammatical or typographical errors. Readers of your business plan may view mistakes or sloppy presentations as examples of poor business or administrative skills. You may use a template such as the one provided at www.liveplan.com.

Be sure to write in the third person. Don't say "I', "me", "we" or "our", instead, say "Castle Child Development Center", "the owner" or "Jane Doe". Be positive and write in the present tense. Don't say, "I hope to care for..." instead, say "The licensed capacity of the school is 75-90 children between the ages of ...."

Directions: Simply answer the following questions in complete sentences and then separate them into paragraphs according to the topic. New program directors may be unable to answer some questions. Cash flow projections should be calculated for year one to five.

The Sections of the Child Care Center Business Plan

- The Business Introduction
- The Business Organization Section
- The Management/Operations Section
- The Marketing Section
- The Financial Section
- Supporting Documents

EXECUTIVE SUMMARY
Provide a brief overview (highlight and summarize primary elements) of the business plan's contents.

BUSINESS INTRODUCTION
- Provide a history and description of the business
- How and why did you enter the child care field?
- Mission statement

- Who are you and what do you do?
- What services do you offer?
- Who do you serve?
- Why is your program necessary?
- How will you impact the lives of your target audience?
] Research market feasibility
- Is there a need for child care in the area where your business will be located?
- How many children are there in your zip code, county, city? (U.S. Census Quick Facts)
- How many licensed programs are there and what is their licensed capacity?
] How much of a need is there and how much of it will you serve?
] Competition
- Who is your competition?
- What services do they offer; what are their strengths and weaknesses?
- Are they a threat to your business?
] Industry trends
- What does the child care industry itself look like at this time: is it stable or declining? (SBA, USDOL Occupational Outlook)
] Potential market
- Given what's known about the above issues, what is the potential demand/need for your facility?

BUSINESS ORGANIZATION
] Legal
- Will the center be a sole proprietorship, a partnership, or a corporation?
- Will it be profit making or a non-profit organization?
- Will it have a board of directors?
- Will it be employer sponsored or supported, or funded by state or local agencies?
- Who will determine the policies and budget?
- Who will provide legal representation?
] Insurance
- What types of insurance will you carry (liability, fire, theft, health, accident) and through whom?
- What are the coverage limits? *[handwritten: corpal punishment / sexual harrassment]*
] Tax and bookkeeping system *[handwritten: paychex (outside payroll)]*
- What records do you need to maintain?
- What system will you use?
] Regulation, licensing, and/or government issues
- What licensing regulations are there for your industry?
- What are the zoning regulations for your location?
- What local building code requirements must you adhere to?

MANAGEMENT/OPERATIONS
] Personnel/management team
- Who are they?
- What are their qualifications?
- What education have they had?
- Are they competent, capable, and experienced?
] Benefits
- What benefits are being offered to employees, if any?
] Employee requirements and job descriptions
- What are your hiring practices?
- What is your wage scale?
- How is your payscale determined?

© 2014 Penn Consulting

- What are your staffing patterns?
- What will specific employees be expected to do?

☐ Business operations
- How will you actually run your business?
- What are your major business policies?
- What is your schedule of daily program activities and how will they provide you with a competitive edge?

☐ Suppliers
- What equipment and materials do you need?
- Where will they be obtained?
- Provide breakdown of costs by supplier.

☐ External partners
- Will a lawyer, accountant, or early childhood specialist's served be used?

☐ Technology needs
- Do you need or will you need any technology to help you, such as computers, telephone add-ons, etc.?

MARKETING

☐ Describe your services
- What do you offer and to whom?
- Do you offer any special services that may not be offered elsewhere?

☐ Describe the target market for you facility
- Who will be served?
- What is the average or median household income level?
- What is the average number of children per household within the targeted age range?
- What is your relative market share projection: the size and fraction of that market that you hope to cover?

Relative market share (RMS): # of licensed slots available + # of slots in your center/# of slots needed

☐ Identify your location
- Where is your facility located?
- Has is met local and state inspections and zoning requirements?
- Does it accommodate special needs?
- What features about your site are desirable for child care and families?

☐ Pricing strategies
- How will fees be determined?
- Will there be late fees, paid holidays and vacations, sick days, etc.?
- Will you charge for special services, i.e., transportation?
- How do your rates compare to your competitor's? Explain differences.

☐ Promotional strategies
- How will you reach your customers?
- What advertising methods will you use?

FINANCIAL

☐ Start-up costs
- If applicable, what will you need to purchase to begin?
- What operating funds will be needed?
- Where will this money be obtained?
- How much, totally, is needed to successfully cover all start-up costs?

☐ Cash-flow projection
- Where will your income come from and where will it go?
- Why will a loan or someone's investment in shares (if relevant) make the business more profitable?

- Anticipate your income and expenses for a two-year period, month by month and by year.
  - Income statement
  - Balance sheet: assets, liabilities, net worth

Break even analysis: "Break-even" occurs when business revenues equal business expenses, i.e., zero profit. The break-even analysis determines the minimum enrollment necessary to make a profit.

Step one-Identify fixed and variable costs. Fixed costs (ones you must pay no matter how many children are enrolled, e.g. salary, utilities, rent/mortgage, insurance, and overhead): For example, they are $4,000 per month. Variable costs are costs that change with the number of children served, such as food, supplies, and extra teachers. Our estimate will be $8,000 per month.

Step two-Estimate income. For example sake we are charging $400 per child per month.

Step three-Divide expenses/costs by the tuition to determine the break-even point. In order to break even we need to make $12,000 per month or enroll 30 children. The break-even analysis is not an exact science. Instead of adding more children, your program could increase tuition or hire fewer teachers (a change in one variable affects the others).

- Revenue versus expenses: how much money do you need to break even?
  - Can you make a profit?
  - Financing plan
- Will you need to borrow money? How much?
- How will you use it and how will it be repaid?
  - Identify sources of funds
- Determine how the program will be funded.
- Will you seek a bank loan?
- How much money can you provide?

SUPPORTING DOCUMENTS
- Personal resume(s)
- Letters of reference
- Accreditations or distinctions earned by the program or its leaders
- Job descriptions
- Contracts, leases, licenses to operate business
- Client lists

Developing a Parent Handbook or Family Manual

One of the most important ways to communicate your program's philosophy (vision and mission statements), objectives and goals is through a policies and procedures manual. Draft policies and develop manuals for both parents concerning the following:

Ages of children served; Months of operation; Days of operation; Hours of operation; Dates the school or center is closed; Health and Safety policies concerning communicable diseases and medication authorization; Philosophy of education, class guidelines; Admission requirements, including parental responsibilities for supplying and maintaining accurate required record information and escorting child to and from center; antidiscrimination statement, Standard fees, payment of fees, fees related to absences and vacations and other charges such as insurance, transportation, etc; Transportation provided, if any; if any transportation is not provided, state this. If a public school bus picks up and delivers to facility, state this. If provided to or from school or home, must include procedures if no one is at drop-off site to receive child; Guidance and discipline techniques. State disciplinary actions used to correct a child's behavior, and guidance technique used; and Emergency procedures (see samples later in the manual).

It is important to review the handbook with parents in an initial interview as well as a group orientation. A parent's agreement to support your policies and procedures will enable you to meet many program objectives.

Sample Parent Orientation Agenda

Welcome and refreshments Introduce Staff
Distribute and Discuss: handbooks, calendars, board of health communicable disease chart, any uniform policies, classroom observation and/or financial policies, meals, daily schedules, nap procedures, field trip policies and schedules, Special care plan forms, discipline and security policies, etc.
Collect enrollment forms, feeding plans, developmental information sheets Parents tour classrooms

Internet Activity: Planning Parental Collaboration and Participation

Thirty years of research confirms that family involvement is a powerful influence on children's achievement in school (Eagle, 1989; Henderson & Berla, 1994; U.S. Department of Education, 1994; Ziegler, 1987).

Log on to the Web site: http://www2.ed.gov/pubs/FamInvolve/resources.html Read the article.

1. Choose one of the topics and summarize the issues that are presented.

2. Discuss why you agree or disagree with the viewpoints expressed.

3. How would this information be helpful to a director? (P. Click & K. Karos, 2010)

Discipline policies
The word discipline, which comes from the root word disciplinare—to teach or instruct—refers to the system of teaching and nurturing that prepares children to achieve competence, self-control, self-direction, and caring for others. An effective discipline system must contain three vital elements:

1) a learning environment characterized by positive, supportive relationships;
2) a strategy for systematic teaching and strengthening of desired behaviors (proactive);
3) a strategy for decreasing or eliminating undesired or ineffective behaviors (reactive).

Each of these components needs to be functioning adequately for discipline to result in improved child behavior. Time-out is frequently used by early childhood educators as a disciplinary method to help children calm down or to change their behavior. Dan Gartrell (2001) refers to professionals who question the usefulness of this technique, especially with very young children. One of the arguments against time-outs is the fact that they do not allow children to develop their own internal controls.

Other arguments against time-outs are that they humiliate children, that teachers expect children to "think about what they have done" at a stage of development when they are incapable of doing so, and that they are sometimes used when the adults can think of nothing else to do. (Click & Karos, 2010)

The American Academy of Pediatrics has published guidelines for developing program polices in the Caring for our Children: National Health and Safety Performance Standanrds manual. You may view them at http://cfoc.nrckids.org/.

REFERENCE
American Academy of Pediatrics, American Public Health Association, National Resource Center for Health and Safety in Child Care and Early Education. 2011. *Caring for our children: National health and safety performance standards; Guidelines for early care and education programs. 3rd edition.* Elk Grove Village, IL: American Academy of Pediatrics; Washington, DC: American Public Health Association. Also

available at http://nrckids.org.

Gartrell, D. (2001). Replacing time-out: Part one–using guidance to build an encouraging classroom. Young Children, 56(6), 8-16.

Reflect:
1. Are there are other reasons why time-out is not an effective tool for helping toddlers to develop discipline?

2. Do you use time-outs in your own classroom? How effective has it been?

3. What other methods have you found to be effective?

Homework
*Review *Microsoft Office or /www.liveplan.com* template for Business Plans and Marketing Plans. Complete business plan questionnaire and draft policies for parent handbook

Session 4 Programs for Infants and Toddlers (birth through three years of age)
The American Academy of Pediatrics recommends the following policies and procedures:

During daily routines (e.g., feeding, play, diapering, hand washing, active play indoors and outdoors), teachers/caregivers comfort children, play and socially interact with them verbally, use positive facial expressions and a pleasant tone of voice and actions, and integrate required health and safety practices. At the time transitions occur for care of the child from the family to a staff member and back again, program staff members and families will use a consistent method to receive and give communication about the child's experiences and routines at home and while in the program. Communication about any unusual event or circumstance occurs promptly no matter when it occurs.

Children less than three (3) years of age shall not spend more than one-half (1/2) hour of time consecutively in confining equipment, such as swings, highchairs, jump seats, carriers or walkers. Children shall use such equipment only when they are awake. Such children shall be allowed time to play on the floor daily. Infants shall have supervised tummy time on the floor daily when they are awake.

Programs should publish minimum age requirements. Children in center-based care who are younger than 3 years have teachers/ caregivers and receive care in rooms that they do not share concurrently with older children unless special arrangements to care for children in mixed-age groups has been made. Children may be combined in mixed-age groups provided that infants and children younger than three (3) years are not grouped with children three (3) years and older except as set forth below. In mixed-age groups, the required staff:child ratios shall be based on the ages of the youngest children in the group if more than twenty percent (20%) of the children in the mixed-age group belongs to younger age grouping(s).

During first hour of the center's operation and last hour of operation, infants and children younger than three (3) years may be grouped with older children so long as staff:child ratios and group size are met based upon the age of the youngest child present in the group.

Children cannot pass through kitchens or laundry areas to reach other parts of the facility or playground. The playground should be adjacent to the facility. If not, a safe route to the playground must be approved by your licensing authority. Children should not cross driveways or parking lots to reach their playground. Children less than 3 years of age may not pass through the rooms of older children to reach the playground. Children 3 years of age and older may not pass through younger children's rooms to reach the playground. The entrance to the center cannot be through the playground unless that passageway is fenced separately from the playground space.

Assignments for teachers/caregivers to specific children minimize the number of teachers/caregivers interacting with each child during a given day and reduce the risk of injury and spread of infectious diseases. Teachers/caregivers should provide consistent, continuous care. No more than 5 teachers/caregivers participate in the infant's/toddler's care during a year. The program administrator designates one of these as the primary teacher/caregiver, the person most responsible for having a long-term, trusting relationship with the child and family, for making sure program policies are followed and communication between staff and family members occurs. Additional specialists may be involved with the child to address special needs or unique learning opportunities as long as the primary teacher/caregiver monitors and supports the child for these experiences.

Toilet learning occurs when the child shows readiness for using the toilet and the family is ready to support the child's involvement in doing so. Readiness indicators include desire to perform self-body care, ability to remain dry for at least two hours at a time, communication skills to understand and express concepts related to toileting, ability to get onto and sit with minimal assistance on a toilet adapted for the child's size or appropriately sized, and awareness of the sensations associated with releasing urine and stool.

Infants should be taken outside two to three times per day, as tolerated, and have supervised tummy time while awake every day. Toddlers (twelve months – three years) receive sixty to ninety minutes of outdoor play, weather permitting.

Parents should understand the importance of early intervention. ***Early intervention*** is a system of services that ***helps babies and toddlers with developmental delays or disabilities***. Early intervention focuses on helping eligible babies and toddlers learn the basic and brand-new skills that typically develop during the first three years of life, such as:
- *physical* (reaching, rolling, crawling, and walking);
- *cognitive* (thinking, learning, solving problems);
- *communication* (talking, listening, understanding);
- *social/emotional* (playing, feeling secure and happy); and
- *self-help* (eating, dressing).

Examples of early intervention services | If an infant or toddler has a disability or a developmental delay in one or more of these developmental areas, that child will likely be eligible for early intervention services. Those services will be tailored to meet the child's individual needs and may include:
- Assistive technology (devices a child might need)
- Audiology or hearing services
- Speech and language services
- Counseling and training for a family
- Medical services
- Nursing services
- Nutrition services
- Occupational therapy
- Physical therapy
- Psychological services

I. Educational services for children with disabilities are provided under IDEA (Individual with Disabilities Act). IDEA is a federal law which requires that a free and appropriate public education be available to children and youth with disabilities in mandated age ranges. This includes special education and related services.

a. Babies Can't Wait of Georgia/Early Intervention. Part H of IDEA (Individuals with Disabilities Act) establishes a system of services from birth until the third birthday, for children with special needs and their families. The law guarantees all children, regardless of their disability, access to services that will enhance their development. Multidisciplinary assessments are provided at no charge to the family. Each family is assigned a Service Coordinator. Access to appropriate services is directed by the child's Individualized Family Service Plan (IFSP). Funds are available to cover mandated services for eligible children when no other resources are available. At age three, eligible children are transitioned to other public and private programs to insure ongoing provision of needed services. Local offices are assigned by county or health district. **Referrals are accepted from parents, hospital nurseries, pediatricians or other medical personnel, child development centers, etc.** http://health.state.ga.us/programs/bcw/

b. Special Needs Preschool. Part B of IDEA (Individuals with Disabilities Act) provides for testing, placement in the least restrictive environment and an individualized education program (IEP) through the local public school system for children with disabilities ages 3 to 5 years. Contact is made through the "director of special needs preschool" or "preschool coordinator" of the local school system. Local phone numbers can be found in the blue pages under "education" or "school system" of the county in which the child lives. Note: It is frequently around age 2 1/2 to 3 years of age that concerns become pronounced and parents and primary health care providers are able to identify problems in development, speech or attention. **Parents should not hesitate to contact the local schools to express concerns and request an assessment to determine eligibility for public school services.**

c. Free and Appropriate Public Education. The public school system is required by federal law to provide appropriate educational services to children with special needs ages 3-21 years at no charge to families. The Georgia Department of Education has a web site at http://www.doe.k12.ga.us.

II. Federal Programs:

a. SSI (Supplemental Security Income). A federal program that provides monthly payments and Medicaid coverage to individuals eighteen years of age and under, who meet eligibility criteria. Babies who are blind or born weighing under 1200 grams are eligible. Two aspects of eligibility are disability (some condition must limit a child's ability to function like other children of the same age to a marked or severe degree) and income. Applications or information can be obtained from the local Social Security office (look in the blue pages of the phone book under US Government) or by calling 1-800-772-1213.

b. Deeming Waiver (Formerly known as the Katie Beckett Waiver). This program is for children who have a marked or severe disability where it has been established that it is less expensive for a child to receive treatment at home than in an institution. The program provides only Medicaid coverage when SSI has been denied due to income. It involves a lengthy, and sometimes intimidating, application process. The Deeming Waiver is generally in place for children with large medical or therapy needs/expenses who are not covered by private medical insurance, or whose medical insurance does not cover the prescribed services at the recommended intensity or frequency. For information or to apply, call the local office of Department of Family and Children Services (DFCS) listed under County Government in the blue pages of the phone book, or call Georgia Medical Care Foundation (GMCF) at 1-800-982-0411.

III. Services for Sensory Impaired Children (Vision and Hearing):

a. BEGIN (Babies Early Growth Intervention Network). This program serves children birth to age five years in a nine county metro Atlanta area. They teach parents developmental activities to help their vision impaired child progress. They also offer family support. For information call 404-875-9011.

b. Georgia PINES (Georgia Parent Infant Network for Educational Services). This program provides information and assistance to families of vision impaired, hearing impaired and multi-handicapped sensory impaired children. Parent advisors make home visits to teach families how to help their child. Georgia PINES also provides audiological assessments and has a loaner hearing aid service. Call 404-296-7101 for information.

c. Atlanta Area School for the Deaf (AASD). This program provides a preschool program for hearing impaired children ages 3 to 6 years from the Metro Atlanta area. Language and communication development are emphasized. They also provide audiology diagnostic services. For more information call 404-296-7101. (AASD sponsors Georgia PINES).

d. Hospital based, community agency based and private audiologists are also available to provide services throughout the state of Georgia. Call your local hospital, the Parent to Parent Central directory, or look in the phone book yellow pages for "audiologists."

IV. Miscellaneous Services:
a. Parent to Parent of Georgia. This program provides trained volunteers who offer emotional support to parents of children with special needs. This is a statewide service and there is no fee involved. For more

information call 770-451-5484 or 1-800-229-2038 outside Atlanta.

This program also maintains a central directory of early intervention services. This is a statewide information and referral source for agencies and individuals providing services to preschool children. To contact this service call 1-800-229-2038. For more information about Parent to Parent visit their web site at http://www.p2pga.org/.

b. Children's Medical Services (CMS). This program provides medical treatment and case management for children with chronic illnesses and disabilities. Eligibility is determined on medical diagnosis and financial status of the family. The programs are located by health district. Contact your local health department for information on the CMS in your area.

c. Georgia Advocacy Office. This is a protection and advocacy system for people with developmental disabilities. This system can provide legal advice and guidance to parents regarding IDEA (the Individual and Disabilities Act). The Georgia Advocacy Office can be contacted at 404-885-1234 (Atlanta) or 1-800-282-4538 (outside Atlanta).

d. Lekotek of Georgia, Inc., is a toy lending library that provides toys and consultation on developing play skills for children with disabilities. The telephone number is 404-633-3430.

ADDITIONAL RESOURCES OUTSIDE GEORGIA

I. Learning Disabilities Resources. For information regarding services for children with learning disabilities, the following may be helpful:

a. LD Fact Sheet: http://www.kidsource.com/NICHCY/learning_disabilities.html

b. National Center for Learning Disabilities: http://www.NCLD.ORG

c. LD Online: (note-there is a link to Georgia resources) http://www.ldonline.org/

Group Discussion - Daily Infant Toddler DAP, Schedule and Equipment needs ECE-1 & 3

Bright from the Start recommends the following minimum standards of care. Early education programs may be recognized for meeting these voluntary standards. Refer to the accreditation criteria of your preferred agency for other standards.

Exhibit A: STANDARDS OF CARE: Birth to 12 Months of Age

	Developmental Characteristics	Goals-Brain Development	Suggested Activities/Materials
Cognitive	Children learn through 5 senses, actively use hands to explore environment, infants will actively explore their environment when they feel secure, develop object permanence (knows objects exist out of sight and will search for them), begin to be aware of cause-effect relationships.	Children learn cause-effect relationships. Use of positive responses by adults when infants seek out and perform new skill will help infants gain self-confidence in their ability to learn. Children realize that out of sight objects exist.	Caregivers should provide times for children to play with toys and rattles, play peek-a-boo and hide and seek, and play on the floor. Musical toys, classical music, books, squeeze toys and rattles that have sound and visual effects with a variety of textures are examples of suggested materials.
Social Emotional	Children develop attachments, trust, learn to smile socially, recognize familiar people and their own self in mirrors. Children will explore their environment in the presence of caregivers.	Children become socially competent individuals. When a child's needs are met consistently, trust, love, and security develops. Children develop and maintain a trusting relationship with the same primary caregivers.	Caregivers should hug, cuddle and rock children often, especially to soothe and calm a fussy baby. Caregivers should refer to children by their name, and talk to them often. Voice tone and volume should be nurturing and encouraging. Mirrors, washable stuffed animals, soft dolls, and puppets should be available for the children.
Communication	Children communicate through crying, coo, gurgles, babbles, squeals, laughs, facial expressions, and respond to human voices. Infants will also imitate the sounds of others.	Children develop self-confidence as they learn to communicate their needs. Two-way communication teaches children that words have meanings and people will respond to their sounds.	Caregivers should talk, sing, read, and name objects on a daily basis. Cardboard picture books, variety of musical tapes, and puppets are example of suggested materials.
Physical	Children have innate reflexes (sucking, grasping), progress from lying on stomach with head raised to sitting alone, develop pincer grasp, reach, learn to transfer things from one hand to the other, learn to crawl, scoot and/or walk.	Children become aware of their own bodies in the environment and develop fine and gross motor skills.	Caregivers should encourage and facilitate fine and gross motor skills. Grasping toys, rattles, teething rings, play gyms, vinyl mats, push and pull toys, and riding equipment are examples of suggested materials.
Self Help	Children's needs are met by caregivers. Begin to encourage older infants to feed themselves and drink from a cup.	Children develop trust and security as needs are met on a regular basis. Older infants develop self-esteem and independence.	Caregivers should meet the needs (feeding, diapering, sleeping, and nurturing) of individual infants on a consistent basis. Provide finger foods and cups with tops to encourage self feeding when age appropriate.

Environment: The infant room should contain 4 basic areas: a sleeping area with cribs labeled for each child; a diaper changing area; an eating area with a place for younger infants to be held and older infants to sit; and a play area with materials/activities listed above to meet the needs of infants at many different stages of development.

Infants should be taken outside on a daily basis weather permitting and according to the parent's instructions. The outdoor environment should include areas of shade and sun, grass, concrete, and resilient ground cover, and may include a garden. In addition to the materials listed above, infant swings, low/soft climbing structures, and a play area with toys can be included. All activities and settings in the child care center will operate under strict supervision to ensure the safety of the children and in accordance with licensing rules and regulations. Individual attention and responsive care giving by the same individual are

Chapter 591-1-1 BFTS Rules and Regulations Child Care Learning Centers (June 12, 2005)

Early childhood professionals must understand the importance of developmentally appropriate learning activities especially during this crucial period of a child's cognitive, physical, emotional and social development. Caregivers must provide responsive and continuous interpersonal relationships and opportunities for child-initiated activities. Diapering, feeding, bathing, comforting and other needs must be met by competent staff members. Caregivers must make efforts to reduce the risk of Sudden Infant Death Syndrome (SIDS). Classrooms must be equipped to provide teachers and caregivers with the tools necessary to engage infants and promote development. The classroom should be divided into centers or interest areas such as: sleeping, feeding, diapering, and playing (manipulatives, dramatic play, reading, art, sand/water play, etc.). Caregivers should provide a consistent daily routine which is guided mainly by the child's feeding and sleeping patterns. The daily schedule should include time for greetings, small and large group play, outdoor play, regular diaper checks and feeding.

Sample equipment list

Cribs with fitted sheets	Diaper pail
Microwave	Sharpie markers
Swings	Refrigerator
Highchairs	Bottle Warmer
Bouncer seats	Velcro fastening feeding bibs
Changing tables and storage boxes	Soft tip spoons
Cubbies for diaper bags and coats	Bookshelves, baskets and board books
Toy storage systems	Mirrors
Rattles	Crawling mats
Music	Playhouse
Colorful educational carpets and quilts	Push and riding toys
Buggy for outdoor play transport	

Review handout or internet site for School Specialty or ABC School Supply Early Learning Planning guides

http://www.abcschoolsupply.com/pdf/2006EarlyLearningGuide.pdf

http://store.schoolspecialtyonline.net/

Internet Activity: Daily Reports Infant/Toddler Information Exchange

As more women enter the workforce, the number of infants and toddlers in child care settings has grown. It is not easy for the parents who place their children in the care of others, and it is sometimes difficult for the caregivers to know what is best for their youngest charges.

Log on to http://www.babycenter.com
Scroll down to "Baby Center Resources," then click on "Topics." Click on "Childcare" in the "Topics" column.
Under "Baby" click on "childcare" and "daily baby activity tracker for parents and caregivers".

1. What kinds of information are available to help caregivers?
2. How would you use the information to help parents?
3. Are there other topics that caregivers or parents would find helpful?
4. How will you communicate with parents regarding their child's daily activities?

Exhibit B: STANDARDS OF CARE: 12 to 24 months of age

	Developmental Characteristics	Goal – Brain Development	Suggested Activities/Materials
Cognitive	Children can follow simple directions, name familiar objects, understand relationships between objects, clearly see cause-effect relationships, and have an increasing desire to explore and experiment.	Children's explorations become increasingly purposeful to find meaning in events, objects, and words as they attempt to discover how the world works. They begin to understand the concept of parts and wholes.	Caregivers should allow children to explore the environment while supervising and encouraging their play. Books, classical music, pattern-making materials, matching manipulatives, interlocking toys that can be taken apart and put back together are examples of materials. Introduce sand and water play and other sensory activities. Provide multiples of popular toys and materials so children will not have to wait.
Social Emotional	Children experience stranger anxiety, look for caregivers response in uncertain situations, express affection for others, imitate others behaviors, engage more in parallel play and simple interaction with others, test limits, strive for independence, and are egocentric.	Children develop identity and a sense of self. They also realize they are separate individuals from caregivers and environment.	Caregivers should nurture children throughout the day both verbally and non-verbally. Caregivers should allow time for dramatic play. Examples of materials include books, play kitchen set, pots, pans, doll clothes, doll carriage, bottles, hats, dress up clothes, and a full length mirror.
Communication	Children progress from saying first words to speaking in simple sentences. They also point to and name objects, play with sounds, ask questions, imitate others' speech, and by 24 months have a vocabulary of 24- 50 words.	Children learn to communicate their needs, learn that words have meaning and power, learn the importance of written words, and develop a vocabulary.	Caregivers should expand on children's words, maintain eye contact, read, sing, and use gestures as well as words to communicate. Books, nursery rhymes, records, tapes, puppets, and flannel board stories are examples of suggested materials.
Physical	Children walk backwards, run, dance, turn the pages of a book one at a time, build block towers, push, pull, throw, empty, fill, open, shut, squeeze, poke, and drop toys.	Children are learning as they discover through physical development. Self-confidence develops as motor skills become better. Children enjoy repetition, such as dumping and filling. Eye- hand coordination is developing.	Caregivers should allow time for children to walk, climb, run, jump, dance, etc., and play with manipulatives that will enhance fine motor skills. Examples of materials include books, puzzles, blocks, stacking cubes and containers, nesting cups, lacing and stringing materials, musical instruments, wagons, push and pull toys, balls, finger paint, large markers, crayons,
Self Help	Children are still working on feeding themselves with a fork and spoon and drinking from a cup. They can finger feed with ease.	Children develop self-esteem, independence, and a positive attitude on feeding themselves, as well as fine motor skills.	Caregivers should allow children to feed themselves and select foods, and should sit with children during meals and encourage conversation. Provide child size eating utensils and cups with lids.
Environment: The set-up of rooms should be arranged so caregivers see all parts of the rooms. The toddler classroom should contain a sleeping area (older toddlers may use mats); a diapering area as well as a bathroom for children; an eating area; and a play area. The play area should be divided into basic areas such as books, manipulatives/blocks, dramatic play, gross motor, and art. Materials and equipment should be accessible to children as appropriate. The outdoor environment should include areas of shade and sun, grass, concrete, and resilient ground cover, and may include a garden. In addition to the materials listed above, infant swings low climbing structures, and a sand box with toys can be included. All activities and settings in the child care center will operate under strict supervision to ensure the safety of the children in accordance with child care licensing rules and			

Chapter 591-1-1 BFTS Rules and Regulations Child Care Learning Centers (June 12, 2005)

Reflect

The teachers in the toddler classes asked to meet with their program director, Mr. Washington. They were all feeling a lack of enthusiasm for what they were doing with the children and were not sure why. They felt the children were bored and that parents were beginning to question whether the children were really learning anything.

1. Define curriculum.
2. What do you think might be causing the teacher's feelings?
3. If you were Mr. Washington, what would you suggest?
4. What are the typical cycles (or scope and sequence) of learning activities in a toddler curriculum?
5. What can the teachers do to help parents understand what happens in the classroom?

Vendors
Day Care Group Purchasing Organization
www.dcgpo.com
- Insurance/Benefits
- Group Purchasing
- Food and Beverages
- Food Program Sponsorship
- Technology Solutions

Great deals can be found at surplus warehouse auctions
GA Department of Administrative Services-Surplus and Supply 404.756.4801
Government online surplus auctions www.govdeals.com
Local Department of Education surplus sales (call your local DOE surplus supply warehouse)

Purchasing a Center in the Southeast region
Contact Judy Mims, CFA (678) 277-9951 www.bullrealty.com
"Specializing in Merger & Acquisition Advisory Services"

Session 5 Programs for Preschool Students (three to five years of age)

The preschool program should be designed to enhance and encourage the cognitive, language, early literacy, and mathematics development of children through activities in the classroom. Teachers/caregivers plan and provide a balance of guided and self-initiated play and learning indoors and outdoors. Children observe, explore, order, and reorder, make mistakes and find solutions, and move from concrete to abstract learning. Teachers should possess the skills necessary to manage disruptive behavior as well as identify the typical and atypical development for three to five year old children. Teachers must demonstrate the ability to promote the social and emotional development of children, including children's development of independence and their ability to adapt to their environment and cope with stress while considering the cultural backgrounds and distinctions of the families served y the program. To build long-term, trusting relationships, the program limits the number of teachers/caregivers and other adults who care for any one preschool-aged child to no more than eight adults in a given year and no more than three teachers/caregivers in one day. These staff members are considered primary teachers/caregivers.

The curriculum includes expressive activities such as free play, painting, drawing, storytelling, sensory activities, music, singing, dancing, and taking part in drama, all of which integrate thinking and feeling and foster socialization, conflict resolution, and language and cognitive development. Teachers/caregivers encourage children's language development using reading, speaking and listening interactively, responding to questions about observations and feelings, storytelling, and writing. To encourage body mastery, the curriculum includes learning socially acceptable self-feeding, appropriate use of the toilet, and large- and small-muscle activities. Preschoolers should have 90 to 120 minutes per eight-hour day of moderate to vigorous activities. In programs where children made choices and worked at their own pace in a variety of well defined activity settings, children exhibited high levels of social interaction, child-initiated behavior, and child involvement in activities.

Source:
Elizabeth Phyfe-Perkins and Joanne Shoemaker, "Indoor Play Environments",
The Young Child at Play: Reviews of Research, Washington, DC: NAEYC, 1986, p. 184

Classroom arrangements should be inviting and stimulating. The physical layout should be practical and accommodate numerous learning centers equipped with materials and supplies which encourage exploration and discovery.

A few tips for setup of learning centers:
1. Install a loft or pillows and bean bags to define quiet reading space away from active or noisy centers
2. Use bookshelves, table or play equipment (such as kitchen sets) to distinguish learning areas
3. Turn computer screens from windows and conceal cords.
4. Mount or enclose audio/visual equipment in cabinets to hide cords and remove operational buttons from children's reach.
5. Be sure all tables and chairs are the appropriate size to insure comfort
6. Allow enough seating for small groups to work together
7. Use walls for posters, display shelves and supply storage in cabinets, etc.
8. Suggested centers: art, manipulatives (legos, geo boards, puzzles or blocks), language or reading, listening, large motor, math and science, dramatic play, music and movement.

Exhibit C: STANDARDS OF CARE: 24 - 36 Months of Age

	Developmental Characteristics	Goals - Brain Development	Suggested Activities Materials
Cognitive	Children respond to simple directions, begin to imitate adults, have a limited attention span, begin to sequence and match objects, identify objects and ask questions.	Children develop reasoning and problem solving skills. Children begin to think for themselves, problems begin to be worked out mentally rather than by use of trial and error, creativity and logical thinking are expanded.	Caregivers should let children attempt to work out problems on their own, create, and explore. Suggested materials include books, large pegs to group, sort, and stack, large crayons, markers, paints, paint brushes, paper, and classical music.
Social/ Emotional	Children are protective of their possessions, want to be independent, are self- centered, they play near and watch other children, occasionally joining in play with others, and they begin to engage in imaginative and dramatic play. They say no often.	Children develop social skills (getting along with others).	Caregivers should encourage cooperative and individual learning opportunities (sharing and taking turns) as well as creative expression. (But caregivers should understand that Twos do not do this well.) Provide opportunities for dramatic play with simple themes and props such as doctor's office or restaurant. Caregivers should allow children to make choices on activities. Multiples of some popular toys and materials.
Communication	Children should engage and be encouraged to begin to use language more in play, ask names of things, make negative statements, and increase their vocabulary.	Children develop fine motor skills and reading and readiness skills (turning pages left to right) Vocabulary, memory, and Speech are increased by labeling items in books and asking questions.	Caregivers should talk clearly to children using simple positive statements and allow children to respond back (two-way communication), expose children to the written word through a variety of literacy based materials, and sing throughout the day Caregivers should allow children to make choices on activities. Caregivers should bend, kneel, or sit down to establish eye contact when talking with children. Examples of materials include picture books and short story books with repetition and rhymes, poems, and finger plays. Reading areas should be cozy and inviting for children and include pillows, puppets, stuffed animals, flannel board, etc. Materials, equipment, and real objects should be labeled.
Physical	Children of this age walk upstairs 2 feet on a step, sit on riding toys and push with feet, hop in place and jump from low heights, climb, run, throw objects using forearms, and are increasing fine motor development.	Children develop eye-hand coordination, prewriting skills, large muscle skills, and strengthen fine motor skills and increase gross motor skills.	Caregivers should allow children to run, throw, catch, jump, climb, ride on riding toys and make choices on activities. Low climbing structures, riding toys, balls, modeling clay, blocks, puzzles and books are examples of suggested materials.
Self Help	Children can feed themselves, wash and dry their hands with assistance, and are beginning to be or are toilet trained.	Children develop positive self esteem, independence, fine motor skills, and one to one correspondence. Children also learn to count objects and follow simple directions (cognitive).	Caregivers should allow children to serve themselves and help set the table, and should sit with children during meals and encourage conversation. Provide soap and paper towels for children, as well as child size utensils.

© Penn Consulting

> Environment: The setup of the rooms should be arranged so caregivers see all parts of the rooms. The classroom for this age group should contain a diapering area and a bathroom for the children; an eating area; and a play area divided into centers such as books, manipulatives, sand and water, blocks, dramatic play, large motor, music, and art. Materials and equipment should be on the children's developmental levels. The outdoor area should have areas of shade and sun, grass, concrete, and resilient ground cover, and may include a garden. In addition to the materials listed above, swings, low climbing structures, playhouse, and a sand box with toys can be included. All activities and settings in the child care center will operate under strict supervision to ensure the safety of the children in accordance with child care licensing rules and regulations.

BFTS Chapter 591-1-1 Child Care Learning Centers (June 12, 2005)

Internet Activity-Visit the DECAL site and review the Pre-K materials list www.decal.state.ga.us. Visit lakeshore.com site to use classroom arrangement software. ADM-5
www.lakeshorelearning.com
www.lakeshorelearning.com/classroom_designer/cd_launch.jsp?popup=yes
www.kaplanco.com/resources/floorPlannerIndex.asp

Playground Equipment Providers
Hasley Recreation http://www.hasley-recreation.com/
Miracle Recreation http://www.miracleplayground.com/

Playground Grants

Play Smart – is a collaborative effort between Smart Start, the early childhood division of the United Way of Metropolitan Atlanta, Bright from the Start: Georgia Department of Early Care and Learning, and KaBOOM! Child care providers in the metro-Atlanta area can apply for challenge grants to create high-quality outdoor play spaces.

Contact: Sarah Sheppard, Project Manager, Smart Start, the early childhood division of the United Way of Metropolitan Atlanta, at 404-527-7361 or ssheppard@unitedwayatlanta.org

Other websites for **playground grants**:

http://www.schoolgrants.org/Links/playground.htm
http://www.spreadtech.biz/ playground surfacing
http://www.boundlessplaygrounds.org/partners/foundation.php
http://www.grants.gov/
http://corporate.homedepot.com/wps/portal/Grants
http://www.nikebiz.com/responsibility/nike_giving_guidelines.html
http://www.aad.org/public/sun/grants.html
http://www.christopherreeve.org/site/c.ddJFKRNoFiG/b.4048063/
http://www.atlantafalcons.com/Community/Youth_Foundation.aspx
http://www.lowes.com/lowes/lkn?action=pg&p=AboutLowes/outdoor/index.html
http://corporate.mattel.com/about-us/philanthropy/grantmaking.aspx
http://www.nrpa.org/newsletter/storyViewer.aspx?templateId=3&editionId=276&contentId=2633
http://www.peacefulplaygrounds.com/grants.htm
www.cbocenter.org/docs/policyday/HEALBrochure(4-07).pdf
http://www.legochildrensfund.org/Guidelines.html
http://hiltonworldwide.hilton.com/en/ww/company_info/ContributionRequestApplication.pdf

Curriculum: Most states provide a list of pre-approved prekindergarten program curriculum models. Any curriculum will need supplementation of developmentally appropriate materials in order to engage all learners.

© Penn Consulting

List of curriculum providers
A Beka Book Publishers 1-877-223-5226
Alpha Omega 1-800-622-3070
Alpha Phonics 1-888-922-3000
Bob Jones University Press 1-800-845-5731
Christ Centered Curriculum 1-800-884-7858
Creative Curriculum 1-800-637-3652
Creative Discoveries 1-781- 596-1143
Early Beginnings 1-800-387-4156
Highscope 1- 800-407-7377
Purposeful Design Publications 1-800-367-0798
Rod and Staff Publishers 1-606 522-4348

A few Curriculum Considerations:
Teaching and learning objectives
Teaching and learning styles
Cultural sensitivity
Age appropriate
Research based
Product quality
Cost and return policy
Packaging

© Penn Consulting

Session 6 Programs for School-age children (five to twelve years of age)

Quality school age programs meet the social and emotional needs and enhance the developmental tasks of 5- to 12-year old children. Teachers must be able to recognize and appropriately manage difficult behaviors, in addition to implementing a cognitively and physically enriching program that has been developed with input from parents. The program should provide a safe environment which is conducive to learning. Research indicates effective programs include academic and recreational activities which enrich and promote learning. Programs should be sensitive to the community it serves.

The United States Department of Education encourages the following guidelines for extended c are programs: "The types of activities found in a quality after-school program include tutoring and supplementing instruction in basic skills, such as reading, math, and science; drug and violence prevention curricula and counseling; youth leadership activities (e.g., Boy Scouts, Girl Scouts, academic clubs); volunteer and community service opportunities; college awareness and preparation; homework assistance centers; courses and enrichment in the arts and culture; computer instruction; language instruction, including English as a second language; employment preparation or training; mentoring; activities linked to law enforcement; and supervised recreation and athletic programs and events.

However, many programs allow children to spend far too much time in passive activities such as television or video viewing. One reason for poor-quality after-school activities may be inadequate facilities. Most after-school programs do not have the use of a library, computers, museum, art room, music room, or game room on a weekly basis. Too many programs do not have access to a playground or park." (P. Seppanen, J. Love, D. deVries, and L. Bernstein, *National Study of Before and After School Programs* (Washington, D.C.: U.S. Department of Education, 1993))

"Looking across the constellation of after-school programs--those in schools, those run in the facilities of community-based organizations, or those found in houses of faith--researchers have identified some common characteristics necessary to developing high-quality programs that meet the needs of a diverse population of school-age children. These characteristics of high-quality after-school programs help ensure children's continued growth, development, and learning throughout the pre-adolescent and adolescent school years.

Sources:
(Carnegie Council, 1994; Fashola, in press; Janie Funkhouser et. al., *Extending Learning Time for Disadvantaged Students* (Washington, D.C.: Department of Education, 1995); Institute for Out-of-School Time, Making the Case, Presented at Regional Technical Assistance Workshops for the 21st Century Community Learning Centers Program, Spring, 1998; Janette Roman, ed., *The NSACA Standards for Quality School-Age Care* (Boston, MA: National School-Age Care Alliance, 1998); Elizabeth Riesner and Janie Funkhauser, Designing Effective After-School Programs (Washington, D.C.: Policy Studies Associates, 1998); de Kanter et. al., 1997. Vandell, 1997; White House Child Care Conference, 1997.)

Common elements include:
1. Goal setting and strong management
2. Quality after-school staffing
3. Low staff/student ratios
4. Attention to safety, health, and nutrition issues
5. Effective partnerships with community-based organizations, juvenile justice agencies, law enforcement, and youth groups
6. Strong involvement of families
7. Coordinating learning with the regular school day

8. Linkages between school-day teachers and after-school personnel
9. Evaluation of program progress and effectiveness

The Afterschool Alliance, **Washington, D.C.** http://www.afterschoolalliance.org/

The Afterschool Alliance consists of public, private, and nonprofit groups committed to raising awareness and expanding resources for after-school programs. Initiated and coordinated by the Charles Stewart Mott Foundation, the Alliance's initial partners include the U.S. Department of Education, JCPenney, The Advertising Council, The Entertainment Industry Foundation, and the Creative Artists Agency Foundation. It is the vision of the Afterschool Alliance that by raising national and local awareness about the importance of afterschool programs, all children will have access to quality, affordable after-school programs by 2010.

The National Afterschool Alliance is promoting a new mentoring program. You can read about it at http://www.afterschoolalliance.org/afterschoolsnack/ASnack.cfm?idBlog=DD282365-215A-A6B3-02FBFC914D9FED70. "Earlier this year, President Obama launched the My Brother's Keeper initiative to address persistent opportunity gaps faced by boys and young men of color and ensure that all young people can reach their full potential.

Through this initiative, the Administration is joining with cities and towns, businesses, and foundations who are taking important steps to connect young people to mentoring, support networks, and the skills they need to find a good job or go to college and work their way into the middle class. The President is calling on Americans interested in getting involved in My Brother's Keeper to sign up as long-term mentors to young people at WH.gov/mybrotherskeeper. This effort will engage Americans from all walks of life to sign up to develop sustained and direct mentoring relationships that will play vital roles in the lives of young people. Secretary of Education Arne Duncan recently sat down with 10 Hispanic young men in Denver for an honest conversation, and to discuss My Brother's Keeper.

Many may ask why these programs are needed for minority students...please see the Children's Defense Fund Cradle to Prison pipeline summary fact sheets for the nation and Georgia.

Ten core competencies common to the professionals who work with the after school child are:
1. Child and Youth Growth and Development
2. Learning Environment and Curriculum
3. Child/Youth Observation and Assessment
4. Interactions with Children and Youth
5. Youth Engagement
6. Cultural Competency and Responsiveness
7. Family, School, and Community Relationships
8. Safety and Wellness
9. Program Planning and Development
10. Professional Development and Leadership

INTERNET ACTIVITY: More than 35 million children between the ages of 6 and 16 have both parents working outside the home. Although many of these youngsters are latchkey children (caring for themselves after school), a growing number are enrolled in group programs. Colleges and universities are just beginning to respond to the need for information and training for those who staff these programs. However, several organizations have been established to provide information and to set standards. One of these is the National School Age Care Alliance.

Click on several of the topics listed on the left side of the page.

1. What kinds of information are available?

2. In what ways could this site help professionals working in out-of-school time programs?

3. Which topic did you find the most interesting or helpful? Why?

Marketing
Every school has a history. That history is your brand identity. Some people think daycare or school marketing is as simple as placing a classifieds or yellow page advertisement, and for some, it can be. If you have competition (and you probably do), you can earn a majority local market share by successfully branding your school. Branding is important because people purchase on emotion. Parents choose businesses that share their values, especially when it comes to their children. It's important to identify and promote your branded identity so you can connect with your target clientele at a glance. A well-rounded branded strategy allows you to do just that. Careful critical thinking now pays huge dividends later.

If your daycare or school is not branded, then you're just another daycare or school. There's nothing that separates you from the competition. This reduces your potential customer pool to make choices based on factors such as price, convenience and preconceived notions. Without a branded identity, you have no control over preconceptions and therefore you're forced to either compete on pricing and location alone. This is not a way to successfully grow your business. Cheap does not outsell quality.

Clear, consistent and distinct messaging is what turns a common school into a real brand. If you want to be heard, your brand needs to be speaking in a unique voice. Sounds abstract? …break this down into a few actionable items:

Looks: It's important to cultivate a visual language and aesthetic for your brand. This means that your website, your ads, your products and all of your other brand assets should have a unified style. Use colors, fonts and logos consistently.

Words: If you had to describe your brand with five keywords, what would they be? When you're able to answer this question, use these keywords to guide every piece of content you put out - from the Contact page on your website to the calls to action on your ads.

Answers: To achieve successful branding, you need to determine the question or need that your business fulfills. What do you have to offer that clients won't be able to find anywhere else? This is the key to your branding efforts.

Source:
WIXBlog, How to Get Big-Brand Attention for your Small Business, July 10, 2014 Retrieved from http://www.wix.com/blog/2014/07/

Marketing methods:
- Signs/billboards
- Media Advertising (print (newspaper. Brochures, leaflets, flyers), television, radio, online/website)
- Phone Directories
- Direct Mail
- Trade Shows
- Public Relations Activities

© Penn Consulting

- Informal Marketing/Networking

Practical Applications- ADM-2,3 Develop a program appropriate for each age group including equipment and supplies, daily schedule, marketing material (flyer, postcard and brochure using Microsoft Office publisher templates) Daily schedules must follow Bright from the Start guidelines regarding outdoor play, television viewing, meal service, etc.

Sample Daily Schedules

Infant Daily Schedule (6 to 12 months)

Schedules for infants are used as a guide for the day. Infant classroom schedules are responsive to individual children's needs. Infants who eat table foods follow a schedule, while younger infants eat at appropriate intervals based on their indicators to staff that they are hungry. Infants eating table food follow the program's snack and meal schedule, while younger infants eat at appropriate intervals based on their indicators to staff that they are hungry. Developmental activities including sensory, large motor (both indoors and outdoors), and small motor activities happen throughout the day as children are interested. Routines, such as diapering, eating, and napping, occur throughout the day to meet each child's unique schedule.

6:00-7:00	Staff members greet children and parents and assists with storage of personal belongings. Children are provided opportunities for free choice play in learning centers (reading, listening, dramatic play, art, manipulative play, music).
7:00-8:30	Potty breaks and diaper changes as needed.
8:30-9:30	Breakfast snack for older babies, diaper changing, feeding
9:30-10:30	Circle time -(Prayer and Interactive Bible story) developmental activities and experiences (sensory, small motor, music, and language), diaper changing, naps as needed
10:30-11:15	Large motor/outdoor play time
11:15-11:35	Check and change diapers as needed
11:35-12:15	Lunch for older infants, diaper changing, feeding, floor play
12:15-2:30	Story time and naps, as needed
2:30-3:30	Snack for older infants, diaper changing, feeding
3:30-4:00	Large motor/outdoor play time
4:00-4:30	Check and change diapers as needed
4:30-5:30	Music and movement- developmental activities and experiences
5:30-6:00	Story time
6:00-6:15	Check and change diapers, prepare for supper
6:15-7:00	Supper and departure

© Penn Consulting

Toddler Daily Schedule (13 months to 35 months)

6:00-7:00	Staff members greet children and parents and assists with storage of personal belongings. Children are provided opportunities for free choice play in learning centers (reading, listening, dramatic play, art, manipulative play, music). Potty breaks and diaper changes as needed.
7:00-7:30	Circle time: songs, stories and finger plays. Children develop calendar skills (months/days, seasons and weather). Gross motor skills development through active indoor activities.
7:30-8:00	Prepare for morning snack. Wash hands and faces. Potty break and diaper change.
8:00-8:30	Morning snack-children are encouraged to develop self-feeding skills.
8:30-8:45	Cleanup and wash hands.
8:45-9:15	Circle Time-Devotions (Prayer and Interactive Bible story with the teacher, the children will be a part of the action in the story.)
9:15-9:30	Potty breaks and diaper changes as needed. Wash hands and faces.
9:30-10:15	Early literacy activities: Pre-reading and math lessons. Children learn to recognize the alphabet and numbers (count) 0-10. Art project time - Arts and Craft.
10:15-10:30	Potty breaks and diaper changes as needed.
10:30-11:30	Outdoor play-weather permitting. Explore the outdoors. Children will learn about trees, leaves, grass etc. Gross motor activities: running, jumping, climbing and riding.
11:30-12:00	Potty breaks and diaper changes as needed.
12:00-12:30	Lunch time-occasionally served family style. Cleanup and wash hands.
12:30-12:45	Potty breaks and diaper changes as needed.
12:45-1:15	Music and Movement. Interactive learning songs. Children are introduced to various types of music and songs for play.
1:15-1:30	Story time with teacher and prepare for nap. Potty breaks and diaper changes as needed.
1:30-3:00	Rest period or nap time.
3:00-3:30	Potty breaks and diaper changes as needed. Prepare for snack.
3:30-4:00	Afternoon Snack - Cleanup and wash hands.
4:00-5:00	Outdoor play weather permitting. Play outside on the playground. Potty breaks and diaper changes as needed.
5:00-6:00	Free choice play in learning centers. Teachers interact with the children as they play and are introduced to musical toys and books, alphabet books and blocks, and number concepts. Caregivers facilitate fine and gross motor skills development through play with finger paint, markers, paint and brushes, puzzles, blocks, play gyms, vinyl mats, push and pull toys, and riding equipment.
6:00-6:15	Potty breaks and diaper changes as needed. Prepare for supper.
6:15-7:00	Supper and dismissal

© Penn Consulting

Three and Four Year Old Class Daily Schedule

6:00-7:00	Staff members greet children and parents and assists with storage of personal belongings. Children are provided opportunities for free choice play in learning centers (reading, listening, dramatic play, art, manipulative play, music). Potty break-children are taught proper hand washing technique during each break.
7:00-7:45	Circle time: songs, stories and finger plays. Children develop calendar skills (months/days, seasons and weather). Gross motor skills development through active indoor activities.
7:45-8:15	Wash hands and faces. Potty break.
8:15-9:00	Circle Time and Interactive Bible story with the teacher, the children will be a part of the action in the story. Calendar skills.
9:00-9:15	Cleanup and wash hands.
9:15-9:45	Morning Snack-children are encouraged to develop self-feeding skills.
9:45-10:00	Potty break. Wash hands and faces.
10:00-10:45	Early literacy activities: Pre-reading and math lessons. Children learn to recognize the alphabet and numbers (count) 0-10. Art project time - Arts and Craft.
10:45-11:00	Potty break
11:00-12:00	Outdoor play-weather permitting. Explore the outdoors. Children will learn about trees, leaves, grass etc. Gross motor activities: running, jumping, climbing and riding.
12:00-12:15	Potty break
12:15-12:45	Lunch time-occasionally served family style. Cleanup and wash hands.
12:45-1:00	Potty break
1:00-1:15	Interactive learning songs. Children are introduced to various types of music and songs for play.
1:15-1:30	Story time with teacher and prepare for nap. Potty break
1:30-3:00	Rest period or nap time.
3:00-3:30	Potty break. Prepare for snack.
3:30-4:00	Afternoon Snack time. Cleanup and wash hands.
4:00-5:00	Outdoor play weather permitting. Play outside on the playground. Potty break
5:00-6:00	Free choice play in learning centers. Teachers interact with the children as they play and are introduced to musical toys and books, alphabet books and blocks, and number concepts. Caregivers facilitate fine and gross motor skills development through play with finger paint, markers, paint and brushes, puzzles, blocks, play gyms, vinyl mats, push and pull toys, and riding equipment.
6:00-6:15	Potty break - Prepare for supper.
6:15-7:00	Supper and dismissal

© Penn Consulting

Extended Care Daily Schedule
5-12 years

6:00-7:00	Children are greeted warmly and assisted in storing personal belongings. Opportunities to rest quietly or play in free choice learning centers.
7:00-7:15	Restroom Break
7:15-7:45	Morning Snack and cleanup
7:45-8:00	Gather belongings and load school buses for school attendance.
3:00-3:15	Store personal belongings and restroom break
3:15-3:45	Afterschool snack and cleanup
3:45-4:00	Restroom break
4:00-5:00	Outdoor play (weather permitting)
5:00-5:15	Restroom break
5:15-6:00	Homework Tutorial, guest speakers, group rap sessions, computer lab time and/or free choice play. Reading and Storytelling time, Listening centers.
6:00-6:15	Restroom Break. Prepare for supper.
6:15-7:00	Supper and dismissal

Holiday/Teacher Workday Care 5-12 years of age

6:00-7:00	Children are greeted warmly and assisted in storing personal belongings. Opportunities to rest quietly or play in free choice learning areas.
7:00-7:15	Restroom Break
7:15-8:15	Circle time: Bible Story, Prayer, and Songs, Review rules through story telling, role play, etc., calendar skills and weather
8:15-9:30	Language Arts-Integrated art and language activities (spelling, poetry, reading)
9:30-9:45	Restroom Break
9:45-10:15	Morning snack
10:15-11:15	Outdoor play (weather permitting)
11:15-11:30	Restroom break
11:30-12:00	Math Fun-Integrated numbers, music and computer
12:00-12:15	Restroom break
12:15-12:45	Lunch
12:45-1:00	Restroom break
1:00-1:30	Foreign Language exploration
1:30-3:00	Rest period. Children nap or listen to soft music, play quietly with puzzles or read.
3:00-3:15	Store personal belongings and restroom break
3:15-3:45	Afternoon snack and cleanup
3:45-4:00	Restroom break
4:00-5:00	Outdoor play
5:00-5:15	Restroom break
5:00-6:00	Homework Tutorial, guest speakers, group rap sessions, computer lab time and/or free choice play in learning centers. Reading and Storytelling time, Listening centers.
6:00-6:15	Restroom Break. Prepare for supper.
6:15-7:00	Supper and dismissal

© Penn Consulting

Discuss key components of marketing material: **Sample Flyer** for School Age Extended Care Program

Register today for the STARS Extended Care Program!

The Shepherd's Training Academy Before and After School Program

Our mission is to provide an enriching academic and recreational program which promotes the development of skills to excel in life.
- age-appropriate activities including fine arts and athletic programs, equipment, and curriculum.
- participants develop social and language skills through multisensory learning experiences
- certified educational professionals provide a Christ-centered educational environment
- increase standardized test scores through evidence based interventions

Tuition is due the first of each month.
One Child $140.00 Two Children $260.00
Activity fee $45/month covers:

The program is available all school days and teacher workdays.
Please contact the office in the event of inclement weather.

"Friday Frolic" Fun Days-field trips and parent's night out the last Friday of each month!

Schedule of Activities

A sample schedule could be included…

Register by April 1 for the **Summer STEAM Camp! STEAM** is an exciting multi-sensory learning opportunity for young people with a special emphasis on the *STEAM* curriculum areas (Science, Technology, Engineering, Art, and Mathematics). The camp sessions were created by content specialists to be both fun and full of learning.

Preparing future leaders to impact the world for Jesus Christ… Ephesians 4:12
4120 Presidential Parkway Doraville, GA 30340
770.455.4781 5shepard@bellsouth.net

Federal Copyright Act (17 USC § 101 *et seq.*)
The school must follow the copyright law regarding the use of printed material, music, and other media products.

Prerecorded video cassettes, videodiscs, CDs, music tapes, and records available in stores are for home use only unless a user obtains a license from the copyright owner or its agent to use them elsewhere.

Rentals or purchases of such media products do not carry with them licenses for non-home showings. A separate license must be obtained to show such materials for entertainment purposes in schools, day cares, churches, and other public gatherings even if no admission or other fee is charged. Some copyrighted materials may be used in face-to-face teaching activities because the law makes a specific, limited exception for such uses (17 USC 110.1). This exception is limited to instances when a teacher is present in a classroom and uses home videocassettes for the purpose of teaching students (not principally to entertain them).

Schools may, through organizations representing movie producers (Motion Picture Licensing Corporation [MPLC] http://www.mplc.org/index/worldwide) or recording artists and publishers (e.g., Christian Copyright Licensing International [CCLI]; Broadcast Music, Inc. [BMI]; or American Society of Composers, Authors, & Publishers [ASCAP]) or by the purchase of "right to use" directly from the composer, publisher, or artist, obtain an annual umbrella license affording the opportunity to use any covered copyrighted materials as often as the user chooses.

Christian Video Licensing International (CVLI) is a partnership between Motion Picture Licensing Corporation (MPLC) and Christian Copyright Licensing International (CCLI) created to specifically serve the needs of the religious community. This new independent licensing agency provides an all-encompassing, low-cost license to churches, religious schools, child care centers, and all other church-operated sites. The CVLI license includes over 55 affiliated producers, ranging from Hollywood studios and Christian producers to family values and faith-based producers. The CVLI Family Values License allows you to comply with the US Copyright Act requirement for a license to exhibit copyrighted home videocassettes and DVDs, both simply and affordably. ASCI members receive a 10 percent discount off the license fee. For more information, please visit their website at www.cvli.org or call CVLI at **888/771-CVLI (2854)**.

Visit the website above and indicate the cost of a license for your center/school.

What are the fines for showing videos without a license?

What rating is appropriate for early education environments?

Session 7 Recruiting and Hiring Staff

The key to a successful early childhood program is its staff. Research indicates that "general intellectual aptitude has not typically been linked to higher student achievement. However a positive relationship exists between teachers with high verbal ability and student achievement." *Qualities of Effective Teachers*, James H. Stronge Potential candidates should be professionally qualified, really enjoy children, and possess excellent communication and social skills. Teachers should also understand the importance of pre-service and ongoing professional development.

Highly qualified teachers with specific training in child development improve the quality of care, improve early childhood literacy skills development and increase their student's performance on intelligence tests.

Minimum credential recommendations:
1. High School Diploma or GED
2. Child Development Associate
3. Early Childhood Education Degree and/or coursework
4. Successful Background check
5. Health Assessment

Recommended Pre-service and ongoing staff training topics:
1. Developmentally Appropriate Practices
2. Parent Support and Relations
3. Injury and Illness/Infection Prevention
4. Immunization Requirements
5. Occupational Health and Safety Practices
6. Emergency Procedures
7. First Aid/ CPR
8. Recognition and Reporting of Child Abuse
9. Nutrition
10. Medication Administration Policies and Practices
11. Special Needs Care/Inclusion
12. Behavior Management

Review SMART Start Georgia offers scholarships for continued education and incentive salary supplements. $400-$2K annually

Early Childhood Educators are required to complete **orientation prior** to assignment with children. **Within the first year** of employment educators must complete **10 clock hours of approved training;** 4 hours in the following topics: disease control, cleanliness, basic hygiene, illness detection, illness disposition, and childhood injury control; 2 hours in identifying, reporting, and meeting the needs of abused and neglected or deprived children. Successful completion of a biennial training program in CPR, triennial completion of first aid both for infants and children.

Annually providers are required to complete at least **10 clock hours of training per calendar year** in the following areas of study: child development (nutrition, learning styles, Special needs child care that is compliant with the Americans with Disabilities Act (ADA), behavior management, and injury control); health (common infectious diseases, sanitation, etc.); child abuse and neglect, parent-staff relationships and communication, and recordkeeping.

For further information regarding training requirements or approved trainings visit the websites below:

Bright from the Start: Georgia Department of Early Care and Learning:
http://www.training.decal.ga.gov

Georgia **Teacher Qualification and Training Requirements** are as follows:

A school or day care center must have a designated teacher/lead caregiver for each group of children.
Qualifications of Teacher/Lead Caregiver
Be at least eighteen (18) years of age;
Have either a high school diploma or a general education diploma (G.E.D.) or one (1) year's qualifying child care experience if hired after the
effective date of these rules;
Have current evidence of successful completion of a biennial training program in cardiopulmonary resuscitation (CPR) and a triennial training program in first aid provided by certified or licensed health care professionals and which covers the provision of emergency care to infants and children if the caregiver is to be counted as part of the fifty percent (60%) of the child care staff with the required current evidence of CPR and first aid training;
Participate in the orientation and training required by these rules;
Not be suffering from any physical handicap or mental health disorder that would interfere with the person's ability to perform assigned job duties adequately and in accordance with these rules;
Never have been shown by credible evidence, e.g., a court or jury, a Department investigation or other reliable evidence to have abused, neglected or deprived a child or adult or to have subjected any person to serious injury as a result of intentional or grossly negligent misconduct as evidenced by an oral or written statement to this effect obtained at the time of application;
Not have a criminal record;
Not have made any material false statements concerning qualifications requirements either to the Department or the proposed licensees.

Caregivers/Aides
A center may employ caregivers/aides to assist the teacher/lead caregiver in the care of children in any group within the center. No caregiver/ aide shall be solely responsible for a group of children.
Qualifications of Caregivers/Aides
Be at least sixteen (16) years of age;
Have current evidence of successful completion of biennial training program in cardiopulmonary resuscitation (CPR) and a triennial training program in first aid which have been offered by certified or licensed health care professionals and which dealt with the provision of emergency care to infants and children if the caregiver is to be counted as part of the fifty percent (50%) of the child care staff with the required current evidence of CPR and first aid training;
Participate in the orientation and training required by these rules; would interfere with the person's ability to perform assigned job duties adequately and in accordance with these rules;
Not have a criminal record;
Not have made any material false statements concerning qualifications requirements either to the Department or the proposed licensees.

Other staff members.
The school or center shall have qualified and sufficient direct-care, clerical, housekeeping and maintenance employees to ensure full compliance with these rules without neglecting the supervision of the children. Staff shall supervise all independent contractors, volunteers, chaperons and students in training whenever they are in the presence of the children.
Substitute Employees. The center shall provide for substitute staff when regular staff is absent from work. All substitute employees shall be at least eighteen years of age. Substitute caregiver staff shall be informed of these rules and the center's policies and procedures for the age group for which they will be

providing care. Substitute service staff shall be informed of the center's policies and procedures necessary to the proper performance of their job duties in compliance with these rules. A substitute employee must have a satisfactory criminal records check determination and receive orientation training. If any substitute serves in anyone (1) position longer than six months, the substitute so employed must meet all staffing requirements for that position.

Students in Training. The center may employ students in training, meaning students enrolled in an educational course of study which requires or permits them to observe and participate in the care of children at a child care learning center during a limited period of time, i.e., one (1) quarter, one (1) trimester or (1) semester. Such students must be under the direct supervision of center personnel at all times.

Work Schedules. Staff shall not regularly be scheduled to perform child care duties for more than twelve (12) hours within any twenty-four (24) hour period.

First Aid and CPR. At least fifty percent (50%) of the caregiver staff shall have current evidence of first aid training and cardiopulmonary resuscitation. There must always be an employee with current evidence of first aid training and CPR on the center premises whenever children are present and on any center-sponsored field trip.

Compliance with Applicable Laws and Regulations. Center staff shall comply with all applicable laws and regulations. Authority O.C.G.A. 20-1A-1 et seq. Requirements are changing December of 2012. See PowerPoint slide.

Some credentialing organizations may require additional professional development.

Internet Activity:

Many professionals point to the low wages and lack of benefits as the cause of the high turnover and poor quality of child care workers. One organization is attempting to raise public awareness of the need to provide living wages for the teachers and caregivers who staff child care centers and out-of-school time programs.

Log on to the Center for the Child Care Workforce: http://www.ccw.org Click on "Policy Update."
1. In the Policy Update section Louis Uchitelle, a New York Times columnist, is quoted as saying "Respectable economic theory holds that government spending, properly directed, lifts the private sector and makes it more useful and profitable." Do you agree or disagree with that statement? Why?

2. What part, if any, should government play in upgrading the quality of child care through wage subsidies?

3. What is being done in your community to raise awareness of the need for better wages for child care personnel?

EXPRESSED TEACHER PROBLEMS
Early educators typically complain about the following issues:
Finding time to plan and do paperwork
Getting the supervisor to respect my opinion
Knowing how to handle aggressive or violent children
Handling a child with a physically disabling condition

Handling a child who requires constant attention without neglecting the other children 3
Handling a parent who is very punitive with her child when she picks him up 4
Getting the other adults in the room to do their share of cleanup and "dirty" work 8
Keeping children's attention during group time 7
Motivating myself to be involved with professional organizations 6
Dealing with criticism from my supervisor 5

Select a scenario from the list of expressed teacher problems and complete a staff-training plan that addresses that problem. Then address the following:

What relevant material would you provide in the staff resource room for the staff to read or check out?
- Books
- Journals (give name of articles and authors)
- Audiovisuals
- Web sites

Develop an agenda for a staff meeting addressing the problem. Include:
- Format (panel, speaker, role-playing, and the like)
- Outline of content
- Discussion of the direct steps you would take, as a director, to support the staff as they deal with this problem on a day-to-day basis (P. Click, & K. Karos, 2010)

Keep morale high-inspirational quotes that reinforce your program's mission should be posted throughout the center.

ARE YOU A BOSS OR A LEADER?

"The Boss drives his people; the Leader coaches them. The Boss depends on authority; the Leader on goodwill. The Boss inspires fear; the Leader inspires enthusiasm. The Boss says "I"; the Leader says "We".

The Boss says "get here on time"; the Leader gets there ahead of time. The Boss fixes blame for the breakdown; the Leader fixes the breakdown. The Boss knows how it is done; the Leader shows how.

The Boss says "go"; the Leader says "Let's go". The Boss uses people; the Leader develops them.

The Boss sees today; the Leader also looks at tomorrow.

The Boss commands; the Leader makes time for things that count.

The Boss never has enough time; the Leader is concerned with people.

The Boss lets his people know where he stands; the Leader lets his people know where they stand. The Boss works hard to produce; the Leader works hard to help his people produce.

The Boss takes the credit; the Leader gives it. ALWAYS BE A LEADER!"

Anonymous

Personnel Policies

After planning a program and defining its goal, the program administrator is challenged with the task of hiring qualified staff members. Staffing patterns change continually with the expansion of classrooms. You will find your role has both a leadership component (leading others) and a management component (technical, non-people oriented). "Leadership is the ability to balance the organization's need for productivity and quality with the needs of the staff." (Decker & Decker 2005) Early childhood programs have long existed based upon a shared leadership model of collaboration between parents, and professionals. The leader and staff create and project a climate or culture which helps others develop perceptions about the program that support its vision. "Leaders can shape their organizational environments and transform the lives of those in their program and even the wider community.) Curtis and Carter 1998) A leader is challenged to create and communicate a culturally relevant vision. This is partially done through the development of personnel policies which protect and clarify employee/employer rights and responsibilities in the following areas:

1. Employee Categories/Classifications and Job descriptions
2. Federal and state regulations and forms- income tax withholding (DOL-4, G-4, W-4), I-9, OSHA, Worker's Compensation
3. Job Announcement and Application/Selection process
4. Employment Agreement-including orientation, probationary periods, work schedules (including breaks), calendars, uniform
5. Supervision and Evaluation
6. Discipline-suspension and termination
7. Grievance Procedures
8. Compensation - Salary schedules
9. Attendance-including time off requests, sick leave, maternity leave policies
10. Documentation of Orientation
11. Benefits-including training opportunities
12. Safety Rules and Regulations including Harassment
13. Training Records and Confidentiality
14. Additional policies may be necessary if teachers are contracted annually – intent form, Non-Discriminatory Statement, etc.

"Once you master the hiring process, you may never have to fire anyone again." Author unknown

The policies within your staff handbook will govern the processes that will enable your program to attract and retain the best qualified employees. They guarantee equal opportunity for all candidates and should be consistent with applicable federal and state laws. .

Typical Employee Categories and Classifications within an early childhood program are usually as follows:

1. Full-time permanent employee – works 35 or more hours per week.
2. Part-time permanent employee – works 20-25 hours per week.
3. Intermittent employee – works as needed.
4. Salaried/On-Call – works 32-50 hours per week on various shifts, i.e., 10 hour, 7.5 hour, etc.

In 1984, the governing board of NAEYC approved the following titles and job descriptions for child care personnel:

1. Early childhood teacher assistant is a pre-professional with no specialized early childhood preparation who implements program activities under direct supervision.
2. Early childhood associate teacher is a professional with minimal early childhood preparation (holds a CDA credential or an associate degree in early childhood education/child development who independently implements activities and may be responsible for a group of children.
3. Early childhood teacher is a professional with an undergraduate degree in early childhood education/child development and is responsible for a group of children.
4. Early intervention specialists are teachers or consultants who specialize in the development and learning of children with special needs.

Federal and state employment laws

COBRA

Under COBRA and Georgia law, businesses that employ 20 or more employees and offer a healthcare plan must offer employees and former employees the option of continuing their healthcare coverage if the employee's healthcare coverage is lost or reduced because his or her employment has been terminated, his or her hours have been reduced, or the employee has become eligible for Medicare.

CHILD LABOR

No minor under 12 years of age may be employed. Minors under 16 years of age who have not graduated from high school must have a work certificate (or work permit) from the child's school. In addition, there are also numerous hourly restrictions: Minors under 16 may not be employed between the hours of 9:00 p.m. and 6:00 a.m., more than 4 hours a day during the school year, more than 8 hours a day during vacations and not more than 40 hours a week. (The rules may be different for employers in agricultural industries.) Also, minors under 16 may not be employed in a "dangerous occupation."

DRUG-FREE WORKPLACE

If an employer implements a drug-free work place program, the employer may qualify for certification for a premium discount under its workers' compensation insurance policy. To qualify, an employer must have a written policy regarding its drug-free and drug testing policies, use a testing facility which meets certain criteria, provide an employee assistance program, provide a semi-annual education program on substance abuse, and conduct supervisor training.

WAGE AND HOUR

The Fair Labor Standards Act sets out minimum wage and overtime requirements that apply to any employer who engages in interstate commerce (which is deemed to include any business with revenues of $500,000.00 per year.) Under the law, non-exempt (hourly) employees must be paid a minimum wage which is $7.25 per hour. When a non-exempt (hourly) employee works more than forty hours in a week, the employer must pay the employee one and one half times their regular rate of pay for every hour over forty worked that week. Employees engaged in executive, administrative or professional capacities and paid on a salary basis are exempt from this act. (That is, these employees do not have to be paid overtime). Because the Federal law is more stringent than the Georgia law, an employer who is in compliance with federal law also complies with Georgia law.

WORKERS' COMPENSATION

Georgia law requires employers who employ three or more employees to provide workers' compensation coverage for their employees. Employees injured on the job are entitled to payment of their medical bills and income benefits for any lost time more than seven days. In most cases, workers' compensation benefits are the only source of recovery for an employee and they cannot file a separate lawsuit against their employer. For injured employees who also had a pre-existing permanent impairment, under certain circumstances, employers may be entitled to reimbursement from the Subsequent Injury Trust Fund for a portion of workers' compensation benefits paid.

DISCRIMINATION

Age: The Age Discrimination in Employment Act prohibits discrimination against workers who are 40 years of age or older. The law applies to all private employers with 20 or more employees, employment agencies and certain labor unions. Georgia law provides it is a misdemeanor to discriminate in hiring and employment against individuals between the ages of 40 and 70.

Bankruptcy: Generally, federal law prohibits discrimination in employment decisions against people who have declared bankruptcy.

Disability: Employers are prohibited from engaging in discrimination against qualified individuals with a disability by the Georgia Equal Employment for People with Disabilities Code, The Rehabilitation Act of 1973 and the Americans With Disabilities Act of 1990. A "qualified individual with a disability" is an individual who possesses the requisite skills, experience, education, and other job-related requirements of the position and who can perform the essential functions of the job with or without reasonable accommodation. An "individual with a disability" is a person with a physical or mental impairment which substantially limits one or more major life activities, has a record of such impairment or is regarded by the employer as having such an impairment. The determination of whether a person is "disabled" should be made with reference to measures that might mitigate that individual's impairment, including medicine or eye glasses. Typical "major life activities" are caring for oneself, performing manual tasks, walking, hearing, speaking, breathing, learning and working. "Reasonable accommodation" might include making existing facilities accessible to the disabled, restructuring jobs, reassigning work or otherwise modifying schedules, or revising employment tests. An employer is not required to create a job that does not already exist. An accommodation is not reasonable where it would cause the employer undue hardship (significant difficulty or expense).

Equal Pay: The Equal Pay Act and Georgia law forbid employers to pay different wages to men and women who are performing equal jobs.

Pregnancy: The Pregnancy Discrimination Act prohibits discrimination because of or on the basis of pregnancy, childbirth, or related medical conditions. Women affected by pregnancy, childbirth or related medical conditions shall be treated the same for all employment-related purposes, including receipt of benefits, as other persons not so affected but similar in their ability or inability to work.

Race, Color, Religion, Sex or National Origin: Title VII of the Civil Rights Act of 1964 prohibits discrimination (any adverse employment action) by employers of 15 or more employees, employment agencies, and labor organizations on the basis of race, color, religion, sex or national origin.

Section 1981 prohibits discrimination against employees based on their race.

Retaliation: The law prohibits employers from retaliating against their employees for asserting their rights to be free of discrimination.

Sexual Orientation: There is currently no Federal or Georgia law prohibiting discrimination against employees based on their sexual orientation.

The **Employment Non-Discrimination Act (ENDA)** is a proposed bill in the United States Congress that would prohibit discrimination against employees on the basis of sexual orientation or gender identity by civilian, nonreligious employers with at least 15 employees. The Association of Christian School International (ACSI) maintains a checklist to help faith based (Christian, Muslim, and Jewish) schools and day care centers comply with the law. Legal Compliance Checklist January 2011 www.acsi.org

EMPLOYMENT AT WILL

Georgia recognizes the doctrine of employment at will. Employment at will means that in the absence of a written contract of employment for a defined duration, an employer can terminate an employee for good cause, bad cause or no cause at all, so long as it is not an illegal cause.

FAIR CREDIT REPORTING ACT

Employers have specific duties when using a consumer credit report for hiring or employment purposes. An applicant or employee must give written consent to the employer before the employer obtains a credit report. Additionally, the employer must provide the employee or applicant with a copy of the report and a summary of their rights before the employer can take any adverse action based on the credit report

FAMILY AND MEDICAL LEAVE ACT

The FMLA requires that employers with 50 or more employees, who are employed within a 75 mile radius, provide eligible employees with up to 12 weeks of unpaid, job-protected leave each year to care for a newborn or newly adopted or foster child; to care for a seriously ill child, spouse or parent; or because of the employee's own illness. Employers may, under certain circumstances, require employees to take unpaid FMLA leave rather than accrued paid leave. It is, however, always the employer's responsibility to designate whether an employee's use of paid leave counts as FMLA leave, based on information provided by the employee and it is the employer's responsibility to notify the employee of this designation.

GARNISHMENT

Garnishment is a court-ordered collection method available to creditors. Once the creditor files the garnishment papers, an employee can challenge the validity of the garnishment and the amount. Employers can also challenge the garnishment but they must file an answer within 45 days of the date of the garnishment notice. If an employer fails to file the required answer, the creditor can seek a judgment against the employer for the full amount of the employee's debt. An employer may not discharge an employee on the basis that the creditor is garnishing the employee's wages.

HANDBOOKS

It is advisable for private employers in Georgia to provide their employees with an employee handbook. Under the current state of Georgia law, a handbook will generally not affect employee's "employment at will" status. Any handbook should contain a disclaimer setting forth an express provision that the at will relationship is not affected by the handbook and that the policies set forth in the handbook are subject to change at any time.

IMMIGRATION

The federal immigration laws require employers to complete an INS Form I-9 to verify each employee's authorization to work in the U.S. The laws establish fines and criminal penalties for employers that knowingly hire unauthorized aliens. The laws also establish procedures for hiring on a temporary or permanent basis certain aliens, including skilled workers and professionals in occupations with shortages of qualified U.S. workers.

JURY DUTY

It is illegal to discharge or in any way penalize an employee because the employee is absent for the purposes of attending a judicial proceeding in response to a subpoena, summons for jury duty, or other court order.

MILITARY SERVICE

Under federal and Georgia law, an employee who leaves a position to perform state or federal military service must generally be restored to his or her previous position or a like position.

SAFETY AND HEALTH

Under the Occupational Safety and Health Act, employers have a specific duty to comply with all applicable safety and health regulations and a general duty to maintain a place of employment that is free from recognized hazards that can cause death or serious physical harm to employees.

[Employers in the child care industry are advised to provide Hepatitis immunizations for employees as a universal precaution against blood borne pathogens.]

PREVENTION

Employers should have both an anti-discrimination and a non-harassment policy. The anti-discrimination policy should include language which declares that the employer will not discriminate against any qualified individuals on the basis of race, religion, national origin, color, gender, age, disability, or veteran status. The harassment policy should include not only sexual harassment, but also other forms of harassment, specifically including religious, gender and racial harassment. Additionally, the harassment policy should have a clearly defined procedure for reporting harassment, including a mechanism whereby the employee can bypass his or her immediate supervisor. The harassment policy should also include a provision which states that the company will not tolerate retaliation against individuals who complain about harassment.
The harassment policy should be posted and disseminated to all employees, who sign a receipt acknowledging that they received the policy. Companies who do not have anti-harassment policies could be left without any defenses in the event of a harassment lawsuit.

UNIONS

The National Labor Relations Act provides for employee rights to organize, join unions, and engage in collective bargaining. It is unlawful for an employer to interfere with an employee's right to join a union and engage in union activities, including discharging or otherwise discriminating against employees because they engage in union activities. Employers also are required to bargain in good faith with a union. Georgia has a "right to work" law which prohibits interference with employment to compel any person to either join or refrain from joining a union.

Source:
What Georgia Employers Need to Know, Georgia Bar Association. Retrieved from
http://sos.ga.gov/index.php/corporations/what_georgia_employers_need_to_know

QUICK REFERENCE
EEOC (800) 669-4000
Federal Trade Commission (202) 326-2222
Georgia Chamber of Commerce (404) 223-2264
Georgia Department of Labor (404) 656-3017
Georgia State Boa rd of Workers' Compensation (404) 656-3818
National Labor Relations Board (404) 331-2896
Office of Secretary of State (404) 656-2881
State Bar of Georgia (800) 334-6865
U.S. Immigration & Naturalization Service (800) 375-5283
This information was produced in a brochure by the Employers' Duties and Problems Committee of the Young Lawyers Division of the State Bar of Georgia. It is intended only as an overview of the law as it affects private employers in Georgia and is not a complete statement of the law. Please consult the applicable law or your attorney for complete information.

INSURANCE

Insurance protection is vital to program sustainability. Early childhood educators have a legal duty to act with reasonable care while supervising the children in their custody. Providers have this duty because of childcare licensing laws and because their position as caregivers to children creates a special relationship of dependency and reliance. When a child is injured because a, early educator fails to use reasonable care, the provider is said to have "breached his/her duty of care,"or "acted negligently." If a child is injured while in your care, the parents might sue you and your program if they think your negligence, or that of your staff, caused the injury. If you have general liability insurance, the insurance company will defend you if you are sued. Professional liability and property liability coverage are essential. If the court decides that you are "liable" (meaning that your negligence caused the child's injury and therefore you should pay compensation), the insurance company will pay any money judgment up to the limits of your liability policy. Some states do not require programs to carry liability insurance by law, but it is the best way to protect yourself, your program, and your/its assets. If you are working for a program that does not provide insurance you should obtain a professional liability policy to cover yourself.

- **General Liability Insurance** covers bodily injury or property damage that occurs during the course of or because of your educational organization.
- **Professional Liability Insurance** is separate and insures employees while conducting business.
- **Property Insurance** covers all of the business equipment inside and outside of your program.

Markel Insurers suggest the following types of coverage:
Umbrella Liability: Umbrella Liability insurance provides additional protection that takes effect after you've gone above the limits of your General Liability or Automobile Liability insurance.
Management Liability

Directors' & Officers' Liability
Employment Practices Liability
Fiduciary Liability

Other Liability Insurance
Corporal Punishment Liability: Defends you against allegations of corporal punishment to the children in your care, even when groundless, false, or frivolous. Many insurance policies don't offer this much-needed coverage.
Sexual Abuse and Molestation Liability: Offers critical coverage for situations that can be explosive. Most school insurers claims staff has expertise in handling these types of claims and is sensitive to the needs of all parties involved.
Child Care Providers and Teachers Professional Liability: Allows teachers and providers to perform their professional duties without fear of devastating lawsuits, defense costs, and judgments.
Child Abduction Liability: Pays reasonable and necessary covered expenses the school or center and the child's parents incur to recover the child.
Special Events Liability: Protects you from liability during field trips, fund-raisers, and other special events. Some insurers require you to buy a separate policy for special activities.
Volunteers as Additional Insureds: When your facility uses volunteers, they're acting on your behalf. This insurance defends their unintentional negligent acts as it defends those of your employees.
Property Insurance: If you own the building that houses your child care facility, you need property insurance to protect both your building and its contents. If you rent, you need property insurance to cover your valuable equipment. Some insurer's coverage is available on a special cause of loss basis, which means you're covered for events like fire, burglaries, vandalism, and even frozen pipes.
Systems Breakdown: Protects you when any mechanical, electrical, or pressure system breaks down. This includes heating and air conditioning systems, computers, boilers, refrigerators, hot water heaters, and telephone systems.
Crime: Covers you if an employee steals money, securities, or other property.
Communicable Disease and Food Contamination: Additional coverage that can be included when Business Income is purchased.
Commercial Property Plus Extension: Additional limits and extensions for coverages such as Accounts Receivable, Employee Dishonesty, Ordinance or Law, and Utility Services.
Key Employee Replacement: Helps you get back to business as quickly as possible following the loss of a key staff member. Provides the funds for a temporary replacement, and to find a qualified permanent replacement.
Accident Medical Insurance: Accident Medical insurance will pay children's medical bills if they are injured at your facility or during activities you sponsor and have no insurance of their own, or their bills exceed what their insurance pays.
Automobile Insurance: Automobile insurance provides complete liability and physical damage coverage for the owned, leased, non-owned, and hired automobiles (such as vans, pickups, and buses) used at your facility.

Web addresses for insurance companies and brokers:
www.acainc.org
www.blockinsurance.net
www.cherrycreekins.com
www.mckeerisk.com
www.churchmutual.com
www.thehartford.com/educational-institutions-insurance/
www.travelers.com/business-insurance/mid-sized-business/educational-institutions.aspx
www.aig.com/Education-Industry_3171_418151.html

www.nncc.org/business/liabil.ins.ccc.html
www.forestagency.com/child-care-center-insurance
www.nationwide.com/child-day-care-insurance-hb.jsp
www.childcareinsurance.com/Pages/default.aspx

Some of the statutes and regulations enforced by agencies within the Department of Labor require that posters or notices be posted in the workplace. The Department provides electronic copies of the required posters and some of the posters are available in languages other than English.

Please note that posting requirements vary by statute; that is, not all employers are covered by each of the Department's statutes and thus may not be required to post a specific notice. For example, some small businesses may not be covered by the Family and Medical Leave Act and thus would not be subject to the Act's posting requirements. For information on coverage, visit the Employment Laws Assistance for Workers and Small Business (elaws) Poster Advisor. You may also contact the Office of Small Business Programs, for assistance with these notice requirements.

Download required posters and obtain information about poster requirements or other compliance assistance matters, by contacting the U.S. Department of Labor by telephone at 1-888-9-SBREFA, www.dol.gov and the Georgia Department of Labor http://www.dol.state.ga.us/ or by email at Contact-OSBP@dol.gov.
Minimum way
Unemployment Insurance
Occupational Health and Safety
Equal Pay

Georgia Unemployment Insurance (UI) provides benefits or temporary income for workers who are unemployed through no fault of their own. The program requires that they be seeking employment or are expected to be recalled to their job within six weeks of the last day worked. Unemployment beneficiaries may be in an approved training program. Georgia employers pay the entire cost of unemployment insurance benefits. Contributory employers pay taxes at a specified rate on a quarterly basis. Governmental and nonprofit organizations are considered contributory employers and pay a specified tax rate on a quarterly basis. They may pay quarterly or elect to reimburse GDOL for benefits paid to former employees.

Georgia New Hire Reporting Program

In 1996, Congress enacted a law called the "Personal Responsibility and Work Opportunity Reconciliation Act," or PRWORA, as part of Welfare Reform. This legislation created the requirement for employers in all 50 states to report their new hires and re-hires to a state directory.

New hire reporting speeds up the child support income withholding order process, expedites collection of child support from parents who change jobs frequently, and quickly locates non-custodial parents to help in establishing paternity and child support orders. New hire reporting helps children receive the support they deserve. Employers serve as key partners in ensuring financial stability for many children and families and should take pride in their role.

Who is required to report?
Employers and/or labor organizations doing business in the State of Georgia must report the following employees:

- *New employees*: Employers must report all employees who reside or work in the State of Georgia to whom the employer anticipates paying earnings. Employees should be reported even if they work only one day and are terminated (prior to the employer fulfilling the new hire reporting requirement).
- *Re-hires or Re-called employees*: Employers must report re-hires, or employees who return to work after being laid off, furloughed, separated, granted a leave without pay, or terminated from employment. Employers must also report any employee who remains on the payroll during a break in service or gap in pay, and then returns to work. This includes teachers, substitutes, seasonal workers, etc.
- *Temporary employees*: Temporary agencies are responsible for reporting any employee who they hire to report for an assignment. Employees need to be reported only once; they do not need to be re-reported each time they report to a new client. They do need to be reported as a re-hire if the worker has a break in service or gap in wages from your company.

What do I have to report?

Required Employee Information	Required Employer Information
Employee's full name (Please identify first, middle, and last name.)	Employer's name (please use corporate name)
Employee's address	Employer's address (please provide address where Income Withholding Orders should be sent)
Employee's Social Security Number	Employer's Federal Employer Identification Number (FEIN). If you have more than one FEIN, please make certain you use the same FEIN you use to report your quarterly wage information when reporting new hires.
Employee's date of birth	
Employee's date of hire	
Employee's medical insurance availability (Yes or No)	
Employee's state of hire	
Employee's actual start date	Does Employer provide multiple medical insurances?
Employee's monthly salary	If multiple medical insurances are available, were they offered?

When do I have to report?
Georgia Statute 19-11-9.2 requires all employers to submit their new hire reports within 10 days after the employee is hired or re-hired or returns to work. Employers who submit reports magnetically or electronically shall submit the reports in two monthly transmissions not more than sixteen days apart.

How do I report new hires?
The Georgia New Hire Reporting Program offers many options that make it easy for employers to report new hires. The options available are listed below.

Electronic Reporting

- *Online Reporting*: Use this Web site to report your new hires. This is the easiest and most efficient way to report new hires!
- *Create your own Electronic New Hire Reports*:

Non-Electronic Reporting

Spreadsheet - If your software is unable to export your new hire information in our electronic format, you might be able to have your software create a spreadsheet (e.g. Excel, Lotus 1-2-3, Quattro Pro) containing your new hire data.

The spreadsheet should contain all of the required information on the New Hire Reporting Form, be created using at least a 10-point font size, and have the
- employer's name,
- Federal Employer Identification Number, and
- address clearly displayed at the top of the report.

-OR-

2. *New Hire Reporting Form* You may download, print, fill out, and fax or mail us a New Hire Reporting Form.

-OR-

3. *W-4 Form* - If you choose to submit a W-4 form as a new hire report, please ensure that each W-4 is easily readable and has the employer's name, Federal Employer Identification Number, and address written at the top of each form.

Other Reporting Methods

Payroll Service: If you use a payroll or accounting service, consider asking the service to report your new hires for you. Leading payroll services are already electronically reporting new hires for thousands of employers.

Where do I report new hires?

Electronic Reports - Using our Web site's online reporting feature is a very popular choice for employers. This feature provides a printable confirmation of reports received and is available 24 hours a day, 7 days a week.

Employers can send new hire data files in a variety of ways, including transferring files through this Web site, through internet connection using File Transfer Protocol (FTP), or mail reports to us on diskette.

Non-Electronic Reports - Paper new hire reports may either be faxed or mailed to our Center.

Mail reports to:	Fax reports to:
Georgia New Hire Reporting Program	(404) 525-2983
P.O. Box 90728	Toll-free: (888) 541-0521
East Point, GA 30364-0728	

Please call the Georgia New Hire Reporting Program at (404) 525-2985, or toll-free at (888) 541-0469 for any questions regarding the new hire reporting process.

REVIEW THE FOLLOWING HR FORMS:

Georgia Department of Labor DOL-4 Quarterly Tax and Wage Report*
www.dol.state.ga.us/pdf/forms/dol4n.pdf
Georgia Department of Labor Separation Notice DOL-800*
www.dol.state.ga.us/pdf/forms/dol800.pdf
Internal Revenue Service W-4 Employee's Withholding Allowance Certificate
www.irs.gov/pub/irs-pdf/fw4.pdf

State of Georgia G-4 Employee's Withholding Allowance Certificate*
https://etax.dor.ga.gov/
U.S. Citizenship and Immigration Service Employment Eligibility Verification. Form I-9
http://www.uscis.gov/i-9-central
*Compare to your state's form
Most forms may be completed online.

Staff Records
It is a good idea to assemble employment packets which contain the necessary forms for each stage of the process. New employees must complete all of the personnel and payroll forms and bring them when reporting for work on the first day of employment so that paychecks can be issued in a timely manner.

Applicant
Job Description and Announcement
Application for Employment
Criminal Record Check Form
Reference Check Forms

Upon Job Offer
Offer Letter Employment Agreement
Medical and Physical Examination Form *
Employee Information Sheet
Salary Schedule Medical Benefits list
G-4 - State Withholding Allowance Certificate
W-4 Federal Withholding Form
I-9 Employment Eligibility Verification

Upon Hire
Staff Handbook Documentation of Orientation Training Record
Health Insurance Premium Rates (if applicable) Health Benefit Plan Declination (if applicable)
Direct Payroll Deposit /Debit Master Card Form (if applicable)

* Reference: Pennsylvania Chapter, American Academy of Pediatrics. 2002. *Model child care health policies*. 4th ed. Washington, DC: National Association for the Education of Young Children. This form was adapted from *Model Child Care Health Policies*, 2002, by the Early Childhood Education Linkage System (ECELS), a program funded by the Pennsylvania Depts. of Health & Public Welfare and contractually administered by the PA Chapter, American Academy of Pediatrics.

Employers must withhold the following taxes from your employees pay checks:

- Federal income tax withholding
- Social Security and Medicare taxes
- Federal unemployment tax act (FUTA).

You must report federal income taxes, social security and Medicare taxes on form 941, Employer's Quarterly Federal Tax Return. Taxes/Social Security and Medicare Taxes
You generally must withhold federal income tax from your employee's wages. The federal unemployment tax is part of the federal and state program under the Federal Unemployment Tax Act (FUTA) that pays unemployment compensation to workers who lose their jobs. You report and pay FUTA tax separately from social security and Medicare taxes and withheld income tax. You pay FUTA tax only from your own funds. *Employees do not pay this tax or have it withheld from their pay.*

Report FUTA taxes on Form 940, Employer's Annual Federal Unemployment (FUTA) Tax return or if you qualify, you can use the simpler From 940-EZ instead.

In general, you must deposit income tax withheld and both the employer and employee so Medicare taxes (minus any advance EIC payments) by mailing or delivering a check, money financial institution that is an authorized depositary for Federal taxes. However, some taxpay deposit using the Electronic Federal Tax Deposit System (EFTPS).

Georgia offers several Job Tax Credit Programs to assist employers. Consult your accountant or the Georgia Department of Labor for additional information. Georgia DHS will secure and subsidize jobs within state and local government departments, private companies, and not-for-profits for a minimum of 5,000 adults who meet the program eligibility requirements. The Department will subsidize 80 percent of the wages for up to six months. The remaining 20 percent will be paid by the employer. Applicants will be screened and provided job coaches to assist them in securing positions for which they are qualified.

Reference Checks

Providing references, verifying employment and/or income could lead to a number of issues, such as misrepresentation and defamation claims as well as invasion of privacy civil suits. Schools and their agents have been sued for an employee's behavior at their next job when they were given a glowing recommendation or character reference and then molested a child or worse. Although Georgia has a reference immunity law it is safest to stick to answering to the three questions that you mention. Checking references and verifying credentials is a critical step in the screening processing. It is essential for committees to explore beyond the names of references provided. Ensure that the candidate has signed a waiver permitting the collection of information from collateral references will permit the hiring committee to thoroughly assess a candidate's qualifications. Like the interview process, reference inquiries should be related to the position description and consistent for all candidates. The reference interview should not be done "on the fly," so committee members are encouraged to schedule appointments with prospective references to ensure that there is adequate time to conduct a comprehensive conversation.

As an employer you may answer specific employment verification questions (job title, dates of service, and whether or not the person is eligible for rehire). Availability is the job candidate's prerogative. The Department of Labor provides a list of illegal interview questions and the Equal Employment Opportunity Commission provides a list of prohibited practices [http://www.eeoc.gov/laws/practices/]. The courts protects a person's privacy rights also.

The Privacy Rights Clearinghouse provides background check guides:
Fact Sheet 16: Employment Background Checks: A Jobseeker's Guide, www.privacyrights.org/fs/fs16-bck.htm
Fact Sheet 16a: Employment Background Checks in California: New Focus on Accuracy, www.privacyrights.org/fs/fs16a-califbck.htm
Fact Sheet 16b: Employment Background Checks: A Guide for Small Business Owners, www.privacyrights.org/fs/fs16b-smallbus.htm

Employers should provide check stubs and W-2 forms to verify income. Any other requests that are written should be completed and returned to the employee, who may in turn submit it to the requesting agency.

Search committees should develop specific job-related questions for a telephone reference check or specific criteria for a written reference. Be careful to avoid asking questions in the reference check that you would not ask the candidate during an interview. All questions asked and issues raised must be job-related and similar for all candidates.

The Process
Be thoroughly familiar with the candidate's file before you conduct a reference check. Review any notes you have made from the application, cover letter, vitae, application materials and interview process.

Take the time to tell the person you have contacted why you are doing so and explain the job duties-responsibilities-functions of the position, including the organization, department, and the number of teachers/students and staff.

1. Make sure you have a written plan for the questions you are going to ask and take as many notes as you can.
2. Do not let opinions of others substitute for facts or examples.
3. Do not evaluate information while you're gathering it. Your goal is to learn more about the candidate and collect more information. You can assess what you have learned and gathered when you are done.
4. Be alert to unusual hesitations, ambiguous or evasive responses, overly negative or vindictive responses, or overly enthusiastic responses.
5. Make sure your reference check is tailored to the position.
6. Check as many employment and personal references as possible.
7. Be consistent and ask the same questions of each reference.
8. Avoid asking questions that can be answered with "yes" or "no."

[handwritten: you can ask? but you cannot answer]

Review the duties etc. of the position and review the application materials. Make a list of facts or qualifications to verify and a list of questions to ask. Areas of possible inquiry could include:
- **Sociability** – How well does the candidate get along with and relate to others?
- **Work habits and ability** – How well does the candidate know the work and perform the job?
- **Personal character** – Is the candidate trustworthy, honest, and dependable?
- **Technical/Functional Ability** - Assess technical/functional ability and attitude on the job.

When checking references, note the following information on a form:
- Name and title of the person supplying the reference information for each reference you check.
- The date you talk with the reference and contact number.

The Script
- When conducting reference checks, be friendly.
- Introduce yourself.
- Indicate that you have written consent for the reference check or that the candidate listed that person as a reference.
- Give a basic description of the position.
- Always feel comfortable asking follow-up or clarification questions if something is not clear.
- Listen to the responses – is there hesitation or vagueness? Remember the person on the other end of the phone may be thinking about a question and the best way to answer it.
- At the end of the conversation, ask the reference if they can think or recommend anyone else for you to speak with.

Pitfalls

[handwritten: give forms to employee to verify income]

It is important not to conduct references checks without a signed release from the candidate. A signed release protects the center/school from being sued for invading privacy or for damages in the case where a candidate loses his/her job or fails to receive a promotion because of your reference checking. Many time employers will only give you information regarding the position title, dates of employment, and eligibility for rehire. If you have a signed release, be sure to convey that information to the reference and be careful that you do not ask any questions that you would not ask a candidate during an interview.

Sample Questions

1. How long have you known the candidate? In what capacity?

2. How would you describe the candidate's experience working in a multicultural environment?

3. Please describe your knowledge of the candidate's ability to effectively develop and teach curriculum at the early education level.

4. Has the candidate shown an ability to build connections within an educational community, with local educational partners, and with local community organizations? Could you give an example or two?

5. How would you characterize the candidate's commitment to students? To the best of your knowledge, what do students think of the candidate?

6. What would parents say about this teacher and their rapport with her?

7. How would you describe the candidate's teaching and leadership skills?

8. How would you characterize the candidate's commitment to the center or school? To the best of your knowledge, what do colleagues think of the candidate?

9. Can you describe a time when the candidate experienced conflict with another member of the instructional or administrative team? How was it resolved?

10. How well did the candidate manage crisis, pressure, and/or stress?

11. How would you compare the performance of <candidate name> with that of others who have held the same job?

12. Please describe <candidate name> work ethic, in terms of attitude, dependability and trustworthiness.

13. Do you have any cautions that we should heed (hear?) if we consider hiring this candidate?

14. Are there any limitations or factors that might interfere with this candidate's ability to be an effective early educator?

15. What type of advice would you give his/her next employer to ensure success?

16. If the [name of candidate] were to come and work for us what kind of professional development opportunities do you think we should offer him/her?

17. Is there anyone else you would recommend we talk to regarding this candidate's qualifications?

18. Do you have any other comments you wish to offer?

This data was adapted from an HR article. The questions are excellent for gaining valuable insights.

Job Offer Letter
Date   [Employee name and address]

Dear [employee name]:

We are very pleased to offer you a[permanent/seasonal/term] position as [position title], based on the following terms and conditions:

Position:
You are appointed to the position of [position title] and in this capacity, you will report directly to [name of direct supervisor]. This is a [permanent/seasonal/term position] and as discussed and agreed with you, your start date in the position will be [start date].

In this assignment of [position title], your key responsibilities will be to provide a brief description of the primary purpose of the position (if available, attach the job description, and refer the employee to it)..

Remuneration:
Your base salary $X per month or $X per year (less statutorily required deductions). Your salary is payable once a month at month end in accordance with the school's standard payroll practices.

Your hours of work are based on the normal operating hours of the school and are expected to be for example, from 8:30 a.m. to 4:30 p.m., Monday to Friday, with a one-half hour unpaid lunch break, amounting to 37.5 hours per week.

Bonus Potential:
Effective upon satisfactory completion of the first 90 days of employment, and based upon the goals and objectives agreed to in the performance development planning process with your supervisor, you may be eligible for a bonus. The bonus plan for this year and beyond, should such a plan exist, will be based upon the formula determined by the school for that year.

Benefits and Pension:
As a permanent/seasonal/term employee, you will be eligible to participate in group benefit plans for employees after your first year of employment, according to the terms of the plans. You are also eligible to participate in the [school name]'s Money Purchase Pension Plan in accordance with the plan requirements.

Stock Options:
Spell out any options that may be available for purchase.

Car/Phone/Travel Expenses:
Normal and reasonable expenses will be reimbursed on a monthly basis per company policy.

Vacation:
You will receive X weeks of vacation per vacation year (May 1 to April 30), pro-rated for the current vacation year, according to the terms of the employment agreement. Vacations are to be taken at such time or times as are mutually convenient to you and the center/school. Please note that carry over of unused vacation is not encouraged, and should be discussed with your supervisor.

Professional Allowance:
In addition, you are eligible to receive an annual accountable professional development account in the amount of $X per year (prorated for the current year), to support your on-going career development needs.

Assessment Period:
FOR APPOINTMENTS TO PERMANENT and SEASONAL POSITIONS: Consistent with the probationary period policy for permanent and seasonal appointments, the first X months of your appointment to this position is a probationary period. We will review your progress in the position on a regular basis and provide you with regular feedback. We will be in a position to confirm continued employment upon successful completion of the probationary period.

FOR APPOINTMENTS TO TERM POSITIONS: Consistent with our supervision policies, for Term appointments, we will review your progress in the position on a regular basis and provide you with regular feedback.

Effective Date:
The terms of this offer shall come into effect on your first day of employment with the center/school.

Other Terms and Conditions
Your employment is subject to the terms and conditions set out in the staff handbook, as well as other applicable policies approved by the .

If applicable, add the following section on Confidentiality:
By accepting this offer, you also acknowledge and agree that you shall abide by the following terms and conditions, and that such terms and conditions are reasonable:

Confidentiality: During the course of your employment with the center/school, you will be entrusted with confidential and proprietary information. You agree that such information will not be released or divulged, whether directly or indirectly, unless authorized by school policy, required by law, or through the express written consent of the given under the hand of the proper officer with authority to give such consent.

We ask that you review the contents of this offer carefully. If the terms of employment as set out in this agreement are acceptable to you, please sign and date one (1) copy and return a fully signed copy to my attention by due date.

[Name of employee], We wish to convey our sincere enthusiasm about the possibility of you joining the center/school. We hope that you find the terms of this offer reasonable and attractive.

Please feel free to contact me if you have any questions at [contact phone number].
Yours truly,

Name _____ Title _____

I agree to accept the conditions of employment indicated above, this___day of____, 20___ .

Employee _____
NOTE: Please ensure that you forward a copy of the accepted letter within 90 days to: [name]

Salary Schedule Form

Employee name _____ Job title _____

Schedule M T W Th F S S _____ a.m. _____ p.m.

Breaks _____ a.m. _____ p.m. and _____ a.m. _____ p.m.

S.S. No. _____ Birthdate _____

Hire Date _____

Base salary: _____ Semi-monthly _____ Monthly _____

Credentials: _____
- Eligibility *1-7% 90 Day Probationary Period _____ and Annual Merit Increase _____
- Paid Holidays: Christmas (10 days), Thanksgiving (3 days), Labor Day, Memorial Day, and M.L. King, Jr. Day
- 2 Paid Professional Development Days (Conference)
- 5 Paid Orientation Days
- Christmas and Birthday Bonus as enrollment permits
- Professional Certification Credential Add: (1 year)

Temporary Certification	$50/month	$600/annual
Provisional Level I	$200/month	$2,400/annual
Standard Certification	$250/month	$3,000/annual
Professional Certification	$300/month	$3,600/annual

- Summer Vacation Compensation (50% of salary for 60 days)
- SMART START GA Incentive Bonus - $2,000 annual for Bachelor's degree and continued education credits in Child Development
- Second year 5 paid vacation days and 5 paid sick days
- Paid 30 minute lunch period with students
- Fringe Benefits:

School time Accidental Coverage	$30.00
Health Insurance (individual premium 50%)	$1,170.00 (elg. after 90 days)
Term Life Insurance	$78.00
Pre-paid legal	$28.00 (elg. after 90 days)
FICA/Medicare Contribution	$1,690.50
Conference Registration	$60.00
Worker's Compensation	$236.00
Total Benefits	$3,292.00

Total Renumeration for this contract position _____
Credentials XXXX Cert. $3,600 and Smart Start GA Incentive Bonus $2,000

*3% if average class load is fewer than 12 students.

Whatever you do, do your work heartily, as for the Lord. Col. 3:23,24

Sample Job Announcement and Application/Selection Process

Program administrators must follow affirmative action guidelines in the process used to fill a vacancy. Affirmative action means employers must identify and change any discriminatory employment practices. Programs must e proactive in recruiting and providing comfortable working environments for minorities and women. The Americans with Disabilities Act outlaws discrimination against persons with disabilities. The Employment Opportunity commission reviews job descriptions and determines whether reasonable accommodations can be made. NAEYC's anti-discriminatory policy states that employment decisions must be based solely on the competence and qualifications of persons to perform "designated duties." (NAEYC Business, 1988)

Programs should use brochures and policy manuals in advertising positions. Before making positions public it is wise to inform your staff. Your job announcement should include a brief job description and any non-negotiable terms such as education and experience, salary, how to apply and any deadlines. The method of application depends greatly upon the program administrator's time to screen applicants. Candidates may be screened by requesting they mail a resume initially of complete a brief telephone interview. Candidate should then obtain an application, if you are interested. You could post applications on your website, mail them, or have them available for pick up in the office. If writing abilities are part of the job description, you may want to include essay questions in the application. As part of the application process, applicants should submit transcripts and credentials.

Applicants should submit an application and ten-year employment history, transcripts, documentation of first aid/CPR training and references. The program administrator must verify references and other credentials to determine whether or not to continue with the processing. Teacher recommendations from previous employers may offer some assistance. After the deadline for application, the program administrator for designated staff member should screen applications for credentials and qualifications for the position. Applications no longer considered should be kept on file for affirmative action purposes a minimum of five years. Applicants are notified of the reasons for rejection, by mail or telephone if their application is not being given further consideration. Prior to the interview the administrator contacts the references listed on the application and processes a criminal background check. Sample reference forms follow.

The program administrator shall contact all qualified applicants for an interview after obtaining verification and documentation. Be careful to follow Title VII of the 1964 Civil Rights Act which prohibits discriminatory hiring practices. Program administrators should use check sheets or rating scales as assessment instruments during the interview process. Forms may be obtained through accreditation organizations or employment form providing companies. Many are included in textbooks published by Aspen Publishers. One such resource is *Developing School Programs and Policies*: A Principal's Manual or the Association of Christian School's *Personnel Forms*.

During the interview the program administrator should review any professional teaching portfolios and ask questions to determine the applicant's ideas about children and education to determine if they agree with the programs vision and mission. It is important to address classroom, discipline and relationship issues. Be sure to discuss and answer any questions about your program and the position. The program administrator should practice reflective listening skills by striving to understand content and being attentive to body language, including tone of voice. Be sensitive to the candidate's values and feelings as you reflect on their comments in your responses. Use appropriate assertion when needed. You should set decision making parameters and inform the candidate of the hiring date and contact them to inform them of your decision on that date. Applicants will be notified and either thanked or asked back to proceed further for a possible **Board interview**. Either a second interview or a second person in the initial interview is beneficial.

Employment Agreement

When the employment agreement is issued to the applicant, it must be signed and returned in order to become valid. Afterwards orientation will be scheduled by the program administrator. A Staff Handbook will be issued to the employee at this time. New teachers may also pick up any materials that he/she may wish to study and prepare. If there are several new members joining the staff, portions of this orientation may be done as part of an in-service training. Staff members are to submit to criminal background checks and a physical examination performed by a licensed physician, prior to employment. The program should be furnished with a record of the examination with the physician's certification. Most often it is wise to have a ninety day probationary period to observe the new hire and provide performance feedback. I recommend a ninety day evaluation and pay increase of one to five percent based upon performance.

Staff members are generally advised of any orientation, training requirements, and dress codes, work schedules including breaks and holidays in writing in the handbook and employment agreement.

Supervision and Evaluation

Programs should regularly evaluate effectiveness including measuring staff competencies. The primary purposes of supervision are as follows:
1. To evaluate the fulfillment of the program's objectives.
2. To maintain the standards of excellence set forth in national standards for child care.
3. To ensure the health and safety of the children.
4. To prevent favoritism, child abuse and /or neglect.
5. To anticipate future needs.
6. To provide vision and direction for the future.
7. To reveal staff member strengths and weaknesses.
8. To provide a plan for program and staff quality improvement.

It is also important that annually staff needs are assessed by a written survey and parent/child satisfaction be assessed as well. The input is valuable to the effectiveness of a program. A program's evaluation system should include input from all key players.

1. Staff members should meet annually to set goals and strategize monthly on how best to achieve those goals.
2. Staff members should be observed in the classroom on a weekly basis and provided feedback by the program administrator or peer mentor.
3. Staff members should be are evaluated quarterly one-on-one with the Administrator to review quarterly goals and expectations, receiving feedback which will enhance job performance.
4. Staff members should be evaluated annually in the following areas:
a) Attitude, initiative and job knowledge
b) Oral and written expression with children, parents, and co-workers.
c) Attendance/dependability
d) Appearance
e) Recordkeeping
f) Adherence to the employment agreement
g) Professional development and training needs
5. Staff members typically receive promotions and salary increases based upon performance. The Georgia Department of Labor advertises annual cost of living increase rates, which may be

© 2014 Penn Consulting

appropriate as a guide.

This topic will be further discussed in session 8.

Small Group Discussion
List qualities that would make you consider promotion of an employee to a lead teacher or administrative support position: people skills, smile, supportive of others, empowering, competence in job skills, pleasant, friendly, self-motivated, etc.

Discipline-suspension and termination

Staff members reserve the right to voluntarily resign, by tendering the resignation letter to the administrator and providing a minimum of 10-business days written notice. In the event, 10 days notice is not given, accounting and separation paperwork may take longer to process. In the event a staff member is unable to adequately render services agreed to because of incompetence, physical disability, or conduct detrimental to the program, the employment agreement shall be terminated. The decision of the program administrator and its board of the school shall be final and not subject to review.

If an employee is not performing the given objectives of his/her position satisfactorily, the program administrator should outline procedures to be followed. Sample procedures are as follows:

1. FIRST SESSION - The program administrator is to outline in writing, the specific areas of concern. It is important to document any infractions and conferences. These areas of concern will be discussed with the employee and an attempt made to address the root attitudes or problems, and seek to counsel the employee accordingly. The employee should be encouraged to respond from his perspective. The program administrator should document the meeting by summarizing its content to include:
    a) The specific concerns that need to be corrected;
    b) The root of attitude problems discerned;
    c) The employee's response to the conference and;
    d) The specific steps of action to correct each problem area (with follow-up dates if deemed necessary by the program administrator).

The conference summary is to be signed and dated by the program administrator and the employee. A copy is to be given to the employee and a copy placed in the employee's file. An explanation of the purpose of the file is to be communicated to the employee.

2. SECOND SESSION. The same procedure is to be followed as with the first session with these exceptions:
    a) The teacher and program administrator should report on the progress they each feel has been made in following the corrective action outlines in Session One.
    b) Any new steps of action should also be documented at this time and the teacher informed that failure to implement by a certain date may result in dismissal depending upon the severity of the problem.
    c) Any item not mentioned in the first session will be discussed and a plan of action formulated.
    d) The program administrator may invite a Department Head or a board member to be present.
    e) The Board receives a copy of the meeting summary.

3. THIRD SESSION. The Third Session constitutes the session whereby the employee is informed in writing that his employment will be terminated. Prior to this meeting the program administrator should

summarize the contents of prior conferences and the steps of action not followed and problem areas not corrected.
   a) A letter or separation notice is to be given which details the reasons for termination,
   b) The teacher will be given a copy of the letter and receive an explanation as to how it will be used in future inquiries.
   c) This final session must include the Department Head and/or a board member.
   d) An employee may e provided the option, after his/her notification of termination to appeal the decision directly to the board within seven business days by giving notice to the program administrator. The Board will hear the teacher's and the program administrator's positions and render a decision by majority vote. The Board's decision is final. Failure to request a hearing with the school board within that time frame shall waive the person's right to such a hearing.

Termination and Dismissal
   a) Cause for termination and dismissal may include, but is not limited to, any one or more of the following: immorality, intemperance, abuse to a student, absent without notification and/or approval (abandonment of position), neglect of duty, or any conduct tending to bring discredit upon the program or upon the teacher that causes a diminishing of his/her effectiveness.
   b) It is the responsibility of the Board and program administrator to decide whether the circumstances warrant the use of a Progressive Discipline Program or immediate termination and dismissal. The Progressive Discipline Program (PDP) will be used if it can serve in a redemptive function without jeopardizing the well being of the school in the eyes of its constituency.

Program administrators and their program can benefit from thorough exit interviews in both voluntary and involuntary employment terminations. They may delegate this responsibility to a staff or board member. The administrator should list reasons for the termination and may not be present during the interview. The departing employee should have an opportunity to add his/her comments or rebuttal to the report form before signing the form. Refusal to sign will be noted on the form. The witness conducting the interview should sign the form as well. The employee will be provided a copy of the form and the original is to be filed in the personnel file. The employee will be told that this form may be made available to prospective future employers. The final paycheck will be released as scheduled following the exit interview provided that keys, program equipment, and any other appropriate property is returned.

Grievance Procedures

Typically programs try to avoid legal action. Both parties generally waive their rights to a hearing in a court of law. Efforts are made to mediate the problem, but if such efforts are unsuccessful, arbitration is required. Arbitration shall be conducted by three arbitrators. Each party shall have the right to select one arbitrator. The two arbitrators selected shall jointly select the third neutral arbitrator. If there is a disagreement about who should be selected for the third arbitrator, there are numerous organizations in Georgia which can provide the name of a qualified person to serve as the "neutral" third arbitrator. Each party to the dispute shall be responsible for the fees and expenses of his/her/its arbitrator and one-half of the fees and expenses of the neutral third arbitrator. If the parties have agreed to use only one arbitrator, the fee and expenses shall be shared equally.

Compensation - Salary schedules

Program administrators develop salary ranges and schedules based upon several factors
1. Program budget
2. Federal or Georgia pay scales which can be accessed at;

Georgia Department of Labor Workforce Information & Analysis Division Courtland Building, Suite 300

© 2014 Penn Consulting

148 Andrew Young International Boulevard, N.E. Atlanta, Georgia 30303
(404) 232-3875 or (800) 338-2082
E-mail: Workforce_Info@dol.state.ga.us Website: www.dol.state.ga.us/wp/lmi_publications.htm
Download the Georgia Wage Survey Occupational Wage Reports

3. Job Description
4. Prior experience
5. Job Performance

A salary schedule outlining base wages and benefits should be distributed to new employees upon hire. Typically the owner, assistant director and persons responsible for clerical duties are salaried. Salaried staff members are paid either monthly, semi-monthly or bi-weekly and are eligible for raises at the following service dates:
1. 90 day Probationary Period Ending
2. Annual Evaluation (typically 3-7%)

Preschool Teacher's and Support Staff are usually paid a base hourly wage on a weekly or bi- weekly time period and are eligible for raises at the same service dates as stated above.

Federal employment laws require preschool teachers to be paid on an hourly basis because they are primarily childcare workers unless their job description requires certain qualifications and responsibilities (e.g. college degree and certification, lesson planning and implementation according to prescribed education standards, continued education to remain informed of standards, etc.). The Federal Department of Labor provides the fact sheet found at this link for additional information:

http://www.dol.gov/whd/regs/compliance/whdfs46.htm

Paying teachers a "salary" or flat fee rather than hourly is illegal. Salaried workers typically work a 40+ hour week in order to qualify for the learned professional exemption from overtime pay. They must earn $455/week. You can find this additional information by clicking on the word exempt at the link above. I hope this helps. Unfortunately many Christian schools and churches get in trouble with the state wage and hour board when a disgruntled employee tries to file for unemployment and mentions they were not compensated appropriately or when they file taxes with a 1099 rather than a W-2.

Wage Conversion Table

Weekly and bi-weekly data based on 40-hour work week. Monthly data based on 4.33 weeks per month. Annual data based on 52 weeks per year.

Courtesy of the Georgia Department of Labor

Hourly	Weekly	Bi-weekly	Monthly	Annually
5.00	200	400	866	10,400
5.25	210	420	909	10,920
5.50	220	440	953	11,440
5.75	230	460	996	11,960
6.00	240	480	1,039	12,480
6.25	250	500	1,083	13,000
6.50	260	520	1,126	13,520
6.75	270	540	1,169	14,040
7.00	280	560	1,212	14,560
7.25	290	580	1,256	15,080
7.50	300	600	1,299	15,600

© 2014 Penn Consulting

7.75	310	620	1,342	16,120
8.00	320	640	1,386	16,640
8.25	330	660	1,429	17,160
8.50	340	680	1,472	17,680
8.75	350	700	1,516	18,200
9.00	360	720	1,559	18,720
9.25	370	740	1,602	19,240
9.50	380	760	1,645	19,760
9.75	390	780	1,689	20,280
10.00	400	800	1,732	20,800
10.25	410	820	1,775	21,320
10.50	420	840	1,819	21,840
10.75	430	860	1,862	22,360
11.00	440	880	1,905	22,880
11.25	450	900	1,949	23,400
11.50	460	920	1,992	23,920
11.75	470	940	2,035	24,440
12.00	480	960	2,078	24,960
12.25	490	980	2,122	25,480
12.50	500	1000	2,165	26,000
12.75	510	1020	2,208	26,520
13.00	520	1040	2,252	27,040
13.25	530	1060	2,295	27,560
13.50	540	1080	2,338	28,080
13.75	550	1100	2,382	28,600
14.00	560	1120	2,425	29,120
14.25	570	1140	2,468	29,640
14.50	580	1160	2,511	30,160
14.75	590	1180	2,555	30,680
15.00	600	1200	2,598	31,200
15.25	610	1220	2,641	31,720
15.50	620	1240	2,685	32,240
15.75	630	1260	2,728	32,760
16.00	640	1280	2,771	33,280
16.25	650	1300	2,815	33,800
16.50	660	1320	2,858	34,320
16.75	670	1340	2,901	34,840
17.00	680	1360	2,944	35,360
17.25	690	1380	2,988	35,880
17.50	700	1400	3,031	36,400
17.75	710	1420	3,074	36,920
18.00	720	1440	3,118	37,440

Attendance

In the event a staff member is unable to work due to illness he/she shall notify the program administrator as soon as possible, preferably one hour prior to the begin of the workday. The administrator should have a list of qualified substitutes to refer to. These substitutes may be persons that were considered for employment previously. In case of emergency in route to the center, staff should report to the administrator as soon as possible. All staff members should be required to be at their assigned areas with sufficient time to store personal belongings and wash their hands.. If you are unable to report or will be tardy, you should report to the administrator as soon as possible. Several; unscheduled absences or tardiness should be communicated as grounds for termination of employment.

Bright from the Start requires employees to be healthy to prevent the spread of disease. Paid sick leave is an optional benefit usually awarded after a predetermined period of service. Budgetary constraints must be considered in order to allot funds for substitute compensation. Programs specify the number of sick or personal days which can be taken whether paid or unpaid. Employees should be informed of the number of absences which are considered acceptable or excessive.

Maternity Leave should be granted in accordance with Federal laws outlined previously. Staff members may be granted paid or unpaid leave and their position is guaranteed for a specific period of time for other reasons such as the death of an immediate family member (Father, Mother, Brother, Sister). Proof of relation should be provided within a specified period. Due to the need for consistent care, positions may not be guaranteed after required time periods have elapsed. The Family and Medical Leave Act may not apply to small organizations.

Orientation

Prior to assignment to children or task, all employees must receive initial orientation on the following subjects:
1. The center's policies and procedures;
2. The portions of these rules dealing with the care, health and safety of children;
3. The employee's assigned duties and responsibilities;
4. Reporting requirements for suspected cases of child abuse, neglect or deprivation; communicable diseases and serious injuries;
5. Emergency weather plans;
6. Training requirements; and
7. Childhood injury control procedures.

Staff members and the person performing the orientation, should sign a documentation of orientation form and it shall be filed in their personnel file.

Benefits

Employees must be advised of restroom, lounge, secure storage areas and parking accommodations upon hire. They should also be advised of any disclaimers regarding the loss or theft of personal property. Staff members should be advised of schedules break times and whether compensation is offered. Federal law does not require lunch or coffee breaks. However, when employers do offer short breaks (usually lasting about 5 to 20 minutes), federal law considers the breaks work-time that must be paid. Unauthorized extensions of authorized work breaks need not be counted as hours worked when the employer has expressly and unambiguously communicated to the employee that the authorized break may only last for a specific length of time, that any extension of the break is contrary to the employer's rules, and any extension of the break will be punished. Bona fide meal periods (typically lasting at least 30 minutes), serve a different purpose than coffee or snack breaks and, thus, are not work time and are not compensable

Employees are typically eligible for discretionary/ incentive bonuses, which are awarded for performance in service. Free or discounted tuition for child care may be offered to employees. You must also consider equal pay for employees that do not have children. A cafeteria benefit plan permits employees to receive a dollar value for their benefits and they may choose to use those dollars in selecting various benefits i.e. child care, health or life insurance, pre-paid legal programs, etc.

Paid holidays generally include the following holidays: Christmas, Thanksgiving, Independence Day, Labor Day, M. L. King, Jr. Day and Memorial Day. Some programs choose to provide unpaid time off the day before and after a federal holiday since families tend to travel during this time and the attendance of children is low. Paid vacation periods may be offered. Vacations should be requested a specified period in advance and requested in writing. The program administrator should provide written approval or denial within a specified time period. Time off request forms should be provided for all personal leave requests. Vacations may be awarded on a seniority as is as it is convenient for the program and the employee.

Program administrators may enlist the assistance of a payroll services provider, investment broker or insurance agent in offering Medical and Dental plans, Retirement or Life insurance programs.

Staff members will be provided paid or uncompensated time off to attend training and/or conferences. Employees should be encouraged to join Child Care Professional Associations and obtain Professional Liability Insurance. This may be offered as a benefit.

Premiums for various plans should be deducted from payroll as agreed in writing by the employee.

Safety Rules and Regulations including Harassment

Sexual harassment
Although preschool and early childhood behaviors are evaluated individually in respect to motivation. We must treat any incident seriously and professionally. No staff member or student shall harass another employee or student in reference to sexual relations (touching, kissing, front to front hugging, etc.). Any harassment shall be reported immediately to the administrator, the board of health and the Department of Family and Children Services. Please be sure to contact the parents involved (by phone) and complete an incident report and/or disciplinary notice for all students, parents or employees involved. Students repeatedly committing this infraction shall be considered for expulsion. No staff members shall harass another employee or student in reference to sexual relations. Any harassment should be reported immediately to the administrator or to another authority if the administrator was involved. Employees committing this infraction shall be disciplined appropriately.

Electronic Communications Policy

The center provides telephones and computers for business or educational use. For the safety of our children, computers and internet service should never be used for personal use, including sending and receiving e-mails, "web surfing" or contacting on-line commercial businesses. It is recognized that occasional telephone calls are necessary. These should be kept to a minimum both in frequency and duration. If an emergency telephone call is received for you, you will be immediately contacted. In all others cases, a note of the call will be made and placed in your mailbox as time permits. Except in the case of an emergency, telephone calls should be made only at break time. Teachers should not call parents from the classroom. Please ask children, family, and friends not to contact you by telephone at work unless absolutely necessary.

The growth in the cellular phone, tablet, and pager industry presents many workplace problems. They are distracting to both employees and students, and their use during work time interferes with our responsibility to provide excellence in ministry.

Pagers may be worn at work, so long as they are in silent mode. Paged calls should be returned only during breaks.

Cellular phones are not to be brought in to the school. Personal telephone calls while at the school are to be held to a minimum and, therefore, there is no need to have a cellular phone at work. Staff members may use the telephone during breaks, however you are asked to keep personal calls to three minutes or less in consideration of others.

Child Abuse and Neglect Prevention

Georgia Code Section 19-7-5 states " School teachers and administrators, school guidance counselors, child care personnel, day care personnel or law enforcement personnel having reasonable cause to believe that a child under the age of eighteen has a physical injury or injuries inflicted upon him other than by accidental means by a parent or caretaker, or has been neglected or has been sexually assaulted or sexually exploited, shall report or cause reports to be made in accordance with the provision of this section; provided, however that when the attendance of the reporting person with respect to a child is pursuant to the performance of services as a member of the staff of a…school…or similar facility, he shall notify the person in charge of the facility or his designated delegate who shall report or cause to be made in accordance with the provisions of this section."

1. The initial person hearing the report should listen to the report and document it. The employee shall report the incident to the administrator.
2. The Administrator and one other staff member shall record the victim's allegation. Asking questions to clarify facts only, not to verify or investigate, this is the responsibility of law enforcement officials.
3. The administrator and or staff member shall inform the Board and the Georgia Department of Family and Children Services. An oral repot shall be made as soon as possible by telephone or otherwise, and followed by a written report (in writing). The report shall contain the name and address of the child, his/her parents or caretakers, if known, the child's age,

4. the nature and extent of the child's injuries (including all evidence of previous injuries) and other reasons the children are considered at risk and names of others who witnessed the child's report of injuries. In the event the administrator is being accused, the staff member shall contact the President of the Board who will follow the guidelines for reporting abuse.
5. The insurance carrier and Bright from the Start consultant should be notified as soon as possible.

Important: In order to prevent such allegations, staff members should follow the following guidelines:
1. Complete training to recognize types of abuse:
- Physical Abuse: Non accidental physical injury, self-mutilation.
- Neglect: Failure to provide a child the necessities of life.
- Self-Molestation: The sexual exploitation of a child for the sexual gratification of another person. Emotional Abuse: "The excessive, aggressive, or other parental behavior that places unreasonable demands on a child to perform above his or her capabilities.
2. Be aware of the Physical and Behavioral Indicators of Abuse:
- Observe the communication between parents and children.
- Observe the child for physical indicators such as bruises, burns, lacerations, etc…
- Determine whether the injury is consistent with the child's age, physical and emotional maturity level, medical history and how he/she explains the injury.
- Observe behavioral indicators, excessive or extremely low responsiveness.
- Observe inappropriate knowledge or activity to sexual behavior.

We encourage all staff members to realize that our service to the families entrusting the education of their children to us is a sacred responsibility. We are accountable to one another, the two-adult rule is emphasized when appropriate. Communicate appropriately with parents regarding the child's activities, the child's behavior, etc.. Respect each person's right to privacy, by not discussing a child with anyone other the administrative staff or the child's parents. The above policy applies to allegations of staff/student misconduct as well as non-school related allegations.

CORPORAL PUNISHMENT

Corporal punishment should never be used in the child care setting, even with the parent's permission.

13. Training Records and Confidentiality

Employees must submit copies of all training to the program administrator to include in the personnel records. All personnel records are to remain confidential. Employer should consult legal counsel on information which can be shared when providing employment verification or references.

Reflect

The Shepherd's Training Academy has a staff of 25 teachers and assistants. Staff meetings are held once a month, and there is always much to discuss. Some members hardly ever speak up at the meetings while others often dominate the time. They always want to contribute to the discussions and frequently ask for help with problems they have in their classrooms. As director Mrs. White wants to help her staff members to feel included and get help if it is needed.

The administrator or staff meeting facilitator should avoid anyone monopolizing the conversation. The agenda will surely increase productivity. Every effort should be made to create a system that includes regular staff meetings where positive supervisor-supervisee relationships can grow. Programs must avoid creating a system where supervision only occurs when problems arise.

Staff meetings should be planned events that include time for information sharing, training and clarification of policies and procedures, as well as performance-based feedback. During meetings, communications should be supportive and solution-focused. Key decisions and next steps that emerge from these meetings should be documented and this information may be used to formulate individual professional development goals and assess staff progress in achieving program goals.

1. What would you suggest to Mrs. White so that each staff member is able to participate in the meetings?
2. What could be done before meetings take place so the time could be spent more productively?

If children are untaught, their ignorance and vices will in future life cost us much dearer in their consequences than it would have done in their correction by a good education. - Thomas Jefferson

SMALL GROUP ACTIVITY

Participants will discuss policies they which to adopt in their centers and begin working on handbooks

Session 8 Supervising and Developing Staff

Program administrators are responsible for planning meetings and regular in-service training to build community and climate within the program, in addition to providing vital training and communication necessary for program effectiveness. Training topics were previously discussed. Administrators may rely on outside sources to provide training required by the licensing regulations. Training can be provided onsite. Administrators should guide employees in setting career and education goals. Regular meetings should help teachers plan with eh annual or long range goals in mind. A few in-service training options include, but are not limited to: child development related books, college course, online courses, road trips to other centers, conventions and conferences, teacher led staff meetings, professional committees and professional libraries within the center. Phi Delta Kappa reports that teachers double their professional development when they participate in professional networks outside the school and share knowledge within their school.

Staff members should be challenged to offer solutions to problems they present. Many centers require employees to complete weekly reports in which they are given the opportunity to submit ideas for in-service training or staff meetings. Many programs adopt a peer mentoring program, whereby teaches with great attitudes and competence are assigned newer teachers to meet with on a regular basis. Teachers should be encouraged to pursue credentials as previously stated.

Program administrators should not permit teachers which resist professional development, possess complaining attitudes or display an insubordinate attitude to leadership.

Internet Activity: The Council for Early Childhood Professional Recognition was established in 1985 to increase the status and recognition of early care and education professionals. The Council offers a variety of services and information. A CDA -- a **Child Development Associate credential** -- is a nationally recognized designation awarded by the Council for Professional Recognition in Washington, D.C. This council became a part of the National Association for the Education of Young Children in 1985.

Candidates must complete 120 hours of early childhood education training, covering the growth and development of children aged 3 to 5 years, with no fewer than 10 training hours in each of the following subject areas:

- Planning a safe and healthy learning environment.
- Advancing children's physical and intellectual development.
- Supporting children's social and emotional development.
- Building productive relationships with families.
- Managing an effective program operation.
- Maintaining a commitment to professionalism.
- Observing and recording children's behavior.
- Understanding principles of child development and learning.

The Penn Consulting Child Development Essentials (CDA) Program prepares students for work in the early childhood care and education field. Participants must be working with young children regularly either in a paid or volunteer position to fulfill their coursework requirements.

Learning objectives:

All Program completers will be able to:
- Plan safe, healthy environments to invite learning
- Facilitate steps to advance children's physical and intellectual development
- Create positive ways to support children's social and emotional development
- Develop strategies to establish productive relationships with families
- Facilitate strategies to manage an effective program operation
- Maintain a commitment to professionalism
- Observe and record children's behavior
- Apply principles of child growth and development

Application and registration
The online or classroom face-to-face course is designed to be completed in 12 weeks.

Register online at: http://www.pennconsulting.org/id35.html
Visit www.cdacouncil.org and read about the CDA 2.0 process.
1. Who can obtain a CDA credential?
2. What kinds of requirements must a candidate complete before being awarded a credential?
3. If you did not have a degree, would you consider applying for the CDA? Why or why not?

Group Discussion and Activity

Discuss and list qualities that attract teachers to programs i.e. (friendly co-workers, salary needs are met, benefits package, professionalism, professional development opportunities, opportunity to express faith or values, etc.)

People quit people-before they quit institutions….. Author unknown

Write a job announcement or teacher recruitment brochure for three positions in your center.

Activity Complete a Professional Development Self-Assessment

This is the first step to developing a plan for professional development. Use this checklist to monitor your progress toward becoming an accomplished early educator.

Read the following list of professional development outcomes and score your progress as follows: 3-Fully accomplished 2-Making progress 1-Need to start	
Professional outcome	**Rating**
1. I have written my philosophy of teaching and learning.	
2. I have a professional career plan which includes goals and objectives for the next year.	
3. I engage in training to improve my skills and competence in working with children.	
4. I display a teachable attitude.	
5. I have worked or am obtaining a credential or degree to enhance my personal and professional life.	
6. I engage in self-improvement programs in order to improve my personal qualities.	
7. I practice good moral habits and model ethical behavior. I encourage others to act ethically.	
8. I behave in a professional manner and encourage others to do the same.	
9. I place the best interests of children, parents, and the profession first when making decisions about what constitutes quality teaching and caring for young children.	
10. I am familiar with the history, terminology, contemporary research, issues, and trends of the early childhood education industry.	
11. I intentionally find ways to apply best practices to my teaching.	
12. I belong to a professional organization and participate in activities such as lobbying, celebrations, study groups, committees, and conferences.	
13. I am an advocate for the children I serve and my profession.	
14. I encourage parental involvement in my program and support them in their role as their child's primary caregiver and teacher.	
15. I seek the advice of other early education professionals and work collaboratively with others.	
Total points	
Results 40-45 You are an accomplished professional. You can work on refining your skills and be a strong advocate for others. You can mentor others and help them to develop in their careers. 30-39 You have made some progress in growing as a professional. 0-29 You are ready to embark on a journey in developing as a professional educator. This is a great opportunity to develop your career plans and seek mentors to guide the way.	

Professional Development Plan

Educator's Name: _____

Current Educational Assignment: _____ No. of Years in Current Assignment: ____

No. of Years of Educational Experience: _____

Licensure Renewal Date: _____ License(s) to Be Renewed: _____
Circle one:
Present Licensure Stage: Initial Educator Professional Educator Master Educator
Licensure Stage Sought: Child Development Director Professional Educator
Professional Licensure Category: Teacher Administrator Pupil Services

Step I: Preparing to Write the Plan: SELF-REFLECTION
Select goals from the assessment and/or the code of ethics.

Step II: Writing the Plan: COMPONENTS
If you have identified more than one goal in your plan, follow Step II, A–E, for each goal:
A. Description of School and Teaching/Administrative/Pupil Services Situation
B. Description of the Goal(s) to Be Addressed
C. Rationale for Your Goal(s) and Link to Self-Reflection, Educational Situation, and Standard(s)
D. Plan for Assessing and Documenting Achievement of Your Goal(s)
E. Plan to Meet Your Goal(s): Objectives, Activities and Timeline, and Collaboration
Date goal(s) (including Step II, A–E) submitted to the PDP Team: _____
Date goal(s) approved/not approved by the PDP Team: _____

Step III: Annual Review of Your Plan
(to be completed in years two, three, and four of the licensure cycle)
A. Completion dates for objectives and activities completed during each year
B. Reflection summary of your growth made throughout the year
C. Description of any revisions made in your goal(s), objectives, or activities

Step IV: Documentation of Completion of Your Plan
(to be completed at the conclusion of the licensure cycle)
A. Three to five pieces of evidence
B. Reflection and summary of your professional growth and its effect on student learning

Also include your Annual Reviews and, for the initial educator, your approved and signed Goal Approval Form.

Date plan submitted to the PDP Team or Administrator: _____

Date plan verified/not verified by the PDP Team or Administrator: _____

Session 9 Recruiting, Training, and Supervising Interns and Volunteers

Student Teachers, Teacher Aides, Parent Volunteers and Student Helpers must complete a criminal background check and orientation before being assigned duties or children. Aides, volunteers and helpers can make an important contribution to your program In order that we may make good use of this type of contribution it will be important to follow these general guidelines:

Prospective aides, volunteers, and helpers shall be approved in advance and assigned to classrooms by the responsible administrator. No payment or other financial benefits will be given for their services. These volunteers will be caring, dependable and effective with children. They should be willing to work cooperatively with a teacher and under a specific teacher's supervision.
The teacher must meet with them outside of hours supervising students to provide these individuals with clear information regarding the classroom management program, curriculum and his or her teaching style. Teachers need to schedule some uninterrupted time to plan with the volunteer. Teachers and volunteers will need to work closely together and be attuned to each other's needs.

Parent volunteers increase the safety of children while participating in activities and chaperoning children on field trips. They tend to be non-professional individuals who are willing to assist a teacher on a regular basis. Children tend to respond to them better if they serve often. Under the direction and supervision of the teacher they may make copies or construct learning materials, games or reinforcement materials, read to the class, students or clean and organize materials (vacuum, sweep, disinfect) in cabinets, closets or restrooms. They may also be instrumental in improving parent communications by offering to type materials for teachers or post notices. Parents should not be left alone with children.

Student interns may perform the same duties as parent volunteers however, they will require very close supervision. They must meet Bright from the Start guidelines regarding age. Students who are assigned must keep their schedule commitment. Students may not be left alone with children.

Teacher aides are individuals who qualified professional educators. Under the direction and supervision of the teacher, that may perform all of the duties listed for volunteers and helpers. Additionally they may:
Provide some instruction, which is planned by the teacher.
Answer student's questions or help students complete assignments.
Monitor independent activities to keep students on-task.
Supplement direct learning centers for example, teach and play assigned games.
Aides and volunteers should not be given regularly assigned teacher duties without approval from the program administrator.

Reflect

Gloria is a mother of five children ranging in age from 3 to 12. She volunteered when each of her children attended your preschool. She is presently helping in her youngest daughter's class. Problems have arisen between Gloria and Consuela, the young teacher, who has been with the class less than a year. Many of the parents and the children already know Gloria and think of her as the teacher in the group. Consuela feels that she is not given the authority she should have as the college-educated professional she is. Gloria also feels that Consuela does not give her credit for the many years experience she has had with young children. They have found it difficult to express their frustrations and feelings with each other, but know they need help or the partnership will not work.

1. Where would you start to help these two adults?
2. Are their widely disparate backgrounds a help or a hindrance in this kind of setting? Explain.

© 2014 Penn Consulting

Adapted from Administering Programs for Young Children (2010), Phyllis click and Kim Karos

Internet Activity: Research professional development opportunities and identify three professional organizations for support. Establish a Professional Development Registry profile. ADM-9

Often volunteers are recruited from people already known to the staff in child care programs. However, sometimes it is necessary to seek outside sources for finding volunteers. In addition, many directors have little experience of working with unpaid staff and may need help. Three web sites were listed at the end of this session, each of which offers different kinds of information or help.

Visit one of the following volunteer organization sites and post a volunteer job description. Be sure to use the organization with a mission that is aligned with your organization's mission.

Volunteer match www.volunteermatch.org
Hands on Atlanta www.handsonatlanta.org
American Association of Retired Persons www.aarp.org
Volunteer Today www.volunteertoday.com
Teach for America www.teachforamerica.org
Americorps www.nationalservice.gov/programs/americorps
United Way www.unitedway.org

Complete Practical Applications-ADM4 & 8 personnel handbook draft & OSHA, DOL poster downloads, and organizational chart

Session 10 Budget

Program administrators must develop a start up budget and annual operating budget which serves as a financial plan for a specified period of time. It is best to hire an accountant or payroll service with experience in laws which pertain to the child care industry. A recent study by the University of Colorado at Denver's Cost, Quality and Child Outcomes Study Team (2005) found that:

"...fiscal tasks and planning account for approximately fifty percent of a program administrator's time."

"....most child care is mediocre in quality, sufficiently poor to interfere with children's emotional and intellectual development."

"...there are few economic incentives for centers to improve quality."

"FINDING 1: Child care at most centers in the United States is poor to mediocre, with almost half of the infants and toddlers in rooms having less than minimal quality."

"...cash costs for centers meeting minimal standards (but not those with good to excellent ratings) was $2.11 per child hour ($95 per child week, or $4,940 per child year)."

"In most states, average child care center fees for an infant are higher than a year's tuition and fees at a public college. (Parents and the High Cost of Child Care: 2013 Report, 2013)

"Factor in two kids, and the study finds average fees higher than the median rent in all states, and higher than the average food bill in all regions." (Parents and the High Cost of Child Care: 2013 Report, 2013)

Fifty percent of the centers were for profit and fifty percent of them were not for profit. The U. S. General Accounting Office (1999) estimated that the cost of care in accredited centers was about $7,000 per year for 50 weeks of full time care. The amount is cost to operate a program and the cash cost ore amount charged and paid for services are different. Quality enhancements are assumed to be the difference.

The increase in two-family household incomes has created a huge demand for childcare related services. Established childcare facilities generally attract parents of infants, preschool children and school-age children who are looking to place their children with daycare providers because of their need to work outside the home. According to Entrepreneur, the start-up costs for a childcare center range from $10,000 to $50,000. (Huntington, 2014)

Program administrators must consider the following costs:

1. Start-up expenses for building, licensing, equipment, supplies, planning and six months operations expenses.
2. Fixed expenses such as those incurred when planning.
3. Variable costs which are contingent upon number of children served.
4. Marginal expenses are those per unit or per person costs incurred in order to increase services beyond a given enrollment.
5. Capital costs are one time costs such as building and land acquisition.

6. Operating expenses are recurrent such as salaries, occupancy, insurance, etc.
7. Hidden expenses are those which cost the program nothing, but are paid by someone else, for instance someone that donates a vehicle or facility.
8. Joint costs are those shared by someone else, for instance a child care center shares space with a Church's Sunday school program or computer and audiovisual equipment with an evening training program.
9. Foregone expenses are income produced by in-kind gifts or services provided a program.

The figures contained in this section are available on the companion textbook website. (P. Click & K. Karos, 2010).

FUNCTIONAL AREA	RANGE
Child Care and Teaching (salaries, FICA, health insurance, training, vacancies, substitutes, classroom equipment)	50% - 60%
Administration and Supervision (administrative salaries, accounting fees, office supplies, phone, licensing fee, advertising, legal fees)	12% - 20%
Food Program (food, kitchen, supplies, kitchen staff)	6% - 19%
Occupancy (rent/mortgage, taxes, maintenance, repairs)	10% - 20%
Other (health consultation, social services, transportation, field trips)	5% - 20%

(Operating Budgets for Child Care Programs, 2001)

Sample Budget Form

INCOME	
Registration fees	
Books and materials fees	
Tuition	
Gifts and contributions	
Fund-raising	
Investment income	
Government Subsidies	
Grants	
Rent	
Total Income	
EXPENSES—Personnel	
Staff salaries	
Total	
Fringe benefits *(10–15% of total)*: Workers' compensation, FICA, FUTA, health insurance	
Discounted staff tuitions	
Total Salaries and Fringe Benefits	
EXPENSES—Controllable	
Advertising	
Banking fees	
Bookkeeping/Audit	
Cleaning service	
Consultant services	
Custodial Supplies	
Discounted sibling tuitions and vacancies	
Educational	
Educational	
Equipment	
Food	
Housekeeping	
Internet service	
Office	
Office	
Paper products (kitchen, bathroom, office, etc.)	
Supplies and materials	
Transportation	
Uncollected tuitions	
Website domain	
EXPENSES—Fixed	
Insurance	
Marketing	
Space costs (rent/mortgage)	
Taxes	
Telephone	
Utilities	
Other costs	
TOTAL EXPENSES	
Cost per child (total expenses _ number of children)	
NET (income minus expenses)	

Handwritten notes: 75% (bracketing Registration fees through Rent); Alarm/Cell phone (next to Space costs); 50 weeks; Only count 75% of kids

Sample **breakeven analysis**: Please see the business plan for an explanation:
- ☐ Yearly expenses are $390,000
- ☐ 64 students - 4 students=60 X $6,500= $390,000
- ☐ Profit $26,000/ by tuition $6,500=4 students

© 2014 Penn Consulting

Operating Budget Worksheet:
School-Age Child Care Program

Directions: Use this worksheet to calculate the operating expenses.

Personnel
Administrative Salary $_____
Benefits $_____
Instructional Salary $_____
Benefits $_____
Support Salary $_____
Benefits $_____
Professional Fees & Contractual Services
Consultants $_____
Transportation $_____
Publicity/Advertising $_____
Insurance $_____
Consultant/Training $_____
Independent Contractors $_____
Other Contracts $_____
Facility
Rent $_____
Telephone $_____
Security system $_____
Utilities $_____
Janitorial Services $_____
Renovations $_____
Other $_____
Supplies and Equipment
Office Supplies $_____
Office Equipment
Program Supplies $_____
Program Equipment $_____
Food $_____
Books and Magazines $_____
Transportation
Vehicles $_____
Maintenance $_____
Fuel $_____
Administrative Costs
Postage $_____
Printing and Copying $_____
Cell Telephone $_____
Other $_____
Total Expenses $

© 2014 Penn Consulting

Most programs obtain financing from private donors, foundations or the government. Some financing is conditional. Bright from the Start (DECAL) offers a list of funding sources in Georgia on their website. It is wise for program administrators to take a grant writing course and/or visit the Foundation Center and Center for Non Profit Organizations before opening the facility.

There are numerous grants available especially at the preschool level. The United States Department of Education's acronym "STEM" (science, technology, engineering, and mathematics), one of the past decade's most prominent educational buzzwords, is quickly becoming out-of-date. Taking its place is the successor term "STEAM" (science, technology, engineering, **arts**, and mathematics). The argument for the integration of arts into the STEM curriculum is based on evidence that children learn in a variety of ways and need to develop creativity and design capabilities in order to create new technologies and make new discoveries.

To see examples of grants that have been awarded for STEAM research and development, such as the Wolf Trap Foundation for the Performing Arts, you may wish to visit Education Week's article "STEAM: Experts Make Case for Adding Arts to STEM."

Below are examples of Funding Agencies
Federal agencies funding STEAM include the following:
- National Science Foundation
- National Endowment for the Arts
- US Department of Education
- US Department of Agriculture (HSI Education Grants Program)

A few of the many major Foundations that have recently funded STEAM education initiatives include:
- AT&T Foundation
- MacArthur Foundation
- American Honda Foundation
- Silicon Valley Community Foundation
- The Abell Foundation

There are plenty of resources, studies, and ideas about students' learning and how the arts can have a positive effect on the STEM curriculum.

Under the Individuals with Disabilities Education Act (IDEA)—the United States Department of Education provides students with special education services until his twenty-second birthday. IDEA is intended to improve educational results for all children with disabilities. Therefore, it provides benefits and services to children with disabilities in public schools and requires school districts to make services and benefits available to children with disabilities enrolled by their parents in nonpublic (private) schools and day care programs. The law includes language requiring state education agencies (SEAs) and local education agencies (LEAs) to ensure the equitable participation of parentally placed children with disabilities in Christian school programs assisted by or carried out under the equitable participation requirements that apply to them. Parentally placed children with disabilities do not have an individual entitlement to services they would receive if they were enrolled in a public school. Instead, the LEA is required to spend a proportionate amount of IDEA federal funds to provide equitable services to these students. Many preschool directors overlook this funding which provides computers and other assistive technology to programs that serve students with disabilities (e.g. ADHD/ADD, Autism, Asperger, Dyslexia, and so forth). Programs can provide tutoring services through the Supplemental Educational Services/Flexible Learning Plans and receive funding from the Department of Education also.

You may obtain other sources of sample business documents and management tools from the following sources:

Bush, J. (2001). Dollars & Sense: *Planning for profit in your child care business.* Albany, NY: Delmar.
Pruissen, C. M. (1998). *Start and run a profitable day care: Your step by step business plan.* North Vancouver: Self Counsel Press.

Hands on Activity- Begin completion of Budget Form
Group Discussion-Review Bright From the Start Grant or Funding Source Handout

Other creative ways to collaborate with the community to fund your program.
www.usda.gov/ Department of Agriculture Food Programs
www.ed.gov/ Department of education Even Start, Title I, Special Education, Parent Assistance Centers
www.hhs.gov/ Department of Health and human Services TANF, Child Care and Development Block Grant, Early Learning Fund, Head Start, Grants Net
www.doi.gov/bureau-indian-affairs.html Indian Child and Family Education
www.ed.gov/pubs/KnowAtGrants/ Department of Education's Grants
www.sba.gov/womeninbusiness/wnet.html
http://fodncenter.org Foundation Center
Child Care Aware www.childcareaware,org
Local Initiatives Support Consortium www.lisnet.org
Online shopping programs which give back to the school. http://www.onecause.com
Campbell's Soup Labels Publix Partners Cards

Internet Activity: Visit the sites and answer the following questions.

1. What kinds of information did you find?

2. Was there anything that would help the director of a child care center?

3. Should government agencies be involved in subsidizing private businesses? Explain your answer.

Surviving Economic Crises
Tuition is the main source of income for many early childhood programs. During economic hard times when parents lose their jobs, enrollment may decline drastically. Directors cut back on expenses as much as possible and some try to organize fund-raising activities. These two measures may solve the problem temporarily. However, if the job picture continues to be bleak, they may not be enough. (P. Click & K. Karos, 2010)

REFERENCE
Neugebauer, R. (2002, January/February). Surviving tight times. Child Care Information Exchange, 143, 10-16.

DISCUSSION
1. What do you think are the first things a director should do when expenses are greater than income?
2. If parents leave for reasons other than job problems, what might be the causes?
3. Read Neugebauer's article to find other solutions to the problem.

Program administrators should keep a finger on the pulse of certain data by monitoring consumer needs, customer satisfaction, and managing costs. The temporary fixes never address the root fiscal problem. Line-item budgeting is a great solution, because it offers decision-makers an incremental, or step-by-step, approach to budgeting. Budget makers can use a line-item budget to make specific decisions, such as changing funding levels of programs being phased out to provide money for new programs or making cuts to budgeted expenses because of changes in organizational policies. Line-item budgeting is easy to model after past budgets and other historical data. When writing a line-item budget, the budget maker can consider whether specific categories (food, paper, utilities, and the like), programs, activities, and departments should receive the same level of funding as the previous year or an increase or decrease by line item.

Historical data might include sample budgets from other organizations. For example, the director of a new school could begin with the budget of another program in the same region with the same enrollment and curriculum offerings. Many organizations provide historical data. Also most vendors have websites that permit you to assemble a shopping cart to get estimates of equipment costs. Please see the websites below:

http://childcareaware.org/child-care-providers/business-plan/preparing-a-budget
www.ccc-oc.org/Resource/.../Operating%20Budget%20Basics.pdf
www.mdchildcare.org/mdcfc/pdfs/budg1-centeroperations02.pdf
www.gsa.gov/graphics/pbs/startupguide.pdf
www.buildingchildcare.net/uploads/pdfs/CCCManualFINAL07.pdf

Follow up on leads by completing this form for all calls. Include data in a direct marketing mail list.

Inquiry Report		
Name		Date
Address		Phone
Child's Birthdate	Grade level	
Referred by		
How did you hear about our school?		
Brochure sent		Date
Application packet sent		Date
Interview scheduled		
Interest: (check all that apply)		
Teacher Qualifications		
Curriculum		
Cost		
Location		
Extracurricular Programs		
Other:		
Additional comments:		

*1st ❡ document
2. about what people are interested in

→ monitor consumer needs
→ customer satisfaction
→ cost control

Session 11 Maintenance, Health and Safety

Injury control precautions

Supervision-*critical to child safety and well-being in early childhood educational settings*

1. Children shall be supervised at all times.
2. "Supervision" means that the appropriate number of staff members are <u>physically present</u> in the area where children are being cared for and are providing watchful oversight to the children, chaperons and students in training.
3. The persons supervising in the child care area must be alert, able to respond promptly to the needs and actions of the children being supervised, as well as the actions of the chaperons and students in training, and provide timely attention to the children's actions and needs.
4. During scheduled breaks teachers someone should be designated to relieve teachers. Staff members leaving students unattended open themselves and the school to unnecessary charges of neglect that could lead to serious legal problems.
5. Teachers should enforce playground rules and maintain staff:child ratios. Insure proper behavior on the playground and discipline misbehaving students.
6. The teacher shall assure that field trips are well supervised. They should ask reliable parents to come as chaperons when an activity demands more supervisory personnel that we have school personnel attending. If students return to school after a field trip and the regular after-school supervisory staff has left, the teacher(s) are responsible for staying with the students until the last student has been picked up.

> **Building Blocks** *CFOC National Health and Safety Performance Standards*
> 1. True or False: The younger the children, the lower the staff-to-child ratio.
> 2. In child care settings, are the teacher's own children included in the staff-to-child ratio?
> 3. True or false: It is permissible to leave a child unsupervised while he or she is sleeping, as long as the sleeping arrangements are safe and in compliance.
> 4. When should caregivers count children to confirm the safe whereabouts of every child?

Civitas: *Building Blocks* - Building Blocks was adapted by Civitas with permission from *Caring for Our Children: National Health and Safety Performance Standards, Guidelines for Out-of-Home Child Care Programs*, Second Edition, 2002. These are nationally recognized standards considered best practices in providing healthy and safe child care environments.

National/State ratios are as follows:

Ages of Children	Staff: Child Ratio	Maximum Group Size
0-18 mos. *not walking*	1:3/1:6	6/12
12-24 mos. *walking*	1:4/1:8	8/16
2 yrs.	1:5/1:10	10/20
3 yrs.	1:7/1:15	14/30
4 yrs.	1:8/1:18	16/36
5 yrs.	1:8/1:20	16/40
6 yrs. And older	1:10/1:25	20/50

Water Activity Ratios	
Infants	1:1
Toddlers	1:1
Preschoolers	1:4
School-age Children	1:6

1. A mixed group shall be based on the ages of the youngest children in the group if **more than twenty percent (20 %)** of the children in the mixed-age group belong to younger age groupings.
2. Two year olds and three year olds should not be combined without parental assent.
3. During early morning times of arrival and late afternoon times of departure, infants and children younger than three (3) years may be grouped with older children so long as staff: child ratios are met.
4. Maximum group size does not apply to **outdoor play** on the playground routinely used by the center or for special activities in the center lasting no more than two
5. (2) hours. However, required staff: child ratios must be maintained.

Research indicates that highly qualified teachers with specific training in child development improve the quality of care, improve early childhood literacy skills development and increase their student's performance on intelligence tests.

Professional caregivers demonstrate competency in the following tasks:
Infant and toddler care:
1. Diapering;
2. Bathing;
3. Feeding;
4. Holding;
5. Comforting;
6. Putting babies down to sleep positioned on their back and on a firm surface to reduce the risk of Sudden Infant Death Syndrome (SIDS);
7. Providing responsive and continuous interpersonal relationships and opportunities for child-initiated activities.
8. Managing atypical or disruptive behaviors of children.

Preschool care:
1. Typical and atypical development of 3- to 5-year-old children;
2. Social and emotional development of children, including children's development of independence and their ability to adapt to their environment and cope with stress;
3. Cognitive, language, early literacy, and mathematics development of children through activities in the classroom;
4. Cultural backgrounds of the children in the facility's care by demonstrating cultural competence through interactions with children and families and through program activities.

School-age care:
1. Social and emotional needs and developmental tasks of 5- to 12-year old children,
2. Be able to recognize and appropriately manage difficult behaviors,
3. Implement a cognitively and socially enriching program that has been developed with input from parents.
4. Effectively communicate with parents, administration and children while maintaining confidentiality of records.

Reference:
American Academy of Pediatrics, American Public Health Association, National Resource Center for Health and Safety in Child Care and Early Education. 2011. *Caring for our children: National health and safety performance standards; Guidelines for early care and education programs. 3rd edition.* Elk Grove Village, IL: American Academy of Pediatrics; Washington, DC: American Public Health Association. Also available at http://nrckids.org.

Discipline means to teach or train, not punish. Primarily acceptable discipline measures redirection, positive guidance and time away. Positive discipline involves the parent and includes but is not limited to:
1. Positive guidance
2. Redirection
3. Classroom rules, expectations and activities that are realistic for the age of the children
4. Limits, consequences and choices that children understand, and that promote self - discipline
5. Limits and consequences that are consistent and applied equally to all children
6. Desired behavior modeled by caregivers
7. Minimal use of negative consequences

Note:
Physical punishment should NEVER be allowed - Shaking, spanking, pinching and other physical contact that causes discomfort is never acceptable.
Abusive language should NEVER be allowed - Words that frighten or belittle a child are emotionally damaging and should never be tolerated.
Grabbing and yelling is ONLY appropriate to prevent harm –
Example: If a child is about to throw a heavy toy at another child a caregiver could shout, "Stop! Put that down!"

Playground Safety Considerations
1. Do adults actively supervise all children and organize active physical play?
2. Is the playground surrounded by a 4 ft. fence?
3. Is the sandbox clean?
4. Is the playground equipment safe, with no sharp edges, broken parts, pinching actions or loose bolts/pieces?
5. Are materials used for the surface under equipment checked often for depth (3-6" required, 8-10" recommended cushioning) and hazards?
6. Are there electrical hazards on the playground such as accessible air conditioners, switch boxes, or power lines?
7. Do foreign objects or obstructions exist in the fall zones under and around the fixed equipment?
8. Are collections of contaminated water on the playground?

Playground mishaps are a leading cause of injury to children aged 5 to 14. Many of these occur because of inadequate supervision, although some injuries result when children use equipment that is inappropriate for their age level. Both parents and child care personnel must be knowledgeable about safety issues in order to prevent injury and emergency room visits.

Internet Activity: View the following documents in the Caring for our Children Manual.
CFOC Appendix DD: Injury Report Form for Indoor and Outdoor Injuries 482
CFOC Appendix EE: America's Playgrounds Safety Report Card 484

Visit the National Program for Playground Safety website: http://uni.edu/playground
Click on "Safety Tips and FAQ's." Choose one of the topics listed.

1. In what way would this information be helpful to a director of a child care program?
2. Would you recommend this Web site to parents in your center?

© 2014 Penn Consulting

Reflect

It was the third playground accident of the week. Julito had been on the geo dome climber when he missed his footing and fell to the ground below. He cried loudly as he lay there and then refused to be comforted for a very long time afterward. He wasn't really hurt, but seemed frightened by the incident. At the staff meeting the following evening, Mrs. Gonzalez expressed her concern. She told the staff that the number of playground accidents was unacceptable and that they must all find a way to prevent them.
1. What do you think are the primary causes of playground mishaps?
2. What suggestions might the staff make to prevent future incidents? (Click & Karos, 2010)

Diaper Changing Procedures [http://decal.ga.gov/documents/attachments/DiaperingHandout.pdf]
1. Wash Hands and put on gloves
2. Organize supplies (gloves, wipes, mat and liner, plastic bag, ✓ointments, diaper/pull-ups, cleaning and sanitizing product (s), change of clothing)
3. *Wipe diaper area-always hold the child
4. Remove soiled diaper and gloves-plastic bag
5. Clean hands
6. Place clean diaper on child
7. Dress child
8. Wash child's hands
9. Dispose of mat liner and plastic bag
10. Clean and sanitize diaper changing area
11. Wash your hands
12. Complete the diaper log

Hand washing - When?
1. Upon arrival for the day
2. Changing classes
3. Before and after: Eating, handling food, or feeding a child; Giving medication; Playing in water that is used by more than one person; Diapering; Using the toilet or helping a child use a toilet; Handling bodily fluid (mucus, blood, vomit), Handling uncooked food, especially raw meat and poultry; Handling pets and other animals; Playing in sandboxes; Cleaning or handling the garbage.

How?
Use warm water and soap
Moisten hands, apply liquid soap
Rub both sides (20 sec.) and rinse (sing alphabet song or _____)
Dry with a paper towel
Turn water off with paper towel
Apply hand lotion

Toy and Equipment Safety Basics
(1) Lead free www.cpsc.gov www.consumeraffairs.com
(2) No chipping paint or rust
(3) No broken or chipped pieces
(4) Batteries should be changed often
(5) High chairs/swings (safety straps and safe bases)
(6) No missing parts from cribs or other equipment
(7) Age appropriate
(8) Washable and sanitizable
(9) Disposable towels, rags, etc.

> 📄 Building Blocks
> 1. What should be done with toys that children have placed in their mouths or that are otherwise contaminated by body secretion or excretion?
> 2. List two objects intended for the mouth that should be cleaned and sanitized between uses.
> 3. True or False: Machine-washable cloth toys should be used by only one individual until they are laundered.

Selecting an Appropriate Sanitizer
References: Canadian Pediatric Society. *Well Being: A Guide to Promote the Physical Health, Safety and Emotional Well-Being of Children in Child Care*
Centers and Family Day Care Homes, 2nd ed. Toronto, ON; 1996
Centers for Disease Control and Prevention. *The ABC's of Safe and Healthy Child Care; 1996*
Adapted from Appendix I Caring for Our Children: National Health and Safety Performance Standards

One of the most important steps in reducing the spread of infectious diseases among children and child care providers is cleaning and sanitizing of surfaces that could possibly pose a risk to children or staff. Routine cleaning with detergent and water is the most useful method for removing germs from surfaces in the child care setting. However, some items and surfaces require an additional step after cleaning to reduce the number of germs on a surface to a level that is unlikely to transmit disease. This step is called sanitizing. A household bleach and water mixture, or one of a variety of other industrial products can be used.

Sanitizer solutions can be applied in various ways:
- Spray bottle, for diaper changing surfaces, toilets, and potty chairs.
- Cloths rinsed in sanitizing solution for food preparation areas, large toys, books, and activity centers.
- Dipping the object into a container filled with the sanitizing solution, for smaller toys.

The concentration and duration of contact of the sanitizer varies with the application and anticipated load of germs. More chemical is required when a cloth or objects are dipped into the solution because each dipping releases some germs into the solution, potentially contaminating solution. When you apply the sanitizing solution to a surface, follow the instructions for that solution to determine the dilution and minimum contact time. In general, it is best not to rinse off the sanitizer or wipe the object dry right away. A sanitizer must be in contact with the germs long enough kill them. For example, when you using a properly prepared solution of bleach water applied from a spray bottle to cleaned and rinsed surfaces, the minimum contact time is 2 minutes. For cleaned and rinsed dishes submerged in a container that is filled with properly prepared bleach solution, the contact time is a minimum of 1 minute. The label on industrial sanitizers specifies the instructions for using the special chemicals. Since chlorine evaporates into the air leaving no residue, surfaces sanitized with bleach may be left to air dry. Some industrial sanitizers require rinsing with fresh water before the object should be used again. Label spray bottles and containers in which sanitizers have been diluted for direct application with the name of the solution (such as Bleach Sanitizer) and the dilution of the mixture. Although solutions of household bleach and water are merely irritating if accidentally swallowed, some other types of sanitizer solutions are toxic. Keep all spray containers and bottles of diluted and undiluted sanitizer out of the reach of children.

Household Bleach & Water
Household bleach with water is recommended. It is effective, economical, convenient, and readily available. However, it should be used with caution on metal or metallic surfaces. If bleach is found to be corrosive on certain materials, a different sanitizer may be required. When purchasing household bleach, make sure that the bleach concentration is for household use, and not for industrial application. Household bleach is typically sold in retail stores in one of 2 strengths: 5.25% hypochlorite

(regular strength bleach) or 6.00% hypochlorite (ultra strength bleach) solutions. The solution of bleach and water is easy to mix, nontoxic, safe if handled properly, and kills most infectious agents.

- *Recipe for a spray application on surfaces that have been detergent-cleaned and rinsed in bathrooms, diapering areas, countertops, tables, toys, door knobs and cabinet handles, phone receivers, hand washing sinks, floors, and surface contaminated by body fluids (minimum contact time = 2 minutes):*
¼ cup household bleach + 1 gallon of cool water OR 1 tablespoon bleach + 1 quart of cool water

- *Recipe for weaker bleach solutions for submerging of eating utensils that have been detergent-cleaned and rinsed (minimum contact time = 1 minute):* 1 tablespoon bleach + 1 gallon of cool water

A solution of bleach and water loses its strength and is weakened by heat and sunlight. Therefore, mix a fresh bleach solution every day for maximum effectiveness. Any leftover bleach solution should be discarded at the end of the day.

Your policies should contain requirements for parents and employees to ensure all personal items be labeled: cubbies, cribs, mats, blankets, sheets, jackets, sweaters, cups, bottles, etc. per Bright from the start guidelines.

Emergency Procedures should be written and posted in each classroom and evacuation plans should be practiced during monthly fire or severe weather drills. Contact your local fire department to perform fire safety training for your staff. Emergency phone numbers should be posted next to every telephone.

Sample Emergency Procedures
Modify the procedures to fit your organization size and staffing. Be sure to indicate who, when, and how parent, emergency medical services, law enforcement personnel, and the state licensing authorities are notified.

In the event a child becomes ill: *This policy applies for children with a temperature of 100 degrees or higher or another contagious symptom.*
1. The sick child should be brought to the office. The Administrative staff should call the parents to pick up the child. After the child has been moved to a separate area, the child must be supervised until his/her parents arrive for him.
2. The Director will determine after reviewing the child's condition and a physician's statement, whether or not he/she can be readmitted to class. Note: notify local health department of high number of cases (more than four).

In case of a serious injury to a child: *A serious injury shall include but is not limited to bleeding, broken bones, fractures, head injuries, bites, and objects in the ear, eye, nose, or absence of breathing.*
1. The office staff will call EMS or contact poison control. The teacher will administer first aid.
2. Determine the seriousness of the injury by information gathered from the victim, his/her appearance and responses.
3. Remove all other children and adults with the exception of two persons certified to perform CPR or First Aid.
4. Perform First Aid or CPR until emergency paramedics arrive.
5. Complete an accident report form (describe in detail the activity in which the child was engaged) and submit to the Director and parents within 2 hours.
6. The Director will follow up on the report & notify Bright from the Start within 24 hours.

In the event of a minor injury: *Minor injuries include minor cuts, burns, scrapes and bruises.*
1. Remove the child to a separate area and alert the office (Administrative Assistant).

2. Treat the wound by washing with clear water as needed. Follow basic first aid instructions. Complete an accident report and submit it to the Director within 2 hours. Please do not permit children to administer first aid. Staff members should wear gloves.

In case of severe weather:
1. Seek inside shelter. Stay away from windows! If you're caught outside in case of a tornado, travel at right angles to path of funnel, or lie flat in ditch and protect your head.
2. If inside, take your students to the basement and be seated along the wall.
3. The office personnel will shut off electricity and fuel lines.
4. The telephone should only be used in cases of an emergency.
5. The following basic supplies should be stored: water, non-perishable food, first aid kid, battery powered radio, and flashlights.

In case of loss of electrical power:
1. Office personnel will contact Georgia Power after switching the breaker switch in the electrical room to determine length of lack of service.
2. Staff shall notify parents if the center/school will be without power for more than one hour.
3. In the event of failure of the emergency lighting equipment, evacuate the building.

In case of fire-Emergency Evacuation Procedures:
Teachers are to stop activities immediately.
Line students up and follow practiced exit route if possible.
Count each student and take attendance as you leave the building.
Pick up **attendance record** and **activity and medical permission form** file used for field trips. Teachers should test the doors for danger before opening to exit. Feel the door and the knob for heat, with the back of your hand. If the doorknob is hot, look for an alternate exit.
Exit building and go to the designated meeting place. _____ Check your attendance records. Notify the Director if all children are not present or if someone is missing.
The Administrative Assistant or Director retrieves emergency records/cards from office and cellular phone (two way radio). Calls 911
Designated staff member checks each room in the building for students; Closes each door and window; Upon arrival of fire department notify them of attendance and/or unaccounted staff or students; Approves re-entry of the building after giving approval by the firemen.
If unable to re-enter the Director will notify parents of need to pick up students.
Parents only should be allowed to retrieve their children from the designated Lead teacher
or other staff member. Do not leave children unattended for any reason, nor send a child back into the building. If danger is eminent, students may be taken to_____until parents arrive.

In the event of a bomb threat::
Make note of caller's comments, recording conversation if possible.
Director or Administrative Assistant should dial *69 to obtain caller's number, then dial 911 and report the call. Notify teachers and staff. Employees should follow emergency evacuation plan above.

In case of gas outage/leak:
Notify office personnel. Designated staff member will shut off gas at switch outside and contact the Gas company. Students should be evacuated as above if service is not restored within the hour.

In case of loss of Water:
Notify office personnel. Designated staff member will contact the water company. Parents should be notified to pick up students if service is not restored within an hour.

© 2014 Penn Consulting

In case of loss of child:
1. Notify Director, security and any other accompanying staff members. Search for 5-10 minutes depending upon location. Notify parent or guardian, and call 911.
2. The Director will also notify BFTS, if the child is not located within 15 minutes.

In case of the death of a child:
When a child is presumed to have expired from natural or accidental causes, take the following steps;
1. Notify the Director or office personnel.
2. Remove all other children to a separate area.
3. Contact emergency medical assistance (call 911) in order to verify the presence or absence of vital life signs.
4. The Director or office personnel will notify the parents & the police immediately, and notify BFTS within 24 hours.

Emergency Telephone Numbers

Children's Health Care of Atlanta or nearest emergency care facility	404 250-5437 or 404 250-2007
Georgia Poison Control Center	1-800-282-5846
Georgia Power (Electrical service provider)	404 325-4001
County EMS/Fire/Police	911
Water Emergency Repair	770 822-5061
Gas Company	1-877-427-4321

First Aid Kits should be replenished after use and checked monthly for expiration dates. The following first aid supplies, along with a manual of instructions, shall be maintained in a central location inaccessible to the children: scissors, tweezers, gauze pads, thermometer, adhesive tape, syrup of ipecac (to be used upon the advice of a physician or poison control center), band-aids, insect-sting preparation, antiseptic cleaning solution, antibacterial ointment, bandages, disposable rubber gloves, and cold pack. Syrup of Ipecac should only be administered under the direction of the child's pediatrician or the poison control center. The American Academy of Pediatrics has advised programs to remove it from kits in order to prevent accidental dosage which may cause more harm as students vomit (than the poison swallowed alone-minus stomach acid) causes.

It is wise to place a kit in each classroom and provide backpacks or fanny packs to take on the playground. Teachers should have a cordless telephone or two way radio accessible on the playground as well. Personal use should be prohibited.

Avoid plant poisoning
1. Learn to recognize and name the dangerous plants around your facility.
2. Keep plants and plant parts away from infants and children
3. Teach children to keep unknown plants and plant parts out of their mouths
4. Teach children to recognize poison-ivy and other dermatitis-causing plants
5. Do not allow children to make "tea" from leaves or suck nectar from flowers
6. Do not rely on pets, birds, squirrels, or other animals to indicate non-poisonous plants.
7. Label garden seeds and bulbs and store out of reach of children
8. Be pro-active. If unsure of whether or not a plant around your facility is poisonous consult the Caring for our Children: National Health and Safety Performance Standards Manual.

In case of emergencies
Call a physician or the Poison Control Center immediately!
Be prepared to provide the following information:
1. Name of the plant, if known
2. What parts and how much were eaten
3. How long ago was it eaten
4. Age of individual
5. Symptoms observed
6. A good description of the plant. Save the specimen for identification by medical professionals or a plant taxonomist at a local university.

Animals in educational settings
1. Any pet or animal present at the facility, indoors or outdoors, shall be in good health, show no evidence of carrying any disease, be fully immunized, and be maintained on a flea, tick, and worm control program.
2. A current (time-specified) certificate from a veterinarian shall be on file in the facility, stating that the specific pet meets these conditions.
3. All contact between animals and children shall be supervised by a caregiver who is close enough to *remove the child* immediately if the animal shows signs of distress or the child shows signs of treating the animal inappropriately.
4. The caregiver shall instruct children on safe procedures to follow when in close proximity to these animals (for example, not to provoke or startle animals or touch them when they are near their food). Potentially aggressive animals (such as pit bulls) shall not be in the same physical space with the children.
5. Safe pet recommendations: Betta fish, hamsters or gerbils

Transportation Safety
1. Car/booster seats and seat belts are required for every child
2. Drivers should be aware of pedestrians in the parking lot
3. Staff: Child ratio should be maintained. Trips should be limited to an hour or less and instructors should interact with the children in order to free the driver to drive.
4. Eliminate Distractions: loud music & cell phones
5. Staff members should take the following paperwork on trips: a. Class Roster b. Bright from the Start's Transportation Record c. Permission and Authorization Forms d. Medication and care plans
6. Annual Vehicle Inspections (tires, headlights, horn, tail lights, brakes, suspension, exhaust system, steering, windshields and windshield wipers) are required
7. All primary and backup vehicles should be equipped with a Fire Extinguisher and First Aid Kit

"Buckle, Buckle, Buckle Up" *(Sung to the tune of "Row, Row, Row Your Boat")*
Buckle, buckle, buckle up
Riding in the car.
Always put your safety belt on
Going near or far.
buckle up.
I am very special, and
I take care of me.
seat.
Riding safely in the back's
The safest place to be.

Suggested motions:
1. Hold two ends of safety belt and
2. Hug self.
3. Thumb over shoulder, point to back

"Wear Your Safety Belt"
(Sung to the tune of "Allouette")

Wear your safety belt
Always wear your safety belt
Wear your safety belt
Riding in the car
When I'm riding in the car,
If I'm going near or far,
I buckle up
I buckle up
I buckle up
I buckle up
Oh - oh - oh - oh
(Repeat above)

'Where's Your Safety Belt?"
(Sung to the tune of "Where is Thumbkin?")
Where's your safety belt?
Where's your safety belt?
Here is mine!
Here is mine!
Buckled 'round my hips
Buckled 'round my hips
Where is yours?
Where is yours?
Suggested motions:
Hand against forehead searching. - Pat front of belt. - Pat hips. - Palms up, questioning.

Did you know…
- A child's body warms 3 to 5 times faster than an adult's.
- The temperature inside a car can rise 30° in 20 minutes, and 43° in one hour, even with the windows left open a bit.
- Heat stroke occurs when the body temperature exceeds 104°. A body temperature of 107° is usually fatal.
- 45 minute maximum trip time on bus.

Passenger Checklists/Attendance should be taken to account for loading and unloading children:
- Before leaving the child care center
- When they board the vehicle
- When they arrive at the destination
- Frequently during field trip
- At the end of the field trip make sure all children are accounted for when loading the vehicle
- Once you arrive at the center to unload
- Double check vehicle to make sure no children are left unattended. (Documentation and report by phone)

Vehicles shall be parked or stopped so that no • child will have to cross the street in order to meet the vehicle or arrive at a destination. The center is responsible for the child from • the time and place the child is picked up until the child is delivered to his or her parents or the responsible person designated by his parents. A child shall not be dropped off at any location if there is no one to receive the child.

Other Injury Considerations

1. Daily schedule and smooth transitions
2. Inappropriate climbing equipment
3. Walls and ceilings
4. Heating and water pipes
5. Air conditioning unit
6. Cleaning supplies
7. Windows and glass doors
8. Foot operated or hands free covered, plastic lined trash containers
9. Floors
10. Visitors
11. Gates
12. Cabinet locks
13. Refrigerator and microwave
14. Office/Kitchen
15. Purses
16. Toys – recalled products or from home
17. Rest periods (head to toe, 3' apart)
18. Safe to sleep on backs (infants)

Common Childhood Illnesses Detection and Prevention

Daily health checks should be performed upon each child's arrival (during greeting). The center should be sure each child submits up to date immunization certification or exemption. Staff Hepatitis B immunizations and annual physical examinations are important too! You can keep up with required immunizations by referring to the American Academy of Pediatrics Immunization Dose Counter www.WellCareTracker.org.

You center should develop exclusion policies which prevent the spread of disease, maintain appropriate ratios and prohibit children that are more than mildly ill from attending class if they are unable to participate in activities and your center is unable to provide additional care. Refer to the board of health communicable disease chart to obtain information on common infectious diseases, ways to prevent and treat them, incubation periods and rules regarding notifying parents, pediatricians and the board of health. You may obtain copies from Bright from the Start's website or your local health department.

There are four modes of spreading disease: fecal to oral, direct contact, infestations and airborne agents. You can prevent the spread of colds and flu by
1. Frequent hand washing
2. Proper use and disposal of facial tissue
3. Proper diet and exercise
4. Training staff to distinguishing viruses which have flu-like symptoms and other respiratory conditions such as asthma through close observation

Small Group Discussion: **Allergies and Asthma**
More than 4.4 million children under 18 have asthma, making it one of the leading reasons for visits to physicians or hospitals. In addition, 70 to 80 percent of children who have asthma also have allergies so caregivers need to know as much as possible about these chronic conditions. Asthma causes the bronchial tubes to narrow resulting in shortness of breath and wheezing.

Treatment must be administered quickly or the attacks can be fatal. Allergies cause a wide range of reactions from itchiness, hives, runny nose and eyes, frequent earaches, nausea, and diarrhea. Insect stings may cause a severe and even life-threatening reaction in which the bronchial tube closes up.

As more and more preschool-age children spend long hours in child care, those who care for them need to be knowledgeable about health conditions in order to manage an emergency should it arise. One of the highest incidences of health problems in children is asthma.

According to the American Academy of Pediatrics, currently 4.8 million children under the age of 18 have asthma. If they have support from parents, child care workers, and pediatricians they can lead a fairly active, normal life. One of the best sources of information about managing asthma as well as other information about children's health is the American Academy of Pediatrics.

INTERNET ACTIVITY: Order copies of the Food allergy overview booklet from http://www.niaid.nih.gov/_layouts/niaid.internet.forms/publicationorders.aspx.

Log on to the Asthma and allergy Foundation of America site at: http://www.aafa.org
Search for "Flu/Cold or Allergics" Answer the questions below:
1. Should a child having an allergic reaction have a fever?
2. How could you use the information in the article either to help staff members or parents?
3. How can you get further information on asthma triggers?

DISCUSSION
1. What are the common foods and environmental conditions that cause allergies? If you do not know, read the Aronson article cited above.
2. Given the seriousness of asthma or some children's reactions to allergens, should caregivers be expected to manage children who have these conditions?
3. How can directors help staff members care for children with asthma or allergies?
4. List common triggers and symptoms.

References
Aronson, S. (2002, January/February). Children with allergies. Child Care Information Exchange, 143, 59-61.
Children's Defense Fund (2001). The state of America's children. Washington, DC: Children's Defense Fund.

Staff should be trained to take universal precautions when handling body fluids. The blood borne pathogens of primary concern are the human immunodeficiency virus (HIV), hepatitis B virus (HBV), and hepatitis C virus (HCV). OSHA defines blood to mean human blood, human blood components, and products made from human blood. Other Potentially Infectious Materials (OPIM) means (1) The following human body fluids: semen, vaginal secretions, cerebrospinal fluid, synovial fluid, pleural fluid, pericardial fluid, peritoneal fluid, amniotic fluid, saliva in dental procedures, any body fluid that is visibly contaminated with blood, and all body fluids in situations where it is difficult or impossible to differentiate between body fluids; (2) Any unfixed tissue or organ (other than intact skin) from a human (living or dead); and (3) HIV-containing cell or tissue cultures, organ cultures, and HIV- or HBV-containing culture medium or other solutions; and blood, organs, or other tissues from experimental animals infected with HIV or HBV.

Below are a few universal precautions in caring for children with HIV (AIDS virus) and Hepatitis B/C as outlined in *Caring for Our Children: National Health and Safety Performance Standards* Appendix J

Cleaning Up Body Fluids

Treat urine, stool, vomitus, blood, and body fluids as potentially infectious. Spills of body fluid should be cleaned up and surfaces sanitized immediately.
• For small amounts of urine and stool on smooth surfaces; Wipe off and clean away visible soil with a little detergent solution. Then rinse the surface with clean water.
• Apply a sanitizer to the surface for the required contact time. See Appendix I. For larger spills on floors, or any spills on rugs or carpets:
• Wear gloves while cleaning. While disposable gloves can be used, household rubber gloves are adequate for all spills except blood and bloody body fluids. Disposable gloves should be used when blood may be present in the spill.
• Take care to avoid splashing any contaminated material onto the mucous membranes of your eyes, nose or mouth, or into any open sores you may have.
• Wipe up as much of the visible material as possible with disposable paper towels and carefully place the soiled paper towels and other soiled disposable material in a leak-proof, plastic bag that has been securely tied or sealed. Use a wet/dry vacuum on carpets, if such equipment is available.
• Immediately use a detergent, or a disinfectant-detergent to clean the spill area. Then rinse the area with clean water.
• For blood and body fluid spills on carpeting, blot to remove body fluids from the fabric as quickly as possible.

Then spot clean the area with a detergent-disinfectant rather than with a bleach solution. Additional cleaning by shampooing or steam cleaning the contaminated surface may be necessary.
- Sanitize the cleaned and rinsed surface by wetting the entire surface with a sanitizing solution of bleach in water (1/4 cup of household bleach in 1 gallon of water) or an industrial sanitizer used according to the manufacturer's instructions. For carpets cleaned with a detergent-disinfectant, sanitizing is accomplished by continuing to apply and extract the solution until there is no visible soil. Then follow the manufacturer's instructions for the use of the sanitizer to be sure the carpet is sanitized by the treatment.
- Dry the surface.
- Clean and rinse reusable household rubber gloves, then treat them as a contaminated surface in applying the sanitizing solution to them. Remove, dry and store these gloves away from food or food surfaces. Discard disposable gloves.
- Mops and other equipment used to clean up body fluids should be:
    1. Cleaned with detergent and rinsed with water;
    2. Rinsed with a fresh sanitizing solution;
    3. Wrung as dry as possible;
    4. Air-dried.
- Wash your hands afterward, even though you wore gloves.
- Remove and bag clothing (yours and those worn by children) soiled by body fluids.
- Put on fresh clothes after washing the soiled skin and hands of everyone involved. References:

HOW OFTEN	ITEMS TO BE DISINFECTED
Daily	Hard surfaced or washable toys (as soiled - frequently mouthed)
	Bathroom door knobs, sinks, sink faucet handles
	Bathroom toilets, flush handles, Sink/faucet handles, Soap Dispensers, Diaper Area
	Crib rails, All washable floors
	Trash cans, Drinking fountains, Kitchen counters
	Telephone receivers
	Water tables (if used that day)
	Children's chairs (immediately if soiled)
Weekly	Cot frames (immediately if soiled), door knobs, soap dispensers, light switches, shelves or other hard surfaces touched by children
	Mats, cribs, pet areas, walls, doors (immediately if soiled)
	Cloth (washable) toys, dress up clothes
	Cubbies, shelves (immediately if soiled)
	Refrigerators (immediately if soiled)
Before Use	Food preparation area and food serving tables (eating tables)
After Use	Diapering area surfaces
	Food preparation area
	Food preparation tools, dishes, equipment, and flatware
	Bottles, nipples and nipple covers
Immediately	Any surface that has been soiled with urine, stool, mucous, vomit, blood or nasal discharge

Sources:
Canadian Pediatric Society. *Well Being: A Guide to Promote the Physical Health, Safety and Emotional Well-Being of Children in Child Care Centers and Family Day Care Homes,*
2nd ed. Toronto, ON; 1996.
Centers for Disease Control and Prevention. *The ABC's of Safe and Healthy Child Care*; 1996.
Centers for Disease Control and Prevention. Guidelines for Prevention of Transmission of Human Immunodeficiency Virus and Hepatitis B Virus to Health-Care and
Public Safety Workers. *MMWR.* 1989; 38(S-6): 1-36.

Centers for Disease Control and Prevention. Update: Universal precautions for prevention of transmission of Human immunodeficiency virus, hepatitis B Virus, and other blood borne pathogens in health-care settings. *MMWR.* 1988; 37: 377-382, 387-388.

Four common factors in SIDS per the Institute of Child Health and Human Development
1. second hand smoke 2.5x greater risk
2. tummy sleeping 4-5x greater risk
3. winter months
4. African American 2x greater risk

Other considerations: American Indian or Alaskan native or male or between 2-4 months of age per the National Institute of Child Health and Human Development
http://www.nichd.nih.gov/SIDS/reduce_infant_risk.htm

Medication administration policies – identify steps: separate from children receiving medication from classmates. Many programs have guidelines concerning the time medication can be administered and specific staff that is trained to do so.
1. Check Authorization Form for signature and completion
2. Check name is the same
3. Read label for date, dosage & frequency, relation to meals, pediatrician info
4. Administer prescribed method & dose
5. Observe for rash, dizziness, vomiting, document and notify parents immediately
6. Document time, amount, your name

A written medical emergency plan is VITAL!
1. Serious Injury
2. Food allergy
3. Asthma
4. Diarrheal Diseases

American Academy of Pediatrics Committee on Pediatric Emergency Medicine, January 2001.
Caring for Our Children: National Health and Safety Performance Standards Appendix N

Situations that Require Medical Attention Right Away
In the two boxes below, you will find lists of common medical emergencies or urgent situations you may encounter as a child care provider. To prepare for such situations:
1. Know how to access Emergency Medical Services (EMS) in your area.
2. Educate Staff on the recognition of an emergency.
3. Know the phone number for each child's guardian and primary health care provider.
4. Develop plans for children with special medical needs with their family and physician.

At any time you believe the child's life may be at risk, or you believe there is a risk of permanent injury, seek immediate medical treatment.
Call Emergency Medical Services (EMS) immediately if:
- You believe the child's life is at risk or there is a risk of permanent injury.
- The child is acting strangely, much less alert, or much more withdrawn than usual. The child has difficulty breathing or is unable to speak.
- The child's skin or lips look blue, purple, or gray.
- The child has rhythmic jerking of arms and legs and a loss of consciousness (seizure). The child is unconscious.

- The child is less and less responsive.
- The child has any of the following after a head injury: decrease in level of alertness, confusion, headache, vomiting, irritability, or difficulty walking.
- The child has increasing or severe pain anywhere.
- The child has a cut or burn that is large, deep, and/or won't stop bleeding. The child is vomiting blood.
- The child has a severe stiff neck, headache, and fever. (minigitvs)
- The child is significantly dehydrated: sunken eyes, lethargic, not making tears, not urinating.

After you have called EMS, remember to call the child's legal guardian. Some children may have urgent situations that do not necessarily require ambulance transport but still need medical attention. The box below lists some of these more common situations. The legal guardian should be informed of the following conditions. If you or the guardian cannot reach the physician within one hour, the child should be brought to a hospital. Get medical attention within one hour for:

- Fever in any age child who looks more than mildly ill. Fever in a child less than 2 months (8 weeks) of age. A quickly spreading purple or red rash.
- A large volume of blood in the stools. A cut that may require stitches.
- Any medical condition specifically outlined in a child's care plan requiring parental notification.

Nutrition-Avoiding Food Allergens

The main elements of an action plan are:
1. specific food allergies and steps to take to avoid that food
2. detailed treatment plan in the event of an allergic reaction
3. symptoms and required medication

Four of the most common food allergens are:
1. peanuts
2. seafood, esp. shrimp
3. milk
4. eggs
5. soy and wheat

Building blocks
1. The center should notify parents of suspected allergic reactions, ingestion of and/or contact with problem food(s) only if a reaction occurs. **True or False**
2. All families in the center/school or class should be advised to avoid known food allergens brought into the setting. **True or False**
3. **True or False:** Before a child enters a child care facility, the caregivers should obtain a written history of any special nutrition or feeding requirements for that child.
4. **True or False:** Infants who are unable to sit should always be held for bottle feeding.
5. **True or False:** Containers of human milk should be kept frozen or refrigerated, and opened iron-fortified formula should be refrigerated until immediately before feeding.
6. Prepared bottles of formula from powder or concentrate or open containers of ready-to-feed formula should be discarded after how long?
7. **True or False:** Bottles and infant foods should be warmed in a microwave oven.
8. **True or False:** Children should never be in the kitchen unless they are directly supervised by a caregiver.
9. **True or False:** It is part of the caregiver's responsibility to model healthy eating and behavior.

Civitas: *Building Blocks* - Building Blocks was adapted by Civitas with permission from *Caring for Our Children: National Health and Safety Performance Standards, Guidelines for Out-of-Home Child Care Programs*, Second Edition, 2002. These are nationally recognized standards considered best practices in providing healthy and safe child care environments.

Choking Hazards (children under 4 years of age)
Description: round, hard, small, thick and sticky, smooth, slippery
Foods most commonly involved in choking incidents:
1. Hot dogs
2. Raw carrots
3. Whole grapes
4. Hard candy, mints, lozenges
5. Nuts
6. Seeds
7. Raw peas
8. Hard pretzels
9. Chips
10. Peanuts
11. Popcorn
12. Marshmallows
13. Peanut butter by the spoonful
14. Chunks of meat larger than can be swallowed whole

Feeding plans are required for infants and encouraged for toddlers. It is important to have special care plans on file for children with food allergies and asthma. All staff members should be trained on procedures for the administration of breathing treatments and the epinephrine pen.

Recognizing and Reporting Child Abuse and Neglect
Abuse: to use wrongly or improperly; misuse.
Neglect: to be remiss in the care or treatment of
Deprivation: to keep from possessing or enjoying something withheld.

Considerations:
1. Do caregivers get regular breaks during the day, so that their own stress is manageable? Protect holidays and vacation time.

2. Has the program developed prevention measures to help reduce the likelihood of abuse and neglect? (Cameras, buddy system, probationary periods, low child:staff ratios, etc.)

3. Have all staff members (including substitutes) had a background check?

4. Some children with brown skin have a common bluish-gray birthmark called "Mongolian Spots". Sometimes these birthmarks are mistaken for child abuse. To view a Mongolian spot - http://www.fwcc.org/mongolianspot.htm.

5. Updated drop off/pick up authorization list with current phone numbers (work, home, cell) in case an unauthorized person or a person under the influence of alcohol or drugs shows up.

6. Discuss questions and concerns related to children openly and regularly - before small irritations become big issues!

7. Does the program have a check-in system to allow authorized persons to enter the facility?

8. Are authorized parents/guardians able to visit the program at any time?

9. Are all outside doors kept locked except for a secure entry door to prevent access from intruders? Example: Back doors are kept locked from the outside, visitors can only enter from one entrance always visible by a program staff.

10. Note: Caregivers and children must be able to exit from the inside in case of fire or other emergency.

11. If emergency exits lead to potentially unsafe areas for children (such as busy streets), are alarms or other signaling devices installed on these doors to alert staff in case a child attempts to leave?

12. Is the physical layout (of centers) arranged so that all areas can be viewed by at least one other adult in addition to the caregiver at all times?
Discuss common Risk Factors for Abuse and/or Neglect:
1. Child
2. Abuser's
3. Social/Situational Stresses
4. Triggering Situations

© Penn Consulting

Review Clues to Recognizing Child Abuse and Neglect
The following signs may signal the presence of child abuse or neglect.
The Child:
- Shows sudden changes in behavior or school performance
- Has not received help for physical or medical problems brought to the parents' attention
- Has learning problems (or difficulty concentrating) that cannot be attributed to specific physical or psychological causes
- Is always watchful, as though preparing for something bad to happen
- Lacks adult supervision
- Is overly compliant, passive, or withdrawn
- Comes to school or other activities early, stays late, and does not want to go home

The Parent:
- Shows little concern for the child
- Denies the existence of—or blames the child for—the child's problems in school or at home
- Asks teachers or other caregivers to use harsh physical discipline if the child misbehaves
- Sees the child as entirely bad, worthless, or burdensome
- Demands a level of physical or academic performance the child cannot achieve
- Looks primarily to the child for care, attention, and satisfaction of emotional needs

The Parent and Child:
- Rarely touch or look at each other
- Consider their relationship entirely negative
- State that they do not like each other

Types of Abuse
The following are some signs often associated with particular types of child abuse and neglect:
- physical
- neglect
- abandonment
- substance
- sexual
- emotional

Georgia has more neglect reported than anything else. It is important to note, however, that these types of abuse are more typically found in combination than alone. A physically abused child, for example, is often emotionally abused as well, and a sexually abused child also may be neglected.

Signs of Physical Abuse
Consider the possibility of physical abuse when the child:
- Has unexplained burns, bites, bruises, broken bones, or black eyes
- Has fading bruises or other marks noticeable after an absence from school
- Seems frightened of the parents and protests or cries when it is time to go home
- Shrinks at the approach of adults
- Reports injury by a parent or another adult caregiver

Consider the possibility of physical abuse when the parent or other adult caregiver:
- Offers conflicting, unconvincing, or no explanation for the child's injury
- Describes the child as "evil," or in some other very negative way
- Uses harsh physical discipline with the child
- Has a history of abuse as a child

Signs of Neglect
Consider the possibility of neglect when the child:

© Penn Consulting

- Is frequently absent from school
- Begs or steals food or money
- Lacks needed medical or dental care, immunizations, or glasses
- Is consistently dirty and has severe body odor
- Lacks sufficient clothing for the weather
- Abuses alcohol or other drugs
- States that there is no one at home to provide care

Consider the possibility of neglect when the parent or other adult caregiver:
- Appears to be indifferent to the child
- Seems apathetic or depressed
- Behaves irrationally or in a bizarre manner
- Is abusing alcohol or other drugs

Signs of Sexual Abuse

Consider the possibility of sexual abuse when the child:
- Has difficulty walking or sitting
- Suddenly refuses to change for gym or to participate in physical activities
- Reports nightmares or bedwetting
- Experiences a sudden change in appetite
- Demonstrates bizarre, sophisticated, or unusual sexual knowledge or behavior
- Becomes pregnant or contracts a venereal disease, particularly if under age 14
- Runs away
- Reports sexual abuse by a parent or another adult caregiver

Consider the possibility of sexual abuse when the parent or other adult caregiver:
- Is unduly protective of the child or severely limits the child's contact with other children, especially of the opposite sex
- Is secretive and isolated
- Is jealous or controlling with family members

Signs of Emotional Maltreatment

Consider the possibility of emotional maltreatment when the child:
- Shows extremes in behavior, such as overly compliant or demanding behavior, extreme passivity, or aggression
- Is either inappropriately adult (parenting other children, for example) or inappropriately infantile (frequently rocking or head-banging, for example)
- Is delayed in physical or emotional development
- Has attempted suicide
- Reports a lack of attachment to the parent

Consider the possibility of emotional maltreatment when the parent or other adult caregiver:
- Constantly blames, belittles, or berates the child
- Is unconcerned about the child and refuses to consider offers of help for the child's problems
- Overtly rejects the child

Resources on the Child Welfare Information Gateway Website
Child Abuse and Neglect www.childwelfare.gov/can/
Defining Child Abuse and Neglect www.childwelfare.gov/can/defining/
Preventing Child Abuse and Neglect www.childwelfare.gov/preventing/
Reporting Child Abuse and Neglect www.childwelfare.gov/responding/reporting.cfm
Adapted from Caring for Our Children Health and Safety Standards.

Child care professionals are mandated reporters. You can obtain the number for your local Department of Family and Child Services Child Protective Services agency in the blue pages of the local telephone directory.

Other means of intervention:
1. Offer parenting classes
2. Offer professional counseling (check certification)
3. Refer to health consultant or contact pediatrician
4. Recommend accountability or support groups
5. Frequent communication with parents

Reference List

1. American Academy of Pediatrics, American Public Health Association, and National Resource Center for Health and Safety in Child Care (2002). Caring for Our Children: National Health and Safety Performance Standards: Guidelines for Out-of-Home Child Care Programs, 2nd edition. Elk Grove Village, IL: American Academy of Pediatrics and Washington, DC: American Public Health Association. Also available at http://nrc.uchsc.edu.

2. Civitas: Building Blocks - Building Blocks was adapted by Civitas with permission from Caring for Our Children: National Health and Safety Performance Standards, Guidelines for Out-of-Home Child Care Programs, Second Edition, 2002. These are nationally recognized standards considered best practices in providing healthy and safe child care environments.

3. Abby Kendrick, Roxane Kaufmann, Katherine Messenger, (1995), Healthy Young Children, Washington, DC; National Association for the Education of Young Children (NAEYC).

Review the following
Child Care Safety Checklist for Parents and Child Care Providers Provides by the Consumer Products Safety Commission

- CRIBS: Make sure cribs meet current national safety standards and are in good condition. Look for a certification safety seal. Older cribs may not meet current standards. Crib slats should be no more than 2 3/8" apart, and mattresses should fit snugly. This can prevent strangulation and suffocation associated with older cribs and mattresses that are too small.

- SOFT BEDDING: Be sure that no pillows, soft bedding, or comforters are used when you put babies to sleep. Babies should be put to sleep on their backs in a crib with a firm, flat mattress. This can help reduce Sudden Infant Death Syndrome (SIDS) and suffocation related to soft bedding.

- PLAYGROUND SURFACING: Look for safe surfacing on outdoor playgrounds - at least 12 inches of wood chips, mulch, sand or pea gravel, or mats made of safety-tested rubber or rubber- like materials. This helps protect against injuries from falls, especially head injuries.

- PLAYGROUND MAINTENANCE: Check playground surfacing and equipment regularly to make sure they are maintained in good condition. This can help prevent injuries, especially from falls.

- SAFETY GATES: Be sure that safety gates are used to keep children away from potentially dangerous areas, especially stairs. Safety gates can protect against many hazards, especially falls.

- WINDOW BLIND AND CURTAIN CORDS: Be sure mini-blinds and venetian blinds do not have looped cords. Check that vertical blinds, continuous looped blinds, and drapery cords have tension or tie-down devices to hold the cords tight. Check that inner cord stops have been installed. See

© Penn Consulting

www.windowcoverings.org for the latest blind cord safety information.
These safety devices can prevent strangulation in the loops of window blind and curtain cords.

- CLOTHING DRAWSTRINGS: Be sure there are no drawstrings around the hood and neck of children's outerwear clothing. Other types of clothing fasteners, like snaps, zippers, or hook and loop fasteners (such as Velcro), should be used. Drawstrings can catch on playground and other equipment and can strangle young children.

- RECALLED PRODUCTS: Check that no recalled products are being used and that a current list of recalled children's products is readily visible. Recalled products pose a threat of injury or death. Displaying a list of recalled products will remind caretakers and parents to remove or repair potentially dangerous children's toys and products.

Session 12 Food and Nutrition Services

The program administrator is responsible for providing nutritious meals and snacks for children during their time in the program as well as providing educational opportunities for families. Educators should be sure to educate the children on healthy and unhealthy food preparation methods. The USDA provides a helpful tool at https://www.supertracker.usda.gov/default.aspx.

SuperTracker can help teachers, staff, and students plan, analyze, and track their diet and physical activity. Students, parents, and teachers may find out what and how much to eat; track foods, physical activities, and weight. Menus must comply with the nutritional guidelines set forth by the United States Department of Agriculture. "Adequate nutrition is essential for the fulfillment of one's potential for physical or biological growth and development and for maintenance of the body." (Decker and Decker, 2005) The National Food Service Management Institute provides nutrition education material for families. The healthiest programs offer parenting seminars which address the nutrition issue. Developing nutritious eating habits really is a team effort. We have so much media advertising to overcome and then the temptation of the fast food restaurants along the roadside.

Research has shown that well-designed, well-implemented school nutrition programs can effectively promote physical activity, healthy eating, and reductions in television viewing time. Emerging research documents the connections between physical activity, good nutrition, physical education and nutrition programs, healthy child development, and academic performance.

Caregivers must follow state licensing regulations and feeding plans in feeding infants. It is important the teacher washes her hands and the child's hands and face before and after every meal. Feeding bibs with Velcro fasteners should be used. Bottles of formula must be prepared at home and labeled by the program with each child's name and the date and time the bottle is received. It is vital that it be clearly marked if it contains human milk. Attention should be given to children with special needs.

Often symptoms of disorders can be greatly reduced or eliminated by a dietary change. Although the American Academy of Pediatrics has not recommended a gluten free diet, the research in *Autism Spectrum Disorders - Gluten-free and casein free diets in the treatment of autism spectrum disorders (ASD): A systematic review* (2009) found some promise. The systematic review, conducted in 2009, concluded that such diets should only be implemented in the event a child with ASD experiences acute behavioral changes, seemingly associated with changes in diet...and/or a child has allergies or food intolerances to gluten and/or casein." The review identified 14 studies testing the effects of a GFCF diet on autism. Both of the papers ARI references were included in this study. Out of 14 studies, 7 reported positive results, 2 reported mixed results, and 4 reported negative results (that is, absence of statistically significant effects). Among the four studies reporting negative results, none were longer than 6 weeks, with two out of four studying effects of the diet for 4 days and 9 days. There are several food groups and foods that cause allergic reactions in autistic people. It's best to modify your diet and try a combination of various foods, supplements, and medication to control the symptoms.

Many program administrators use catered meal services or pre-packaged meals rather than hiring staff for meal and snack preparation on site. It is imperative that staff members responsible for diapering not prepare meals. Centers with fewer than fifty children should have one full-time child care food service worker and a part-time aide. Centers caring for one hundred twenty five children should have a worker and a full time aide. Once a center reaches 126-200 children a full-time food service manager should be employed. These persons must be trained thoroughly in the state's licensing standards as well as USDA food service guidelines. These standards generally are aligned with those recommended by the American Academy of Pediatrics, the national Resource Center for Health and safety in Child

Care (2002). Careful oversight of food and paper purchases is necessary to control costs and reduce waste. Be sure to review the Bright from the Start (DECAL) Applicant's Guide for Licensing handout from regarding sanitation requirements (dish washing, food storage, etc.).

Internet Activity: Visit the www.usda.gov website and download the meal patterns for infants and toddlers and the weekly menu planning form.

We can help young children eat a variety of tasty, good-for-you foods! The United States Department of Agriculture 1 **Great Plate**™ for Preschoolers program promotes an easy-to-remember healthy equation to help caregivers visualize how to fill preschoolers plates. A good-for-you and tasty meal is pictured showing the divisions of 1/2 fruits and vegetables, 1/4 whole grains, and 1/4 lean protein which makes "1 Great Plate™" and meet criteria for lunch components.

Visit the SuperTracker website and compare the following:
a serving of fresh green beans cooked without fat added
a serving of fresh green beans cooked with butter added

https://www.choosemyplate.gov/SuperTracker/default.aspx

Enter green beans in to the Food-A-Pedia window, then click on the types listed above.

1. Are surprised by the difference in calories?
2. Explain why?

Foods like cheese, butter, sausage, and desserts may taste good to you, but they can have a lot of saturated fat and cholesterol. Eating too much of these unhealthy fats could lead to high cholesterol and heart disease. No more than 30 percent of calories should come from total fat. Less than 10 percent of calories should come from saturated fat.

The Department of Health and Human Services provides a menu planner which provides calorie and carbohydrate counters at http://hp2010.nhlbihin.net/menuplanner/menu.cgi

Bright from the Start offers meal subsidies through the Child and Adult Care Food Program (CACFP) The CACFP is a federally funded nutrition program authorized in section 17 of the National School Lunch Act (42 U.S.C. 1766). Program regulations are issued by the USDA under 7 CFR Part 226. USDA's Food and Nutrition Service(FNS) administers the CACFP through grants to states. In Georgia, Bright from the Start administers the program.

The CACFP is a United States Department of Agriculture (USDA) Child Nutrition Program designed to reimburse providers for nutritious meals served to children or adults in a day care environment. The program provides reimbursement to child care centers, adult care centers, emergency shelters, family day care homes, and after- school programs for providing creditable meals to children or adults in their care. (Emergency shelters receive reimbursement only for meals served to children.) For the most part, the children served in this program must be 12 years of age or younger. However, there is also an after-school "at risk" program that serves school-age children through the age of 18. The adults served in adult programs must be either functionally impaired or 60 years of age or older in a day care setting. No residential programs, except emergency shelters, qualify for the CACFP.

The Child Nutrition and WIC Reauthorization Act of 2004 (Pub. L. 108-265) now permits for-profit child care centers to participate in the CACFP when 25% of the centers enrollment or licensed capacity receive either Title XX or are eligible for free or reduced price meals.

© Penn Consulting

Interim Rule - For-Profit Center Participation in the CACFP (July 27, 2005)
This rule adds a provision to the CACFP regulations that authorizes for-profit centers providing child care or outside-school-hours care to participate based on the income eligibility of 25% of children in care for free or reduced price meal.

Prior to making an application to participate, attendance at Program Training is required for new institutions that wish to sign a direct agreement with Bright from the Start. An application package is distributed at the training, which is held once a month in either the Metro Atlanta or Macon area. Organizations should contact the Administrative Assistant at 404.657.1779 to register for this training.

Child or adult centers that wish to participate under the sponsorship of an approved Administrative Sponsor and day care home providers, which are required to participate under a Day Care Home Sponsor, may obtain a list of approved sponsors from the Administrative Assistant at 404.657.1779. Sponsors will provide pre-approval training and applications to facilities.

	Child Care Center Meal Reimbursement rates			Day Care Homes	
Type of Meal Served	Free	Reduced Price	Paid	Tier I & Tier II Higher	Tier II (Tier II Lower)
Breakfast	1.31	1.01	.24	1.06	.39
Lunch or Supper	2.5675	2.1675	.3975	1.97	1.19
Snacks	.65	.32	.06	.58	.16

Subject to change.

The Enhanced Food-Based Menu Planning Approach is a variation of the Traditional Menu Planning Approach. It is designed to increase calories from low-fat food sources in order to meet the Dietary Guidelines. The five food components are retained, but the component quantities for the weekly servings of vegetables and fruits and grains/breads are increased.

ENHANCED FOOD-BASED MENU PLANNING APPROACH-**MEAL PATTERN** FOR LUNCHES					
	MINIMUM REQUIREMENTS				OPTION FOR
FOOD COMPONENTS AND FOOD ITEMS	AGES 1-2	PRESCHOOL	GRADES K-6	GRADES 7-12	GRADES K-3
Milk (as a beverage)	6 fluid ounces	6 fluid ounces	8 fluid ounces	8 fluid ounces	8 fluid ounces
Meat or Meat Alternate (quantity of the edible portion as served):					
Lean meat, poultry, or fish	1 ounce	1½ ounces	2 ounces	2 ounces	1½ ounces
Alternate protein products1	1 ounce	1½ ounces	2 ounces	2 ounces	1½ ounces
Cheese	1 ounce	1½ ounces	2 ounces	2 ounces	1½ ounces
Large egg	½	¾	1	1	¾
Cooked dry beans or peas	¼ cup	3/8 cup	½ cup	½ cup	3/8 cup
Peanut butter or other nut or seed butters	2 tablespoons	3 tablespoons	4 tablespoons	4 tablespoons	3 tablespoons
Yogurt, plain or flavored, unsweetened or sweetened	4 ounces or ½ cup	6 ounces or ¾ cup	8 ounces or 1 cup	8 ounces or 1 cup	6 ounces or ¾ cup
The following may be used to meet no more than 50% of the requirement and must be used in combination with any of the above: Peanuts, soynuts, tree nuts, or seeds, as listed in program guidance, or an equivalent quantity of any combination of the above meat/meat alternate (1 ounce of nuts/seeds equals 1 ounce of cooked lean meat, poultry or fish).	½ ounce =50%	¾ ounce =50%	1 ounce =50%	1 ounce =50%	¾ ounce =50%
Vegetable or Fruit: 2 or more servings of vegetables, fruits or both	½ cup	½ cup	¾ cup plus an extra ½ cup over a week2	1 cup	¾ cup
Grains/Breads(servings per week): Must be enriched or whole grain. A serving is a slice of bread or an equivalent serving of biscuits, rolls, etc., or ½ cup of cooked rice, macaroni, noodles, other pasta products or cereal grains	5 servings per week 2 –minimum of ½ serving per day	8 servings per week 2 – minimum of 1 serving per day	12 servings per week 2 – minimum of 1 serving per day3	15 servings per week 2– minimum of 1 serving per day3	10 servings per week 2 –minimum of 1 serving per day3

1 Must meet the requirements in appendix A of 7 CFR 210.
2 For the purposes of this table, a week equals five days.
3 Up to one grains/breads serving per day may be a dessert.

The Enhanced Food Based Menu Planning Approach is designed to meet the nutritional standards set forth in program regulations.

Visit the www.usda.gov site. Search for the Infant Meal pattern chart. Answer the questions below:

Reflection Questions
When can cereal be introduced to the infant diet?
When should meat be introduced to the infant diet?
How many ounces of prepared formula does a 7 month old need for a 10 hour day?
How many 8 ounce bottles would that be?

Internet Activity - Calculate Calories
Visit the Healthy Eating Calculator website
http://www.bcm.edu/cnrc/healthyeatingcalculator/eatingCal.html

References
Preventing foodborne illness in child care centers and family child care homes
http://cru.cahe.wsu.edu/cepublications/eb1868/eb1868.pdf
Menus for Heart Healthy Eating
http://www.mayoclinic.com/health/heart-healthy-diet/HB00039
Health Child Care America Promoting Healthy Eating
http://www.healthychildcare.org/PDF/E-NewsSept10.pdf
You Can Prevent Foodborne Illness
http://cru.cahe.wsu.edu/cepublications/pnw0250/pnw0250.pdf

Session 13 New School Year Checklist

Task	Expected Completion Date	Date Completed
Prepare needs assessment		
Contact licensing and zoning agencies		
Seek legal advice		
Survey available sites		
Figure start-up costs		
Choose building or decide to build		
Draw floor/site plans		
Supervise building or renovations		
Develop marketing strategy		
Meet with representatives from all licensing agencies		
Obtain building permits and clearances		
Start licensing process		
Establish a bank account		
Open a post office box		
Obtain insurance		
Prepare budget projections (1, 3, 5 year)		
Order supplies and equipment		
Prepare a brochure		
Advertise for students		
Write job descriptions		
Design family manual and enrollment forms		
Design personnel handbook		
Advertise for staff		
Interview and select staff		
Plan open house		
Interview children and parents		
Conduct orientation for staff		
Conduct orientation for parents		
Prepare for opening day		

Adapted from *the New Program/New Year*
Checklist of tasks needed to open a new school. (P. Click & K. Karos, 2010)

Internet Resources: New and veteran program administrators can benefit from the plethora of information available on the internet. For instance, the CDC site provides invaluable data for parents, experienced directors, and early educators. They have a set of milestone checklists and tips for discussing developmental delays and disabilities with parents that is excellent. They also have fact sheets on a few of the disabilities that should be discovered in early childhood (autism, ADD/ADHD, visual, hearing problems, behavior disorders, etc.). Program administrators should bookmarked the sites. You will find yourself accessing them almost weekly.

American Academy of Pediatrics (AAP)
AAP and its member pediatricians dedicate their efforts and resources to the health, safety, and well-being of infants, children, adolescents, and young adults. The AAP Web site contains links to parenting tips and articles and information on health topics, professional education and resources,

advocacy concerning child and adolescent health, and AAP membership requirements and benefits.
http://www.aap.org

American Dietetic Association (ADA)
ADA, the nation's largest organization of food and nutrition professionals, serves the public by promoting optimal nutrition, health, and well-being. Information regarding nutritional standards for child care programs is available by searching the ADA Web site.
http://www.eatright.org

Centers for Disease Control (CDC)
CDC serves as the national focus for developing and applying disease prevention and control, environmental health, and health promotion and education activities designed to improve the health of the people of the United States. The CDC Web site has a section called Health Topics A-Z that links to articles on a variety of health topics.
http://www.cdc.gov

Child Health Alert (CHA)
The CHA is an organization committed to the health and well-being of all children by helping parents, teachers, and health professionals understand and make sense of health news that affects children. The CHA Web site offers many resources, including a newsletter, a healthy hand-washing poster, and various articles.
http://www.childhealthalert.com

Children's Defense Fund (CDF)
The Children's Defense Fund (CDF) is a non-profit child advocacy organization that has worked relentlessly for more than 40 years to ensure a level playing field for all children. We champion policies and programs that lift children out of poverty; protect them from abuse and neglect; and ensure their access to health care, quality education and a moral and spiritual foundation.
http://www.childrensdefense.org/

Children's Safety Network (CSN)
CSN works with maternal and child health (MCH), public health, and other injury prevention practitioners to provide technical assistance and information, facilitate the implementation and evaluation of injury prevention programs, and conduct analytical and policy activities that improve injury and violence prevention. The Web site has links to CSN publications, resources for injury and violence prevention, as well as links to other organizations dedicated to preventing injury and violence.
http://www.childrenssafetynetwork.org

First Children's Finance (FCF)
First Children's finance tools will support you in your work projecting and analyzing the financial realities of your center. FCF provides financing tools and resources for making a business plan to child care centers and family child care providers. It provides loans to new child care centers and family child care providers in selected areas. It also supports expansion, quality improvements and operations of existing programs.
http://www.firstchildrensfinance.org/businessresourcecenter/centers-2/finance/finance-tools/

Foundation Center Directory
Foundation Grants to Individuals Online is a nonprofit service organization that offers an online listing of grants to individuals in the United States.
http://gtionline.foundationcenter.org/

Gateway to Government Food Safety Information
This site provides useful food safety information.
http://www.foodsafety.gov

National Program for Playground Safety (NPPS)
NPPS is a nonprofit organization dealing with playground safety information in the United States. The NPPS Web site has a safety tip and FAQ section, a quarterly newsletter, and statistical research on playground safety.
http://www.uni.edu/playground/

National Safety Council (NSC)
The NSC is a nonprofit, nongovernmental organization dedicated to providing safety and health solutions for reducing unintentional deaths and disabling injuries. Its Web site provides links to safety events and training, products and resources about safety and injury prevention, and news stories concentrating on what the NSC is doing to reduce accidental death and injury.
www.nsc.org

Answer the following questions below:
1. What kinds of information are available on the site you visited?

2. Which do you think would be the most helpful to an inexperienced director? An experienced one? Why?

3. Did you find information that was new to you? What was it?

Session 14 Family and Community Involvement

Student performance is profoundly influenced by parental engagement in the educational process as well as in school life. There are opportunities throughout the year for parents to support classroom instruction, whether as a mentor for a science class, a speaker on Career Day, or to chaperone on field trips. The parent teacher organization meetings feature speakers, panels and other presentations designed to educate parents about their child's development and the preschool experience. Satisfied parents are the best form of advertisement and educators cannot be successful without this partnership.

Read the following poem and discuss the importance of parent teacher partnerships.

Who's to Blame?

The college professor said,
"Such rawness in a student is a shame.
Lack of preparation in high school is to blame."
Said the high school teacher,
"Good heavens, that boy's a fool.
The fault, of course, is with the middle school."

The middle school teacher said,
"From stupidity may I be spared.
They sent him in so unprepared."
The primary teacher huffed,
"Kindergarten blockheads all.
They call that preparation?
Why, it's worse than none at all."

The kindergarten teacher said,
"Such lack of training never did I see.
What kind of woman must that mother be?"
The mother said,
"Poor helpless child. He's not to blame.
His father's people were all the same."
Said the father at the end of the line,
"I doubt the rascal's even mine.
—Anonymous

Any teacher, any parent, and any child can relate to "Who's to Blame." Why? Because we've all been guilty of it. But the simple fact is that playing the blame game does us no good. It does not move us forward, it does not help children, it does not improve teaching, and it wastes our valuable time and energy. There's only one piece of advice I can give you regarding the blame game: **DON'T PARTICIPATE!**

Every year, we receive a certain group of students. We do not get to "pick" them. We do not get to pick their parents. We do not have a say in their educational experiences prior to teaching them. We do, however, get to take them as they are and help them to grow from there. If we are committed to doing that, then we have no time for blaming. We have only time, and not nearly enough of it, to teach every one of them, to share our gifts, to recognize theirs, and to help them become what they are capable of becoming. *The blame game is a lame game! If you play, then dearly you'll pay!*
-Annette Breaux

Internet Activity: Planning Family and Community Involvement – View the following sites and develop a tentative draft of **parent organization** bylaws. ADM -7

http://www.ptotoday.com/bylaws-nonprofit
www.pta.org <br> ational_pta_bylaws_june2011.pdf
www.plymouthchristian.org/PTF_ByLaws.pdf

What are three purposes that parent teacher organizations serve?

The No Child Left Behind Act (NCLB) of 2001 encourages the use of Title I, Part A funds for preschool programs: Title I preschool programs take into account the experience of model programs for the educationally disadvantaged, and the findings of relevant scientifically based research indicating that services may be most effective if focused on students in the earliest grades at schools that receive funds under this part. [NCLB Section 1112 Local Educational Agency Plans (c)(1)(F)]. A Title I preschool program that provides services to children from low-income families must ensure that those services comply at a minimum with the education performance standards in effect under section 641A(a)(1)(B) of the Head Start Act (ESEA section 1112(c)(1)(G)) (available at http://eclkc.ohs.acf.hhs.gov/ hslc/Head%20Start%20Program/Program%20Design%20and%20Management/ Head%20Start%20Requirements/Head%20Start%20Act/headstartact.html#641A). The funds can also be used to host parent education meetings, reading specialist, literacy programs, and the like. For more information visit: http://www2.ed.gov/programs/preschooldevelopmentgrants/index.html

Check out these free publications provided by NCLB funding:
Learning to Talk and Listen
An oral language resource for early childhood caregivers. This publication is available to download free at http://lincs.ed.gov/publications/pdf/ LearningtoTalkandListen.pdf.

Words All Around
Language Building Tips for Center-Based and Home-Based Child Care Providers. This publication is available to download free at http://lincs.ed.gov/publications/ pdf/language_tipsheet.pdf.

Shining Stars: Toddlers Get Ready to Read: How Parents Can Help Their Toddlers Get Ready to Read
This publication is available to download free at http://lincs.ed.gov/publications/ pdf/ShiningStarsToddlers.pdf.

Shining Stars: Preschoolers Get Ready to Read: How Parents Can Help Their Preschoolers Get Ready to Read
This publication is available to download free at http://lincs.ed.gov/publications/ pdf/ShiningStarsPreschool.pdf.

Typical Language Accomplishments for Children, Birth to Age 6—Helping Your Child Become a Reader
Learning to read is built on a foundation of language skills that children start to learn at birth—a process that is both complicated and amazing. Most children develop certain skills as they move through the early stages of learning language. This publication is available to download free at http://www2.ed.gov/parents/ academic/help/reader/part9.html.

Read the study below. It was published by Dr. John H. Wherry, President of The Parent Institute and identify the one topic which you think will have the greatest impact upon child development and later student performance.

A **National Research Report**:
What Principals Would Tell Parents to Help Parents Help Their Children

---

Here's what elementary and secondary principals said when asked what they would tell parents, "If they could tell parents just one thing to help them help their children":

Take time to talk with your children, and listen to what they have to say. (Overwhelmingly #1)
- Dept. of Ed. study: Average American mother spends less than 30 minutes a day talking to her children. Average American father—15 minutes.
- Talk when your child comes home from school.
- Make a point to talk 1:1 with each child, not always just group talk.
- Talk, pray, sing, laugh, read, listen with your children.

Take an active interest in your child and what he or she is doing in school--and monitor their progress. Don't just ask, "What did you do in school today?" Ask questions like, "How are you doing?" "What are your latest test grades?" "Do you feel you are achieving?" "What was the most interesting thing you did today?" "What did you do best today?" "What is coming up tomorrow?" "What do you think Jesus thinks about his?"

Let your children know you love them. Take the time to show that you care. Help build your child's self-esteem, the opinion she has of herself.
- Let them know that you think they are valuable, capable human beings and that you know they can succeed.
- Give them positive feedback on all areas of their lives.
- Support them in their activities including homework, sports, dealing with life experiences.
- "Don't put children down. If you look for what the child is doing right, you won't have time to see the things he is doing wrong."
- Point out to your child when she is doing something right. Be careful of the words and ideas you say and share with your children. You are one of the most important people in the world to your kids and they want to make you happy. What you say to them and how you say it will set the tone and goals of their lives for years to come. Use encouragement freely and criticism very seldom.

Teach children to be responsible.
- Tell them that you love them and hold them accountable for their decisions. Tell them up- front the positive and negative consequences certain behavior will result in.
- Stand beside your child, not in front of beside them. Help them face life's challenges with you at their side.
- Love them enough to let them hate you sometimes—when you have to take an unpopular stand in their best interest.
- Give your child responsibilities at home.

Read to and with your children everyday.
- Set an example by reading yourself.
- Make reading materials available.
- Encourage your child to start his own library.
- Children are never too young nor too old to read to them. Reading provides time together, reading

© Penn Consulting

practice and good language background.

Make certain kids spend time on homework.
- Provide an adequate place and insist on a set time for homework. (Try "as soon as" technique—you can set your own time for homework as soon as your grades are acceptable.)
- Discuss homework with your child.
- Help your child do homework effectively. SQ3R (Survey, Question, Read, Restate, Review).

Adapted from a study by Dr. John H. Wherry, President of The Parent Institute.

Session 15 Accreditation and Networking

Internet Activity - develop three potential community networks (local stores, vendors, resource and referral agency, associations and child care programs)

Accreditation of programs has greatly improved the quality of programs for young children. Since accreditation became available, a growing number of schools and programs are taking advantage of this method of upgrading quality. Although NAEYC has accredited more than two hundred programs in the state of Georgia, there are numerous national accreditation organizations for early childhood programs.

Accreditation is a voluntary process designed to improve the quality of early care and education programs. Achieving accreditation involves extensive self-study and validation by professionals outside the program to verify that quality standards are met. Research has demonstrated that accreditation positively impacts early care and education program quality, including benefits to children, staff, and families. Accreditation systems require early care and education programs to meet standards that exceed minimum state regulatory requirements.

A number of organizations have developed accreditation systems to recognize early care and education programs that generally meet higher standards than are required by State regulations.

Listed below is a sample of **national accreditation systems for early care and education programs**, listed in alphabetical order.

Association of Christian Schools International (ACSI) Early Education Services
P.O. Box 65130
Colorado Springs, CO 80962-5130 719-528-6906, ext. 228
World Wide Web: http://www.acsi.org E-mail: earlyeducation@acsi.org
ACSI is a nonprofit organization, founded in 1978 through a merger of three Christian school associations. Programs and services are designed to assist Christian schools at every grade level including early education and higher education. Information about ACSI accreditation is available on the Web at http://www.acsi.org/web2003/default.aspx?ID=883.

Council on Accreditation (COA)
120 Wall Street, 11th Floor
New York, NY 10005
212-797-3000 or 866-COA-8088
World Wide Web: http://www.coanet.org E-mail: coainfo@coanet.org
COA is an international, independent, nonprofit, child- and family-service and behavioral healthcare accrediting organization. Founded in 1977 by the Child Welfare League of America and Family Service America, COA partners with human service organizations worldwide to improve service delivery outcomes by developing, applying, and promoting accreditation standards. Originally known as an accrediting body for family and children's agencies, COA now accredits 38 different service areas, including substance abuse treatment, adult day care, services for the homeless, foster care, and inter-country adoption.

COA's accreditation process involves a detailed review and analysis of an organization's administrative operations and service delivery against national standards of best practice. All of an organization's programs for which COA has standards are subject to review—COA reviews and accredits the entire organization, not specific programs. As is fitting with its mission and values, COA's accreditation process is designed to facilitate organizational improvement. COA views accreditation as a

structured means of achieving positive organizational change.
Additional information about accreditation is available on the Web at http://www.coanet.org/front-end/page.cfm?sect=3.

National Accreditation Commission for Early Care and Education Programs (NAC)
National Association of Child Care Professionals (NACCP)
P.O. Box 90723
Austin, TX 78709
800-537-1118 or 512-301-5557
World Wide Web: http://www.naccp.org E-mail: admin@naccp.org
NACCP is a membership organization for child care owners, directors, and administrators.
NACCP manages NAC. The components of NAC standards include the following: program philosophy and goals, health and safety, administration, parent communication, curriculum, and interaction between staff and children. Additional information about accreditation is available on the Web at
http://www.naccp.org/displaycommon.cfm?an=5.

NAC has a faith-based component as a response to weekday programs seeking to extend their ministry and/or to improve the relationship with a sponsoring organization of faith. Additional information about the faith-based component of NAC is available on the Web at
http://www.naccp.org/displaycommon.cfm?an=1&subarticlenbr=77.

National Accreditation Council for Early Childhood Professional Personnel and Programs (NACECPPP)
3612 Bent Branch Court
Falls Church, VA 22041 703-941-4329
NACECPPP is a national, nonprofit organization established in response to needs identified by the center-based, private-licensed, and religious early childhood community
nationwide under the sponsorship of the Child Care Institute of America, the national association representing that community. For additional information, contact William Tobin, Executive Director, Early Childhood Development Center Legislative Coalition at 703-941-4329.

National Association for the Education of Young Children (NAEYC) NAEYC Academy for Early Childhood Program Accreditation
1509 16th Street NW
Washington, DC 20036-1426
800-424-2460 or 202-232-8777, ext. 11360
World Wide Web: http://www.naeyc.org
E- mail: accreditation.information@naeyc.org
Founded in 1926, NAEYC is the world's largest organization working on behalf of young children with more than 100,000 members and a national network of nearly 450 local, State, and regional Affiliates. In 1985, NAEYC established a national, voluntary accreditation system to set professional standards for early childhood education programs and to help families identify high-quality programs. The NAEYC Academy for Early Childhood Program Accreditation administers a national, voluntary accreditation system to help raise the quality of all types of preschools, kindergartens, and child care centers.

The NAEYC Accreditation Criteria address all aspects of an early childhood program, including interactions among teachers and children, curriculum, interactions among teachers and families, administration, staff qualifications and professional development, staffing patterns, physical environment, health and safety, nutrition and food service, and program evaluation. Significant growth in and demands on the accreditation system led the NAEYC Governing Board to establish a

© Penn Consulting

project to reinvent accreditation by developing new program standards, criteria, and assessment procedures and by taking immediate steps to improve the reliability and accountability of the system while better managing the demand for accreditation. The transition to the next era of NAEYC Accreditation is now underway, with full implementation scheduled to occur by 2006.

The new NAEYC Early Childhood Program Standards and Accreditation Performance Criteria were approved by the NAEYC Governing Board in April 2005. They take effect in September 2006, replacing the current ("1998") Accreditation Criteria. New self-study materials based on the new standards and criteria will be released at the NAEYC Annual Conference—December 7–10, 2005 in Washington, DC. Information about the NAEYC Early Childhood Program Standards and Accreditation Performance Criteria is available on the Web at http://www.naeyc.org/accreditation/050415.asp. Additional information about accreditation is available on the Web at http://www.naeyc.org/accreditation/academy.asp.

National Association for Family Child Care (NAFCC)
5202 Pinemont Drive
Salt Lake City, UT 84123
800-359-3817 or 801-269-9338
World Wide Web: http://www.nafcc.org E-mail: accreditation@nafcc.org
NAFCC is a national membership organization working with more than 400 State and local family child care provider associations across the United States. The mission of NAFCC is to support the profession of family child care and to encourage high-quality care for children. The focus of NAFCC is to provide technical assistance to family child care associations. This assistance is provided through developing leadership and professionalism, addressing issues of diversity, and promoting quality and professionalism through NAFCC's Family Child Care Accreditation.

Accreditation was designed to promote and recognize high-quality, professional family child care. NAFCC Accreditation standards cover the following content areas: relationships, environment, activities, developmental learning goals, safety and health, and professional and business practices. Quality Standards for NAFCC Accreditation, Third Edition 2003, sponsored by the National Association for Family Child Care, developed by the Family Child Care Accreditation Project, Wheelock College, is available on the Web at http://www.nafcc.org/books/qual03.pdf. Additional information about accreditation is available on the Web at http://www.nafcc.org/accred/accred.html.

National Early Childhood Program Accreditation (NECPA)
The NECPA Commission, Inc.
1150 Hungryneck Boulevard, Suite C305
Mount Pleasant, SC 29464
800-505-9878
World Wide Web: http://www.necpa.net E-mail: info@necpa.net
NECPA is a voluntary accreditation for programs serving children ages 0–5 years. The NECPA program is an Automated Accreditation Indicator System (AAIS). This system and the instrument itself were developed by Dr. Richard Fiene, in conjunction with the Early Childhood Education Programs Department of Pennsylvania State University at Harrisburg. The NECPA self-assessment instrument is based upon criteria in the following component areas: administration and general operations, professional development and work environment, indoor environment, outdoor environment, developmental programs, parent and community involvement, formal school linkages, and health and safety.

National Lutheran School Accreditation (NLSA)
The Lutheran Church—Missouri Synod

1333 South Kirkwood Road
St. Louis, MO 63122-7295
888-843-5267 or 314-965-9000
World Wide Web: http://lcms.org E-mail: NLSAoffice@lcms.org
NLSA is available for every school operated by a single congregation, by an association of congregations, or by a Recognized Service Organization of the Lutheran Church—Missouri Synod or the Lutheran Church—Canada. NLSA is a national accrediting process designed to evaluate schools based on their unique purpose as Lutheran schools. NLSA is for early childhood, elementary, and secondary schools.
The NLSA Standards Manual is available on the Web at http://www.lcms.org/graphics/assets/media/DCS/standards.pdf. Freestanding early childhood centers that desire accreditation also with NAEYC may use the "Guide for Evaluating the Mission of Freestanding Early Childhood Centers," which, when completed, allows centers to be accredited by NLSA through an abbreviated process if they gain NAEYC accreditation.
Additional information is available on the NLSA Web site at http://www.lcms.org/pages/internal.asp?NavID=1741.

National AfterSchool Association (NAA)
1137 Washington Street, 2nd Floor Dorchester, MA 02124
617-298-5012
World Wide Web: http://www.naaweb.org
NAA (formerly the National School-Age Care Alliance), founded in 1987, is a professional association with membership that includes more than 7,000 practitioners, policy-makers, and administrators representing all public, private, and community-based sectors of after-school and out-of-school time programs, as well as school-age and after-school programs on military bases, both domestic and international. NAA provides a voice for the after-school profession, and is dedicated to the development, education, and care of children and youth during their out-of school hours. Information about NAA's accreditation is available on the Web at http://www.naaweb.org/accreditation.htm.

Additional Information
Accreditation systems require early care and education programs to meet standards that exceed minimum State regulatory requirements. However, the steps between State licensing and achieving national accreditation are often significant. Eleven States have developed a Statewide Quality Rating System (QRS) as a method to assess, improve and communicate the level of quality in early care and education settings. Ten of these States include accreditation in their QRS, although how it is included varies. Additional information about QRS is available under the Quality Rating Systems topic in the Popular Topics section of the NCCIC Web site at http://nccic.org/poptopics/index.html#qrs.

Child care programs wanting to earn or renew national accreditation can receive services funded by Bright from the Start to help them prepare for and complete the application or renewal process. Through a competitive grant process, Bright from the Start funds technical assistance organizations to help child care programs meet national standards of quality including National Association for the Education of Young Children (NAEYC) for child care centers; National Association of Family Child Care (NAFCC) for family child care providers; the Council on Accreditation (COA) for after school programs; and other comparable national accrediting organizations.

Accreditation facilitation services, provided free of charge to child care programs, include site visits to assess the program's readiness to participate; assistance to help each program develop an improvement plan; on-site technical assistance; and coaching to help program staff develop skills to achieve and sustain program improvement goals.

© Penn Consulting

Program administrators should purposefully network with professional organizations in order to stay up to date on current research and strengthen their programs. **Child care resource and referral (CCR&R) agencies** provide technical assistance and additional accreditation facilitation services in their regions. A few programs are listed below:

Georgia Association for Young Children
404-222-0014
gaycdirector@algxmail.com
http://gayconline.org

Quality Assist, Inc.
404-325-2225
info@qassist.com
http://qassist.org

Helping child care learning centers, group day care homes, family day care homes, and school-age care programs earn or renew national accreditation:

REGION 1- Child Care Resource and Referral Agency of North Georgia- Quality Care for Children, Inc.
770-387-0828
1-800-308-1825
http://www.qualitycareforchildren.org

REGION 2 - Child Care Resource and Referral Agency of Metro Atlanta- Quality Care for Children, Inc.
404-479-4200
1-877-722-2445
http://www.qualitycareforchildren.org

REGION 3 - Child Care Resource and Referral Agency of the Central Region at Macon-Medical College of Georgia
478-751-3000
1-877-228-3566
http://www.mcg.edu/ccrr

REGION 4 - Child Care Resource and Referral of Southwest Georgia at Albany-Darton College
229-317-6834
1-866-833-3552
http://ccrr.darton.edu

REGION 5 - Child Care Resource and Referral Agency of Southeast Georgia at Savannah - Savannah Technical College
912-443-3011
1-877-935-7575
http://www.ccrrofsoutheastga.org/

REGION 6 - Child Care Resource and Referral Agency of East Georgia- Quality Care for Children, Inc.
706-543-6177
http://www.qualitycareforchildren.org

Professional Development Course Evaluation

Rate the following statements by checking **AGREE (A)** or **DISAGREE (D)**.   DATE

PLANNING	A	D
Individual Needs Assessment Completing this training meets my professional growth interests or my individual needs for professional development.		
Content (1) This session focused primarily on program administration.		
Content (2) Content and concepts were thought provoking and relevant to my needs.		
DELIVERY		
Learning Strategies The training used learning strategies that applied knowledge of human development and learning.		
Relevance of Professional Development The training objectives reflect my professional growth objectives.		
Materials The textbook, assignment handout, Powerpoint presentations, etc. were useful.		
FOLLOW-UP		
Transfer to Job I will be able to use the knowledge and/or skills learned in the training.		
Support Activities I plan to participate in follow-up activities with Penn Consulting and my colleagues.		
EVALUATION		
Implementation (1) I plan to apply newly learned knowledge and/or skills.		
Implementation (2) I would be interested in additional training.		
Implementation (3) I would recommend this workshop to others.		

Please complete the following sentence:
I will use the information or training that I received to . . .

List below the services you are interested in obtaining further information regarding:
- ☐ General consulting
- ☐ Training
- ☐ Grant writing
- ☐ Licensing
- ☐ Corporate Document Drafting
- ☐ Tax Exempt Application
- ☐ Room Arrangement

Please email this form to apenn@pennconsulting.org.

© Penn Consulting

get book section on special needs

References

1. Administration of programs for young children, Thomson Delmar Learning Online companion Retrieved from www.delmarlearning.com/companions/content/140182644Xactivities/index.asp?isbn
2. American Academy of Pediatrics, American Public Health Association, and National Resource Center for Health and Safety in Child Care (2010). Caring for our children: National health and safety performance standards: Guidelines for out-of-home child care programs, 3rd edition. Elk Grove Village, IL: American Academy of Pediatrics and Washington, DC: American Public Health Association. Also available at http://nrc.uchsc.edu. *(free online)*
3. Aronson, S. (2002). Model child care health policies, Compiled by The Early Childhood Education Linkage System, National Association for the Education of Young Children. *(training on allergies)*
4. Association for Supervision and Curriculum Development, (2008). Educating everybody's children, Alexandria, Va. , Association for Supervision and Curriculum Development. http://www.ascd.org/publications/books/107003.aspx
5. Bredekamp, S., & Copple, C., eds. (1997). Developmentally appropriate practice in early childhood programs. Rev. ed. Washington, DC: NAEYC.
6. Click, P. and Karos, K. (2010). Administration of programs for young children. 8th ed. Albany, NY: Delmar Publishers.
7. Crown Career Direct Tools, Personality i.d. assessment online http://www.crown.org/Tools/Career/
8. Decker, C., and Decker, J., Planning and administering early childhood programs, 8th ed., Upper Saddle River, NJ, Pearson Prentice Hall, 2005.
9. Feeney, S. and Freeman, N.. (2005). Ethics and the early childhood. Washington, D.C.: National Association for the Education of Young Children.
10. Foundation Center Retrieved from http://foundationcenter.org/. *(Grants)*
11. Franklin Covey Leadership Roles – Free Assessment of Leadership Skills Retrieved from http://www.franklincoveycoaching.com/.
12. Georgia Child Care Market Study Retrieved from www.caresolutions.com.
13. Huntington, M. (2014). The average start-up cost for a childcare center. Retrieved from The Small Business Chronicle: http://smallbusiness.chron.com/average-startup-cost-childcare-center-16097.html.
14. Kidder, R. (1995). How good people make tough choices: Resolving dilemas of ethical living. New York, NY: Fireside.
15. Kipnis. (1995). How to discuss professional ethics. Young Children , 42 (4): 26–30.
16. MacDonald, S., (1997), The portfolio and its use: A road map for assessment. Little Rock, AR: Southern Early Childhood Association.
17. Maxwell, J. (2005). The 17 indisputable laws of teamwork assessment, and REAL - SELF-EVALUATION QUIZ (measure your relationship, equipping, attitude and leadership skills) http://www.injoy.com
18. National Association for the Education of Young Children, (1998). Accreditation criteria & procedures, Washington, D.C., NAEYC.
19. National Center for Education Statistics. Retrieved from http://nces.ed.gov.
20. Operating budgets for child care programs. (2001). Retrieved from Child Care, Inc.: www.childcareinc.org/pubs/OperatingBudgets.pdf.
21. Parents and the High Cost of Child Care: 2013 Report. (2013). Retrieved from Child Care Aware: http://www.usa.childcareaware.org/costofcare.
22. S. Feeney, N. F. (2008). Professional ethics: Applying the naeyc code. Retrieved from National Association for the Education of Young Children: www.naeyc.org
23. United States Department of Education. Funding, Grants, Publications, and Teaching Resources. Retrieved from www.ed.gov/fund/landing.jhtml, www.ed.gov/programs/landing.jhtml, www.ed.gov/nclb, www.ed.gov/pubs, www.ed.gov/free/index.html
24. Webster, N. (1828). Teaching, Learning. Retrieved from American Dictionary of the English Language: http://webstersdictionary1828.com/

ABOUT THE AUTHOR

Althea Penn, M.Ed.Adm., NAC, PDS is a conference speaker and professional development specialist with over thirty years of experience in education as a teacher, principal, and Children's ministry leader. She has a passion for children and those who serve them. She is an inspirational communicator and has served as a conference speaker and seminar leader for The Georgia Preschool Association, the National Black Child Development Institute, Kid's Advocacy Coalition, Quality Care for Children, the Association of Christian Schools International, and other organizations which share her passion for intentionally cultivating potential. As an educational consultant, she has trained thousands of educational organization program administrators and educators. Althea is married to her best friend and high school sweetheart. They are the parents of two adult children.

Penn Consulting is an education consulting firm specializing in professional development for early childhood educators. We provide motivating staff development and business consulting for administrators and teachers of programs for young children. Our objectives are to ensure optimal development of children by developing programs that engage every learner and to improve processes and performance in order to promote student achievement and program sustainability. We provide organization development services (including strategic planning, licensing, and accreditation consultation) for those seeking to start private schools, preschools, afterschool programs, and other educational institutions.

Congratulations to those completing the 40-Hour Director's Training Credential
School leaders at all levels of education can use the resources and strategies in the 40-hour Director's Training course to strengthen their efforts to ensure that their programs are sustainable and their students learn with high quality teachers. Every school should have a mission statement and a vision based upon shared values and beliefs. This course encourages leaders to engage all stakeholders in the process of developing a mission statement and vision for the school that provides focus and direction for all involved. Administrators must be familiar with available resources in order to support the diverse needs of its stakeholders (students, families and staff). They must know how to access additional support in order to ensure appropriate education for all students and support for teachers. Hopefully we answered the following questions:
Where are you now?
Where do you want to be?
How will you get there?
What resources do you need?
How will you know you are there?
The curriculum focused on translating theory into effective leadership practice at the early education/primary school level. Through the course work program administrators build the leadership, management, and problem-solving skills needed to become ethical and innovative leaders who can meet the challenges of an ever-changing early education system. I hope to hear great things about your programs.

Connect with me online at:
Twitter: http://twitter.com/pennconsulting
Facebook: http://www.facebook.com/althea.penn
Website: http://altheapenn.tripod.com or www.penntraining.com
Email: penntraining@yahoo.com

Book Order Form
Equipping early educators

Title	Regular	Discounted Price	Quantity	Amount
Christian Education Mandate	$19.99	$10.00		
Disorder Fact Sheet Booklet	$9.99	$5.00		
Early Education Program Administration Toolkit	$49.00	$30.00		
Subtotal				
Shipping $4 first book, $1 each additional				
Subtotal				
Tax (Georgia residents only 6%) $5.00=$.30 $10.00=$.60 $15.00=$.90 $20.00=$1.20 $25.00=$1.50 $30.00=$1.80 $35.00=$2.10 $40.00=$2.40 $45.00-$2.70 $50.00=$3.00				
Total Due				

Please make checks payable to: Penn Consulting

Check enclosed: Amount _____ No. _____

Credit Card Authorization (Please print)

Cardholder name _____

Card number _____ Exp. Date
_____

CSC/CVV # _____ Circle one: American Express   MasterCard   Visa
☐ Shipping address same as billing (otherwise write both below)

Billing/Shipping Address _____

City/State _____ Zip _____

Phone _____ Email _____

Penn Consulting
Child Development: Cultivating a love of learning and fostering competence in young children.

Professional Development: Training teachers whose lives and scholarship become a living textbook to their students.

Organization Development: Enhancing educational program sustainability and success through best practices in administration and program planning.

Organization Development Services
† Articles of Incorporation/Bylaws Drafting
† 501© 3 Tax Exemption Applications
† BFTS Licensing Application
† CAC Food Program Application
† Grant writing
† Student and Exchange Visitor Program (SEVP) I-17 Student Visa Application
† Marketing (Website, Brochures)
† Employee Orientation-Personality Styles in the Workplace, Policy and Procedure Review
† Mock Inspections
† Teacher Observations
† Parenting Seminars-see topics below!

Professional Development Services
Child Development Associate Courses and CDA Council Verification Visit

Workshops
Healthy and Happy Children – (6 hours or 3 2-hour sessions)
Injury Control, Infectious Diseases, and Child Abuse and Neglect
The Way Kids Learn – Learning Styles (2 hours)
Reading is "Fun"-damental - Early literacy birth-nine years (4 hours)
Effective Discipline Principles and Techniques – (4 hours)
Professionalism (21st Century Parents and Teachers) - (4 hours)
Administering and Planning Educational Programs for Young Children - (40 Hours) *** 4 PLUs**
Classroom Management Strategy Toolbox - (4 hours)
Every Child Learns Differently - **Differentiated Instruction PreK-3rd grade (6 hours)**
Shining Stars (Differentiated Instruction-6 hours and Classroom Management-2 hours) *1 PLU
Artistic Encounters - Integrating art across the subjects-S.T.E.A.M. (2 hours)
Purposeful actions - Building trusting relationships (parents and teachers) (2 hours)
Money, Money, Money [Basic Grant Writing for Educators] - (4 hours)
Kids Count on You - Strengthening Families and Protective Factors Initiative - (2 hours).
Moral Development (2 hours)
Planning Healthy Meals (3 hours)
Infant and Toddler Development (30 hours)
Child Development - the Preschool Years (30 hours)
The workshops listed above are approved for early childhood educators pursuant to the University of Georgia's contract with Bright from the Start: Georgia Department of Early Care and Learning. All workshops are available onsite, many are available online.
* Also approved for Professional Learning Units by the Georgia Department of Education Office of Professional Learning.

Parenting Seminars
Positive Discipline is Teaching - 90 minutes
Bringing up Healthy Children – USDA Nutrition Guidelines – 90 minutes
Literacy Begins at Home – Phonics Instruction Primer 90 minutes
Raising Spiritual Champions – Biblical Discipline 90 minutes

Penn Consulting Standardized Testing Services *(primarily for home school students)*

Spring Achievement Testing
The *Stanford 10 Achievement Test®* is a multiple-choice assessment that helps educators and parents find out what students know and are able to do. This testing instrument is a reliable tool which provides objective measurement of achievement and guidance for instruction. The Stanford Achievement Tests are also available in combination with OLSAT (*Otis-Lennon School Ability Test®*). The OLSAT measures the cognitive abilities that relate to a student's ability to learn in school. By assessing a student's abstract thinking and reasoning abilities, OLSAT supplies educators with information they can use to enhance the insight that traditional achievement tests provide. Combining the Stanford achievement tests and the OLSAT learning ability test will help you develop reasonable expectations for your student's progress, based on his or her abilities. Once you are able to discern whether your student is reaching his or her academic potential, you can understand how to tailor your teaching to your child's learning style.

Testing Price
- Stanford 10 Achievement Test and OLSAT combination (Spring-April)—$60/$80 per student (includes testing preview materials, test taking materials, postage, computerized scoring report, diagnostic consultation)*
- Wide Range Achievement Test (Year round)—$25 per student (includes scoring report, diagnostic consultation)

The Stanford 10 Achievement Test Evaluates:
1. Word study skills
2. Reading skills/ comprehension
3. Vocabulary
4. Mathematics
5. Language
6. Spelling
7. Social studies/science
8. Listening

Parents receive confidential results:
1. Norm-referenced scores: scaled, grade equivalent, stanine, and percentile rank
2. Graphed achievement percentiles
3. Content cluster skills evaluations
4. Skills performance ratings
5. Score interpretation brochure

Year Round Standardized Testing
The widely respected *Wide Range Achievement Test®* (WRAT) accurately measures the basic academic skills of word reading, sentence comprehension, spelling, and math computation. This quick, simple, psychometrically sound assessment of a student's important fundamental academic skills serves as an excellent initial evaluation, re-evaluation, or progress measure for any student—especially those referred for learning, behavioral, or vocational difficulties. Assessments can be obtained in as little as 45 minutes for younger children (K-3rd) and as little as one hour for older students (4-12th grade). The test can be administered and scored at a local library individually.

Student Eligibility—*Homeschool students*—For a student to be defined as "homeschooled," the majority of his education must be privately funded and provided at home rather than in a traditional classroom setting. Students whose education is home-based but provided by a publicly funded school would not be considered "homeschooled" for these testing purposes.

ADA Accessible—Special accommodations can be made upon request for students requiring a wheel-chair accessible desk or other special arrangement.

Private Testing Session—Private testing sessions are available upon request, for an additional charge. (*This may be necessary if your child has an IEP and diagnosed learning difficulty.-additional $15*)

Test Results Consultation—Up to one half-hour consultation sessions on score interpretation and curriculum recommendations are available at no extra charge. (Scoring SAT10/OLSAT-10 business days and WRAT-immediately)

Testing Dates—SAT10/OLSAT April of each year-Computerized results and diagnostic feedback are available ten days after test administration.

Registration—To sign up, simply register your student(s) at www.pennconsulting.org. Register early as space is limited. Early bird discount available for students registered by March 1 of each year.

PLEASE NOTE: All test materials are secure and confidential and may not be viewed by anyone other than the student(s) and approved administrator(s) *during testing*. The test questions or answers may not be discussed with any parent, student, or other individual before, during, or after testing.

Test Administrators—Penn Consulting representatives adhere to all guidelines for implementing test security, while ensuring that its highly qualified staff maintains a thorough knowledge of testing procedures and professional conduct. Mrs. Penn, the test administrator and all proctors meet the qualifications for administering the paper and online assessments. They are credentialed, experienced, have attended test administration training, and completed assessment college coursework. They understand the concepts of standardized testing, security importance, and the implications of testing irregularities.

Benefits of Standardized Testing
1. It provides students with reliable feedback about their own level of knowledge and skills.
2. It helps students to associate personal effort with rewards and motivates them to work harder.
3. The testing and its feedback identify teaching and learning objectives.
4. It motivates educators to work harder and more effectively.
5. It helps educators to identify areas of strength and weakness in their teaching plans and methodology.
6. The tests yield quantifiable information (scores, proficiency levels, and so forth).
7. The tests can be used to assess students' progress over time
8. The tests can be used to register your child for TIP - Duke's gifted program or the Davidson Institute.
9. The test can be used to meet the Department of Education's assessment requirement (Students should be evaluated at least every three years beginning at the end of the third grade).
10. They help educators to identify learning styles, unknown talents or abilities

"Test scores do not indicate whether children are learning to think from God's point of view or whether they enjoy what they are doing and are starting on the path of lifelong learning. And tests cannot tell the overall story of how a child's experience in school is preparing him for life. Such results—the results that matter most—must be evaluated by parents and teachers along the way, using a multitude of tools of which a standardized test score is only one." James Deuink, *The Proper Use of Standardized Tests*

Made in the USA
Lexington, KY
21 June 2015